Anthony Blizzard

Chorley Wood. 15

THE CHURCH HESITANT

To R. M. M. G. and C. E. E. M. G.

THE CHURCH HESITANT

A Portrait of the
Church of England Today

Ysenda Maxtone Graham

Hodder & Stoughton
LONDON SYDNEY AUCKLAND

British Library Cataloguing in Publication Data

Maxtone Graham, Ysenda
  Church Hesitant.
  I. Title
  283

ISBN 0-340-56906-9

Published by Hodder and Stoughton,
a division of Hodder and Stoughton Ltd,
Mill Road, Dunton Green, Sevenoaks, Kent TN13 2YA
Editorial Office: 47 Bedford Square, London WC1B 3DP

Typeset by Hewer Text Composition Services, Edinburgh
Printed in Great Britain by Mackays of Chatham plc.

Contents

Acknowledgments

Clergy and lay hospitality was lavish and generous: I am immensely grateful to the people I visited, who invited me to watch them at work and did not insist on the presence of a diocesan press officer. I would especially like to thank the people who took an active, consistent and highly encouraging interest in the book while it was being written. They are, in alphabetical order, Mr Richard Cohen, my editor at Hodder & Stoughton; Miss Caroline Dawnay at Peters, Fraser & Dunlop; Mr and Mrs Dane Halling; The Most Reverend Richard Holloway, Bishop of Edinburgh and Primus; the Revd David Hutt, vicar of All Saints, Margaret Street; Canon Roger Job of Winchester; Mr and Mrs Robert Maxtone Graham, my parents; Mr and Mrs Patrick Rance, my aunt and uncle; the Revd Mark Roberts, Rector of Sandwich; the Revd and Mrs Bruce Ruddock at St Michael and All Angels, Barnes; Mr Michael Smith, who became my husband a month before publication; and Mr Jim Swanton. The kind monks at St Edward's House in Westminster let me write in their library, and so did the librarians of Sion College on the Embankment.

Ysenda Maxtone Graham

Introduction

Writing This Book

The thickness of *Crockford's Clerical Directory* is daunting. How can one write a portrait of the Church of England today, and leave unvisited whole blocks of surnames? There are twenty-two clergymen called Hewitt and I have only visited one of them, on the North Yorkshire moors.

'It's a big animal you're tackling.' Lots of people said this to me. The Church of England is seen, by its members who shut their eyes, as a great bear-like creature with jowls and claws, which moves. My aim in writing this book is somehow to capture it, if only for a minute; to pick arbitrary points on its massive body and scrutinise them before the great beast moves on again.

Systematic examination would require a hundred authors, all working simultaneously and recording signs of health and illness on an assessment sheet. I am a single author and my examination is haphazard. It is not a report but a portrait, and portrait-painters are allowed to make much of the characteristics that fascinate them and be sketchy about the bits that leave them cold. There is more than strictly necessary about nuns in this book, and less than necessary about the Anglican Cycle of Prayer. I don't, in general, write things that you can look up in a book.

Hodder gave me an advance of £10,000 and that has all gone. It was spent largely on the following: train fares to remote dioceses and parishes, and the leaf-tea and British Rail banana cake needed to make those journeys bearable; stamps, paper and envelopes to write letters to the characters in the book; and the collection. I went to an average of three church services a week and, at first, put in at least a pound each time. Usually I had just talked to the vicar and he had told me how desperately the church needed ordinary money from the congregation's pocket; but towards the end of the year I became mean and put fifty pence in, or sometimes two tens which made a clinking noise.

'You'll lose your faith.' That is another comment people made. Well, I haven't lost it. I have never been sure what 'my faith' is, anyway, and I suppose it is hard to lose something if you can't even describe what it is. My family is not a churchgoing one and I was not a Sunday-school child. My grandmother, Jan Struther, did write the hymns 'Lord of all hopefulness, Lord of all joy' and 'When a knight won his spurs in the stories of old', but only because she was commissioned to by Percy Dearmer, and she had such a good imagination that she could imagine what it must be *like* to be a Christian.

In the sixth form at the King's School, Canterbury, I shared a study with boys who had been trebles in cathedrals. They had a tape, written on in loopy eleven-year-old writing, of Choral evensong recorded in their time: 'Responses: Smith. Psalms: 84, 85. Mag and Nunc: Rubbra in A flat.' That was my first brush with the psalms, and for a term I was drunk on the Parry chant for Psalm 84: 'I had rather be a doorkeeper in the house of the Lord: than to dwell in the tents of ungodliness.' None of the ex-trebles was a believer, much as they loved the Smith Responses and 'Rubber bra in A flat'. Nor was I, and we used to talk sadly about a really nice blond boy, good at everything, who had become a Born Again Christian and was now out of reach, his eyes distant and glazed over with a new and sickly light.

At Cambridge I sang in choirs and was a King's College Choir groupy, in love with a few choral scholars, keen to distinguish the sound made by King's from the sound made by St John's, and to hear the Allegri *Miserere* sung by as many choirs as possible on Ash Wednesday.

I felt sorry for Christians because they looked so pale. Then, after

Cambridge, I was given driving lessons by a rosy-cheeked Christian friend called Andrew Makower. After changing lanes in the dark on a one-way system off the Upper Richmond Road, I broached the subject of God. Andrew said it was *loopy* to believe that the world wasn't made by Him. We went back to his parents' house for supper and the whole evening was cosily and comfortingly Christian. They said Grace and sat round a simple table drinking water out of mugs.

They gave me C. S. Lewis books for Christmas and now I have a row of them in my house: meanly produced yellow paperbacks bought at Christian bookshops. They were delicious to read, each sentence clear, honest about what human beings are like and impossible to disagree with. I started needing to go to church: not to the same one every week, but to different ones. I went to hugging services at Pentecost, bare and ill-attended evensongs on Sunday evenings, gaunt mattins at seven thirty in Westminster Abbey. It was the beginning of the menu mentality, and I still haven't managed to shake it off. I have All Saints moods and All Souls moods. This, I now realise, is not a thing to boast about. It means you never have to lift a finger to help anyone. Lots of parish priests have asked, 'Where do you worship?' and I have developed nervous answers. 'I'm still shopping around, actually.' 'I have an excuse to go to a different one every Sunday because I'm writing a book.' 'I sometimes go to a red-brick one in Barnes.' '*I* was a butterfly when *I* lived in London,' is about as compassionate a reaction as I got. 'It's not what you *get* from going to church that matters, it's what you *give*,' was the more usual reply.

Churches seemed to be the most peaceful buildings left in England and I thought how sad it would be if they weren't there any more or were turned into recording studios. London on Sunday nights made me heavy with dread and sadness. Going to evensong somewhere made it slightly more bearable.

An ex-missionary in Hammersmith, Canon Alan Page, prepared me for confirmation when I was twenty-three. There were photographs of him and his wife in a hot country in front of a rickety church; we sat at right-angles at a small table with a Bible each. Never have I come across such a quick finder of references: he could go from a closed Bible to John 16, verse 8 in just over two seconds. The corners of the Gospel pages – especially the St John's Gospel pages – were brown with years of hurried licking and flicking. He taught me what the Holy Spirit was, and his wife brought us tea. Then I thought they were just Christians; now I realise they were evangelicals.

The Bishop of Dover confirmed me in a row of fourteen-year-olds in white dresses. (Priests ask, 'Where do you worship?' Bishops, I have found, ask, 'Who confirmed you?' They long to know, in the way that a hairdresser longs to know who cut your hair last time.) Then the kind Makowers tried to plant me in a friendly local congregation: the congregation of St Dionys, Parson's Green. It didn't work. I carried on flitting, and reading the 'Church Services Tomorrow' section of *The Times* with the avidity with which one reads the television pages for Christmas Day and Boxing Day. 'I *must* go to that.' 'I *must* hear him.'

Now it is even worse. Every Sunday morning the awareness of what I am missing in some church somewhere in England makes me fidget and unable to concentrate. Going to an exposition of a bit of Luke by John Stott means missing a sermon by Martin Israel in South Kensington, the Byrd Five-Part Mass in Winchester Cathedral and countless gaudy Masses in the north. Bits of England, previously unknown to me, now beckon. At Easter I was shut up in a convent while every single bishop was preaching in his full and listening cathedral. This book can show only a thin slice of what is going on.

One of the dangers of researching a book like this is that you get sent to see only the good people. One inspired, intelligent, self-sacrificing and devout Anglican sends you to see another. You miss out the dull ones. Every now and then I made an effort at randomness, putting my finger on a name in Crockford's and writing to it. Thus I met the vicar of Duxford and the vicar of St Andrew's, Southgate. I compiled lists of randomly linked clergy, such as ones with adjectival surnames:

John *Nice*, Warrington
Christopher *Sly*, Essex
Leonard *Small*, Leatherhead
Peter *Strange*, Newcastle

Charles *Keen*, Deal
Linda *Smillie*, London N5
Leslie *Slow*, Bradford
John *Tidy*, Burley-in-Wharfdale
Derek *Stiff*, Sudbury
George *Meek*, Hove
Joseph *Humble*, Regent's Park

and ones whose surnames sounded like ecclesiastical preferments:

Donald *Deacon*, Birmingham
Bishop *Bishop*, Malmesbury
Canon Desmond *Dean*, East Sussex
David *Vicars*, Bridgend
David *Priest*, Pimlico
Miss Christian *Nunn*, Salisbury
Nicholas *Monk*, Swindon
Roger *Reader*, Islington

but it would have been unkind to go across England to visit clergy, pretending you had heard of them, but really only because their surnames fitted into a list. As it happened, I met some of them anyway.

'Be careful not to turn into one of those churchy women,' is another comment people made. A second bass in my choir thought that a year spent living and breathing the life of the Church of England would make me join the women who make twenty pounds of lumpless marmalade and then make covers for the lids of the jars by cutting circles of cloth with pinking shears. There certainly is a danger of becoming one of these churchy women, but the flitting from church to church has so far prevented me from joining anything, except at Brighton, where I have agreed to give three pounds a quarter for the rest of my life to maintain a roof. Yet in certain ways the year has changed me. A thick layer of churchiness now covers the surfaces in my drawing-room. The books on top of the piles are the *Church of England Yearbook*, *Evangelicals on the Move* and *Walsingham Way*. Propped up against candles and lamps are holy postcards sent by friends who have tried to find the apt thing. St Dominic, tonsured and haloed, stands between the parish church of Fotheringhay in Northamptonshire and an Edwardian postcard with the caption, 'They all loved the curate'. In this way my house now resembles a vicarage – or rather, a canon's house, where beautiful or funny objects sent by other canons are on display among hand-outs and minutes. The Bible is always out, open at a text someone has just quoted at me: today it is Deuteronomy 18, verses 9 to 12, about how fortune-telling is an abomination unto the Lord.

Vicarages have photocopying machines, potties, cassocks above the downstairs lavatory, funeral-fee charts, unopened diocesan mail, winking answering machines and crosses on the wall. So far I have kept my house free from these.

Gardening never interested me before but this year it did for the first time. Quite a few people, lay and ordained, gave me cuttings to take back to London. I would set out in the train with an overnight bag containing the *Church Times*, my smart notebook and the improving book I was trying to read – the biography of Cosmo Gordon Lang, for example. I would come back two days later exhausted, inspired and laden with stuff: this month's parish magazine and last month's, a service sheet, two books lent to me – *Tensions* and *Consecrated to Prayer: A Short History of St Mary's Portsea*, for example – and three flower-pots full of wet soil a different colour from Fulham soil, with a small green plant taking root in each. A bit of my garden is now known as the Young Evangelical Garden.

Hymns have been stuck on my mind for weeks on end, and their auras and scanning truths have insinuated themselves into my deepest self. The hymn I have sung most often this year is the staunch classic 'Christ is made the sure foundation'. It is sung all over the country in churches of all sizes at the beginning of important services, and it is a relief to discover that people are still singing 'Consubstantial, co-eternal' at the tops of their voices, although in some places it has changed to the safer but no more understandable 'God the one and God the trinal'. The stately pace and reassuring words of this magnificent hymn have been a constant presence at the back of my mind. I suppose this is what hymns are meant to be. The second-most-sung piece of music has been not a hymn but the Creed set to its new wild and confident tune. The words are not so much sung as spat out:

> We!
> believe!
> in God the Father,
> Ma-!
> ker of!
> the universe

and so on. Evangelical churches love it. It has a meditative refrain and is so catchy that I could sing nothing else for days.

I am getting better at counting in sevens. This is a skill I learned from vicars. They can name the coming Sundays in the month, leaping with astonishing agility from odd to even numbers: the fifth, the twelfth, the nineteenth, the twenty-sixth. I became so used to being among bishops, priests, deacons and regular communicants that when, in early June, I found myself for once at a secular dinner party in Clapham I could think of nothing to say and was shocked by the conversation, which was about writers and their dissolute pasts. 'How lovely your garden is!' was all I could manage. 'Did you know you lived round the corner from a branch house of the Wantage nuns?'

More than half the priests I visited were genuflectors. It is something they learned to be at school or at theological college. Very few Anglican parishioners seem to genuflect: the habit has not seeped through to the laity. I do cross myself sometimes now, up, down, left, right, and that seems natural. No one has ever taught me to do the special criss-cross rubbing of the forehead, mouth and chest that comes before the Gospel but I sometimes have a go at doing it anyway, if everyone else is.

'God!' is still my most-used expletive. 'God, how terrible!' 'God, how do you manage?' I constantly hear myself saying in vicars' studies. It is inexcusable, and sometimes I see the expression of pain on people's faces. It is hard to drop the habit. 'Good heavens!' I have tried, and 'Goodness!' but at moments of genuine surprise or shock 'God!' still comes out. I still swear on my bicycle and am, in fact, no nicer in any way than I was before the year's basking started.

Sometimes, at the end of interviews, the person I was visiting put his hand on my head and prayed that I might write a good book, to the glory of God. Before lunch, the more low-church hosts would say Grace in a laid-back way: 'Lord, we thank you for giving us a chance to talk together, and we ask that you would give your blessing to this writing commitment. And we thank you for this food before us. Amen.' I can't be rude about *him*, I thought after such prayers. It is impossible to write a cold-blooded analysis of the Church of England because this kind of thing happens. God breathes down your neck.

Rather than putting microphones under devout people's mouths and sitting there while they speak for the whole of side A and half of side B about why they are Anglicans, I have tried to spend *time* with people, to see them at work and to get a sense of what their life is like. There is quite a lot of pure talking as well, because after the assembly in the church school or the weekday Mass you usually sit down to discuss parish life. I have got used to milky tea in mugs at strange times of day, such as twelve and six, when most secular people are having drinks. These are the reflecting times of day. The willingness of clergymen and women (I refuse to write 'clergypersons') and lay people to talk to me has been moving and uplifting. There has been a great deal of welcome and very little shiftiness. I have slept under duvets in the spare rooms of Christian strangers, who have collected me from the station and given me a clean towel. Most were clearly longing to talk: some remote vicars had never been asked, by an outside recording source, what they actually did all day and whether their congregation was getting bigger or smaller.

Often it was getting bigger. One expects this with an evangelical church – everyone knows that *they* are growing and re-seeding themselves all over the place. But small, musty churches are surviving robustly in tucked-away places off main roads. The fact that church attendance is diminishing in general, but stable or rising at almost any church you happen to visit, is one of the many mysteries of the Church of England.

I

The Spectrum

lergymen and women, trained in waist-high pulpits, use
their arms a great deal while speaking. The two most
common arm movements are the great enfolding gesture
– large symmetrical circles from the breast, which demonstrate
an urge to gather and include – and the wide arm-span. The
wide arm-span can be either gentle or abrupt, and it is used
in argument, to demonstrate the enormous distance from the
extreme evangelical to the extreme Anglo-catholic wing of the
Church of England. The abrupt arm-span is used for the infuriated
or despairing argument: 'How can you call it one church? It's
hundreds. No coherence any more. I mean, you've got those
clap-happies at one end, speaking in tongues, and those others at
St Mary's, Bourne Street, aping Rome. They're not related.' The
gentle, more ballet-like arm-span is used for the calm argument:
'The Church of England affirms more than it denies. It can *take*
the Bishop of Durham. We are blessed in belonging to a church
which includes rather than excludes. People *are* different and it
would be dreadful if we all had to be squeezed into a box.' (A
squeezing gesture is followed by a box gesture.)

As one more central fact of the Gospel is declared not to have
happened after all; and as one more priest claims that he cannot, in
conscience, accept the ordination of women, the spectrum widens.

Sometimes people fall off the end. Extreme evangelicals fall off and go to house churches in school gyms, or the nearest lively Baptist church. Disgusted Anglo-catholics 'go over', or suddenly choose the simple Quaker life. Extreme liberals gradually find that they don't believe anything at all any more, except that there might have been a census once but it certainly wasn't in AD 0.

The spectrum sometimes seems to be groaning and sinking under its load, rather as the Isle of Wight would if you really did stand everyone in the world on it, as is said to be possible. Retired churchgoers keeping warm on the outskirts of towns, and people who live in SW7, are some of the most vociferous despairers. The old churchgoers remember the time when you could go to any church in the whole country and be given Holy Communion in beautiful Book of Common Prayer language. People in SW7 remember Holy Trinity, Brompton, when it was a normal parish church doing normal Anglican things like mattins. Some of them still call it Holy Trinity, Brumpton. 'Have you been there recently?' they ask. '*What* a change! A parade of microphones! Frightful music – guitars. I do *not* want to take my Holy Communion at a Happy Eater.'

Violently opposing beliefs are held by the Church of England's ordained members, and this is shocking to the troubled laity. You would have thought that, by now, it would have been unanimously decided whether or not the Bible contradicts itself. But it hasn't. Liberal catholics[1] are relaxed in admitting that the Bible is riddled with contradictions, while the young evangelist Paul Weston, who teaches at Oak Hill Theological College, has yet to be persuaded that the Bible does contradict itself. The answers to enormous questions, such as what a priest is, whether the Resurrection really happened, whether Buddhists are saved and what Holy

---

[1] The word 'catholic' with a small 'c' means, in this book, Anglican catholic. It would be wrong to call all high-church Anglicans Anglo-catholics, because some of them aren't. They would hate to be branded as Anglo-catholic when what they are is Anglican catholic. Some of them are liberal catholics, some just catholics. But none of them is a Roman Catholic. The small 'c' is proof that I am talking about Anglicans. For consistency's sake, evangelicals will have a small 'e', liberals a small 'l' and charismatics a small 'c'. I will only use the word 'charismatic' in its Christian sense, meaning 'filled with the gifts of the Spirit'. It does not necessarily mean, in this book, attractive to people, fun-loving or popular.

Communion is, rather than being clear and unanimous, are scattered in fragments across the spectrum and as a lay person you can choose which answer you like and go there on Sundays.

A stricter church would sack people all the time. It would have spies in plain clothes, like Michelin diners-out, going around testing churches for Anglicanness. Insufficient use of the Alternative Service Book would be reported, as would excessive use of the Roman Missal. Cohabiting ordained men would be sniffed out, and anyone caught doing wicked things, or not believing that on the third day He rose again, in accordance with the Scriptures, would be suspended. But the Church of England stretches itself to include such people. It gives them the benefit of the doubt. It trusts them to sack themselves if they really feel that they are living a false life. 'Judge not, that ye be not judged', is the guiding text. And the guiding principle is, 'Do what Jesus would have done'. All arguments in the Church of England involve a quick shutting of the eyes to imagine a compassionate man with a beard and sandals walking about in the Middle East 2000 years ago. *He* would have forgiven them, and given them the benefit of the doubt. What mattered to *Him* was whether people loved their neighbour.

In the old days, clergymen were put in prison for their Romish behaviour and sacked for not believing enough. The *Encyclopedia Britannica*, under England, Church of, tells you more than you want to know about this. But now the Church of England is glad to have people who are willing to be bishops, priests or deacons at all, and is not quick to condemn. If a priest says he doesn't believe in a bodily Resurrection but he believes in the Christ Reality behind it, and still feels like a Christian, the most practical solution is to leave him alone.

There are more non-despairers than despairers about the width and depth of the Church of England's spectrum, though the despairers are louder. The English love classifications and subtle gradations, and if you manage to persuade yourself that all are trying to worship the one true God the mad differences in the way they do it seem just to be another example of the richness of creation. As long as they don't destroy each other, the two wings are at liberty to flap about as much as they like, and get further and further apart.

London is the best place for learning about the wings, because it is there that they are at their most extreme. The vicar in one parish is too visible – standing on a huge central platform and reproduced on eight hanging televisions in the galleries – and in the next he is totally lost to view in a cloud of incense. The Revd Stephen Coles, at St Thomas's, Finsbury Park, is lost. 'You can never *see* the vicar,' a member of the congregation whispered to me as we shuffled, squinting, round the church during the Epiphany Mass procession. Outside it was the dark and damp sixth of January. Inside it was a blaze of warmth, light and smoke. The red-brick wall glowed and a distant biretta could occasionally be seen, in the lead. We sang a long, obscure Victorian hymn about God made manifest, our thin English voices drowned by the beefy voices of the Barbadians who made up most of the congregation. We prayed for Deogratius, for Joshua and for Bethany. The visiting preacher, from another tradition, was out of his depth.

Stephen Coles lives at a vicarage near Finsbury Park station which he has named the Cardinal's Hat. It is a beautifully decorated house, with invitations to Stephen and Russell on the chimneypiece. 'In this deanery', he said, 'there's not a single church that could be described as middle-of-the-road Anglican.'

The Revd Richard Bewes, three miles south at All Souls, Langham Place, is highly visible. At the central place where in a catholic church you would find a nave altar with a starched white table-cloth, at All Souls you find a giant modern pulpit, jagged and metallic so it looks like a sculpture. The pews and galleries are packed with well-dressed Christians who have come a long way, knowing that at All Souls they will be given a good, strong dose of Bible. 'Put on the Lord Jesus Christ, Romans 13:14!' we are asked to chant: upstairs first, then downstairs. 'Louder this time!' 'Put on the Lord Jesus Christ, Romans 13:14!' Heidi, lithe and blonde, sings, 'All I ever do is love you'. Then Richard Bewes, in a suit and tie, preaches loudly for a long time, holding a gilt-edged Bible and sometimes waving it in the air. His sermon is being instantaneously taped and printed out of a machine, so that at the end of the service you can leave with the Word tucked under your arm rather than the Body and Blood in your digestive system. Today's text is 1 John 5, verses 1 to 12, and we are taken through each verse, digging deeply. The three confirming tests of the true believer, faith, love and obedience, turn out to be buried in the first verses. So they are! We stare at our pew Bibles, riveted, while Richard Bewes sucks the juice from the passage. (I never find it embarrassing to take notes during evangelical sermons. Lots of people take notes.) After the biblical exposition comes a more general bit of sermon about living the Christian life: 'If you are ever in a position of doubt, just read the Gospel. And if that doesn't help, you are not really a believer at all.' 'We can be in Heaven *now* if we love as He loves, give as He gives.' Then comes a lowering of the voice for prayer, which has the same soothing effect as the quiet music that you stretch to at the end of a hard aerobics class. After that comes a deafening and uplifting hymn accompanied not only by the clean organ but by the piano, drums, violins, flutes and cymbals. You leave fizzing.

All Souls is a staunch church. It speaks in one tongue rather than in many, and the worshippers don't raise their arms in a trance-like way as they do at, for example, St Andrew's, Chorleywood, the home of the charismatics just outside the M25. St Andrew's looks like a barn but is centrally heated and rich with hot-water urns. On Sunday evenings parked cars swamp the village. The vicar, Bishop David Pytches, ex-Bishop of Chile, Bolivia and Peru, spoke to me in a tongue once after the Sunday evening service, with his hand on my head. It sounded African and holy. He did it in a spirit of selfless prayerfulness and I didn't ask him, 'What did that mean?' because it would have broken the benign spell which the Holy Spirit had cast.

Doing the Knowledge of English churches and churchmanship takes years. Crockford's helps. In the tiny abbreviated entry for each ordained member of the Church of England you can suck almost as much juice as Richard Bewes did from that bit of 1 John 5. Compare the following two entries:

HUNT, Kevin. b.59. St Jo Coll Dur BA80. Ox Univ BA83 MA88. St Steph Ho Ox. d 84 p 85. C Mansfield ST Mark S'well 84–85; C Hendon and Sunderland *Dur* 85–88; V Sunderland Springwell w Thorney Close from 88. *The Clergy*

House, Springwell Road, Sunderland SR3 4DY (091-528 3754).

PIPER, Gary Quentin David, b.42. Nottm Coll DipEd 71. Oak Hill Th Coll 75. d 78 p 79. Hon C Fulham St Matt *Lon* 78–85; RD Hammersmith from 86. *St Matthew's Vicarage, 2 Clancarty Road, London SW6 3AB (071-731 3272).*

Their names, English and un-posh, don't tell you much except that they are probably really nice English chaps doing their best. Kevin Hunt did two degrees; Gary Piper thought he wanted to be a teacher. It is at the next fact that the two clergymen diverge. St Steph Ho in Oxford is very high-church and Oak Hill Th Coll in north London is very low-church. Suddenly, in your imagination, you see one in black clerical dress and the other in what old-fashioned bishops call 'mufti'. Kevin did two curacies, the second in Sunderland where he is now a vicar. Gary was an honorary curate – non-stipendiary, perhaps – at St Matthew's, Fulham, which is the church on the Wandsworth Bridge Road which had a sign outside it for months saying

What is missing from this CH   CH?
UR!

He has been vicar there since 1985 and he is obviously good at it because he has been made Rural Dean. Kevin is probably a bachelor because he lives in something called The Clergy House. Other clergy might live with him, in the Roman Catholic way. 2 Clancarty Road, London SW6 sounds nice: I would rather be Gary.

Measuring surmise against fact is a thrilling exercise and this is the kind of thing I spent my advance on. Kevin Hunt was wearing black clerical clothes and he introduced himself as Father Kevin. 'And this is Father Philip, who lives here as well.' The Clergy House is roomy and characterless, built in the 1950s when the middle of Sunderland was knocked down and its inhabitants placed in new, identical outskirts. All the roads in Springwell begin with 'S', all the roads in Thorney Close with 'T', all the roads in Grindon with 'G' and all the roads in Pennywell with 'P'. Young curates take weeks finding their way around. Fr Philip was Fr Kevin's new curate: he had been ordained deacon three days ago and he was getting used to his new title and life. The table in the living-room ('lounge' was not the word, but nor was 'drawing-room') was thick with congratulations cards – 250 of them, full of love and good wishes. The vicar of Pennywell and his wife came to supper; they live in Parkhurst Road, Pennywell, and their curate, Fr Simon, lives in another 'P' road, not with them.

The next day was Thursday and Fr Kevin and Fr Philip got up early to say Morning Prayer together in the church. Then Fr Kevin said Mass and Fr Philip, in his new alb and green stole, did all the things the deacon is allowed to do, such as read the Gospel and say 'Let us proclaim the mystery of faith!' There were twelve in the congregation, all loyal and old, and afterwards we had tea and biscuits in a pink room at the back. The milk-bottle top was pierced with a thumbnail rather than gently sunk in and taken off. The old people talked for a long time about past happiness and present diseases, and Fr Kevin and Fr Philip listened attentively and made encouraging and loving replies. In the evening they were both off to York to see the Mystery Plays as a post-ordination treat. (Fr Philip had been on a pre-ordination *re*treat conducted by the Bishop of Durham, who almost cried, he was so moved.)

Gary's mufti was a yellow Lacoste-ish T-shirt, pale summer trousers and training shoes. His vicarage, 2 Clancarty Road, Fulham, is even nicer than it sounds. (It is not a house in an ornate Victorian terrace but a farmhouse – the only farmhouse left in Fulham from the days when it was full of market-gardens. The windows are large and low and the rooms are irregularly shaped, borrowing light from one another. 'I believe in home-grown leadership,' he said, looking out at the fertile garden, now badly overgrown and in need of weeding. He has a happy face and his attitude to the priesthood is relaxed. He lets lay people take his services, in any way they like as long as there is a Creed and a confession. He prefers ordained people to preach because they know the Bible better. 'We've got a teaching programme at the moment: on Sunday mornings we're doing Proverbs and in the evening we're doing Characters in the Bible.' House groups meet in the week to talk informally about what Proverbs was trying to tell them on Sunday.

The sad play on letters which filled the church's noticeboard for so long has now been changed to, 'Jesus Christ requests the pleasure of your company here on Sunday!' That is less sad. 'Gary Piper's doing *very* well down on the Wandsworth Bridge Road,' other vicars in the neighbourhood say. He himself has had his horizons greatly widened by being made Rural Dean. (It is lovely that you can live in a farmhouse in London and be a Rural Dean – you don't have to be an Urban Dean.) He acts as a kind of foreman for the clergy in the deanery and he has seen extremely high things going on in Hammersmith. They have convinced him that there are many ways of worshipping the Lord.

Church noticeboards are always informative, and the beginner's part of doing the Knowledge is learning to tell, while driving at the speed limit past a given church, precisely where it falls in the spectrum. Gary Piper's church is easy: its plea that you should come in, and its reminder that Jesus is the host, could only be informal evangelical. To find the other end of the spectrum in Fulham you have to go past Fulham Broadway to the church at the traffic lights. There the noticeboard is dark red with exquisite gold lettering, telling you the hours of Mass on Saturdays, Sundays and weekdays. The general noticeboard rule is: it's catholic unless the name of the priest is dwarfed by a blown-up text or plea for attention. Rather as sweet-shops are now called 'Benson & Hedges' twice in huge gold-backed lettering, and 'S. Patel' once in minute lettering, so evangelical churches have sacrificed the man in charge's name for a louder message.

Here the spectrum starts to fill up with its large, multicoloured middle. There are not two but five Anglican churches in Fulham. The other catholic one, All Saints, is the one on Putney Bridge, waving across at the Diocese of Southwark which starts on the other side of the river. Its vicar, Prebendary Kenneth Bowler, believes in the Real Presence (rather than 'the Real Absence', which is what some Roman Catholic priests jeeringly imagine that Anglicans spend their time celebrating). But he is not so catholic and traditionalist that he is against the ordination of women. He marries people that other, stricter, clergymen refuse to marry, and says, 'The sacrament's God's, not mine'. (The man behind the red and gold noticeboard, Fr Martyn Webster, presents people who come into his church with a shelf-full of anti-ordination of women leaflets. I found him sinister. His office had a cheeseplant in it and stank of air-freshener.) Between Putney Bridge and the Wandsworth Bridge Road there are two more churches, one formal evangelical and one sad evangelical.

Categories blur. In Hounslow there lives a clergyman who is a charismatic catholic. This is confusing. We are brought up to believe that 'charismatic' and 'catholic' belong in different boxes, and it is an effort suddenly to have to combine them, just as it was an effort to grasp at school that someone was doing a strange mixture of A-levels, such as English, French and Chemistry. But why shouldn't they? And why shouldn't he? The Holy Spirit landed on him, and him a Mass-sayer. The spectrum is not simply getting wider: bits of it are being blended with others, and optimists see this as a sign of hope.

Bishops help this blending to happen. Out of the evangelical pool, the good clergy are plucked, consecrated and put in charge of a diocese. Experience soon makes them unshockable. The Archbishop of Canterbury who, in his past, ran a charismatic church in Durham and then an evangelical theological college in Bristol, now sees the point in monks. He speaks to them in an affirming way, as he does to all catholics. At some point in the address or essay he usually reminds us that he came from another tradition; but he does not deride. He had to be taught how to swing a censer when he first became Bishop of Bath and Wells. He was a willing learner.

Suddenly, in the coach on the way back from Walsingham, the congregation of the Anglo-catholic church of St Michael's, Brighton, started singing chorussy, pop-songish, devotional pieces of music which I had only ever heard evangelicals sing before. We were on the M11 and it was just after six: on the dot of six we had said the Angelus. 'I really can't bear this one,' the prebendary I was sitting next to whispered, when we came to a soppy tune about a girl with wind in her hair (supposed to be Mary), sung to the tune of 'Scarborough Fair'. But he sang it all the same, not to be churlish.

The traditions are learning from one another. If you ask Eric Kemp, the aged and reactionary Bishop of Chichester, what his favourite hymn is, he will tell you it is 'Shine, Jesus, shine'. Evangelical churches are more sacramental than they used to be; catholic churches, more sacramental than ever, are also more laid back. Exchanging the Sign of the Peace is an example of friendliness in church services wafting up into the higher regions. It is a habit still deplored by many, but again, you have to ask, 'What would *He* have done?' and picture a man in a nightshirt-like garment. *He* would have shaken hands.

High-church and low-church ordinands are generally kept apart. When you are deciding to go to theological college you tend to have firm ideas about whether you are a catholic or not, and you wouldn't dream of applying to the wrong kind of place where they would teach you strange beliefs and unnatural gestures. Cuddesdon is liberal catholic, up-to-the-minute with issues. St Stephen's House: Anglo-catholic, nice to homosexuals. Westcott House: Catholic but less extreme. Wycliffe Hall: evangelical but in Oxford. Ridley Hall: intellectual evangelical. Oak Hill: nearly all married families. Trinity College, Bristol: Dr Carey used to be Principal. Chichester: Anglo-catholic, but homely rather than slick. And so on. You, and your director of ordinands, pick the most suitable one. Salisbury & Wells is the one you would choose if you were an in-betweeny. There, at the weekly Friday evening College Eucharist, you are greeted with a dog's dinner of liturgical language and behaviour. Some say 'thee' and some say 'you'. Some say 'men' some say 'mankind' and some say 'humankind'. Some genuflect, some lift their arms in a trance of worship. This prepares you for real life but it can be confusing while you are there.

The traditions are brought face to face at the ordination. After that, you are put in a Post-Ordination Training (P.O.T.) group, which in some dioceses is a laughable affair because you don't learn anything, and is known as 'potty training', but in others is useful because it tells you things you never learned at theological college, such as what a quarterly marriage return is, how to anoint and what to say when an ill person in hospital asks if she is going to be healed. Evangelicals, catholics and in-betweenies sit in a room together, some on chairs and some on the floor, and discuss things. 'In *my* tradition', says one. 'At *my* end of the market', says another. 'I don't wear black. It's not my tradition.' 'I have difficulty with that. It's my tradition, I suppose.' People much prefer to say 'my tradition' than to name the tradition. 'I *hate* labels', is something often said.

Pam Wise and Jane Wilson have met through their ordination and P.O.T. group. Pam was at Cuddesdon and Jane was at Wycliffe Hall and they are now both curates in north London. We sat drinking Diet Coke in Pam's garden in Wembley two days after the huge anti-ordination of women rally in Wembley Arena called the 'Festival of Faith'. Pam was still recovering from the shock of discovering that her very own vicar had attended it. 'I found myself slipping down the candle pretty quickly after Cuddesdon,' she said. She had been put off by the ponciness of Anglo-catholicism that she had come across: the obsession with vestments and length of candles, the kissing of the new priest's hands at his first Mass. God seemed to be being lost in all this and the priesthood elevated beyond its proper place. 'I believe in the royal priesthood of all believers,' she said, and those are the words of someone who is slipping down the candle, or spire. At Evening Prayer in her church they say the Hail Mary and she finds this a revolting denigration of women. She now finds it offensive when language is gender-specific.

Jane was having a lovely time at her evangelical church, Emmanuel, Northwood, working with Gary and Derek. 'Derek is just *so* good,' she said. 'He's asked me to oversee all the pastoral work in the parish.'

'I'm allowed to run the mothers and toddlers group on the housing estate,' said Pam.

They talked about homosexuals. Pam knew lots of practising ones at Cuddesdon and for her it is not a problem or a worry. 'I have difficulty with that,' said Jane.

'Wearing a deacon's stole is like having to continue to wear L plates,' said Pam.

'*We* all wear a black preaching scarf and hood,' said Jane.

The traditions wave at each other across a chasm. But human beings from each side make friends.

*   *   *

In the deep countryside, churches can't be as extreme in their highness or lowness as they can in London, Surrey and the Green Belt. Country vicars have got to satisfy the needs and tastes of the very people whose souls they have the cure of, and who might not be able to drive. 'You've got to be all things to all men in the country,' the Hewitt on the North Yorkshire moors told me. He is called Francis Hewitt and is vicar of Lastingham, Appleton-le-Moors and Rosedale. 'On Sundays I do Sung Eucharist with vestments at Lastingham, then I go to Rosedale and take my guitar. I do six services some Sundays. The only thing that keeps me sane is that we have the same readings and I give the same sermon.' 'Within three parishes', said the vicar of Duxford, Ickleton and Hinxton in the diocese of Ely, 'we provide everything that's legal in the C of E.' If you have only got one church, and are a sensitive rather than a bulldozing vicar, you tend to mould your services to suit all tastes – mattins one week, Book of Common Prayer early in the morning, Rite A most weeks, Rite B sometimes, guitars sometimes, organ usually. If you have got two or more churches, as many rural vicars have, the tendency is to give each one a character of its own – not violently contrasting incense with tongues, but gently contrasting vestments with guitars.

Expressions for where you stand on the churchmanship spectrum tend to be woolly and inoffensive in the country: 'In rural areas, churchmanship tends to be low-ish Protty,' said the vicar of Burbage in Wiltshire. 'Straightforward sunny side of middle, I would say!' is another common rural position. The distinguishing features of country churches are not so much whether they are high or low but whether they are full or empty, damp or dry, rich or poor, old-fashioned or modern, living or dying.

A spiritual revival is going on in the small town of Burbage, near Marlborough. But at East Grafton, the tiny village next door, the congregation just carries on going to church every Sunday, getting neither bigger nor smaller. I shadowed the vicar, Nicholas Leigh-Hunt, on a cold morning in February. He drove to East Grafton at ten for a Book of Common Prayer communion service. The congregation was sparse, over forty-five and dressed in woolly coats. The organ console was covered in blue polythene and the service was musicless. The vicar stood with his back to us, as the altar dictated, and read Cranmer's beautiful, sin-laden words. We meekly kneeled upon our knees.

He hardly had time to say goodbye at the end. The family service at Burbage was starting at eleven. In the two-mile drive he had to change his mood from stiff to groovy. The parish church of Burbage was packed, loud and waiting. Jerry Lynas, a good man of the parish, stood behind a deck of buttons to man the hissing amplifier. Choruses were already being sung by the seated congregation. (The etiquette of standing or not standing up to sing is changing. Pre-service choruses are nearly always sung sitting down.) Nicholas Leigh-Hunt's tone of presentation was that of a man thirty years younger than the word-perfect celebrant at East Grafton. He sat back a great deal and let the people of the parish take over. Ann, an inspiring lay preacher, gave 'the talk'. It was addressed to the children and she had a large supply of visual aids – seeds, an avocado stone, wellington boots, an anorak. 'What was the sower *like*?' she asked.

The children didn't answer. A grown-up churchwarden had to: 'Prolific.'

'*That's* a big word,' said Ann.

'When we try to have a family service at East Grafton,' Nicholas Leigh-Hunt told me later, 'either the very old ones stay away or they sit there stiffly, hating every minute.'

The *Church Times* is never called the C. T. The *Church of England Newspaper* is frequently called the C. E. N., partly because it is more in need of shortening, partly because it is the low-church newspaper, and abbreviations have spread more thoroughly through the evangelical world than they have through the Anglo-catholic. (Our Lady of Walsingham is, it must be admitted, known as O. L. W., but only on signposts and leaflets, not verbally.) The C. E. N. uses a *Guardian*-like mixture of italic and roman script in its titles: WORLD *News*, CLASSIFIED *Adverts*, *The* INSIDE *story*. The *Church Times* still looks as if it is typeset in hot metal, even though it isn't. It has very few misprints: the employees scour it for literals and inconsistencies. The C. E. N. is worse for misprints. It is particularly bad on apostrophes: 'Jesus victory', it says. 'St Giles Church'. (Surely it should be St Giles's, or, at the very least, St Giles'.)

Its paragraphs are often short. 'There is indeed a scandal here,' is one. Leaders say direct, chatty things such as 'He may well have a point'. Forthcoming events in the *Church Times* are special high-church services: in the week of the Feast of St Barnabas, for example, churches called St Barnabas's advertise their patronal festival in a tasteful, black-edged box. In the *C. E. N.* the week's events are not services but courses, seminars and roadshows: 'Beating Burnout: How to survive in a stress-filled world.' Details are called 'info'.

Both newspapers are trying to shed their reputation for representing only one wing. They are crossing over slightly, but what remains is a strong feeling that one is upmarket and the other downmarket. Readers of one are rarely readers of the other. You can't afford to be as choosy as that with the two Church of England bookshops behind Westminster Abbey. The Faith House Bookshop is high and the Church House Bookshop is low, but they are both often out of things so you have to go to the other and ask the woman nicely if *she* has heard of the book you want.

The English cling to these subtle differences. It would be boring if the Church House Bookshop and the Faith House Bookshop were exactly the same. We don't want to be standardised by a central Church of England body any more than we want to be made to eat clean cheese by Brussels. But the wings can threaten each other. They can become factions. *He* would not have wanted factions in His church; but what more can you expect of human beings who are dealing with infinitely important questions to which *He* does not seem to be giving a clear answer? If you do believe that we are members of one holy catholic and apostolic church, you have every right to mind if the Church of England goes off and ordains women to the priesthood without waiting for the Pope to agree. If you go by everything in the Bible and believe that sodomy is an abomination unto the Lord, it is no good sitting still: you must bear witness. These are not light matters. Theatres for argument are provided: the General Synod gives its members five minutes to have their say before the red light comes on. Pushing and shoving for votes can take place and be noticed. Dioceses have annual conferences held at enormous venues, and here powerful visiting speakers can change stubborn Christians'

minds. The signatures of letters to the *Church Times* are often
as long as the letters: like-minded people sign them in a gang.
It is an ugly sight. The short open letter which fell out of the
Church Times in 1991 about how we, the undersigned, think that
multifaith services are a bad thing was signed by so many people
that it needed a whole supplement of its own; the signatures were
packed together in minuscule print, as small as the grey writing
on the pages of a passport which says 'United Kingdom of Great
Britain and Northern Ireland' again and again.

Poorly attended churches going about their business can wake
up one day and find that another church has come and planted
itself next door. Church planting is seen by some as a saintly and
miracle-wreaking occupation which has been going on since Acts,
bringing salvation and music to dead patches of the globe; and by
others as the next horror which is going to smother the delicate
parish system.

Church planting is this: a congregation prays for another venue,
to which some of its members can move, in order to bring Jesus
closer to the doorsteps of the unchurched. It sounds harmless
enough; it is harmless if the venue is within the boundaries of the
parish. There is a vicar with a church-planting data-base in Deal,
George Lings, and he can call up lots of church plants which have
happened because of the problem of IPP – Inadequate Penetration
of the Parish. New housing estates on the other side of the ring road
need a worshipping venue nearby, and the school gym, smelling of
weekday sweat though it is, is a more magnetic place than the
distant parish church.

If you are a growing church you can fill up the new venue
quickly and it, too, must seed itself. The parish of Cranham, near
Uxbridge, is bursting with planted churches and needs to spill out
of the boundaries and plant in another parish. To do this a church
should ask the permission of the invaded incumbent. He might say
'No', and the bursting church might feel that God is calling it to
move in all the same. Thus, on George Lings's data-base, you can
also call up examples of 'Cross-boundary, without permission'.

Dead or dying churches have been woken up with a jolt.
Congregations rise from nought or six to 300 within weeks.
St Paul's, Onslow Square, in South Kensington was actually

redundant and had to be re-consecrated. The Queen had to sign twice. Now it is one of Holy Trinity, Brompton's plants, and the east end is crowded with drums, trailing wires and singing Christians. Families pile in on Sunday mornings.

'Nothing is further from our intentions than to poach people from other churches, as we say again and again and again and again and again,' said Mark Elsdon-Dew, the bright-eyed Resources and Communications Director at Holy Trinity, Brompton. 'We're just desperate to reach the thousands and thousands of people who don't go to church at all. What we say to bishops is please, please don't close a church down without asking us first. We *need* churches.'

What worries the worried is that church plants are all *that kind* of church – drums and trailing wires, low-grade but addictive pop music, laid-back messages of salvation, not a dog-collar in sight. Oh no, says George Lings's data-base; there has been one Anglo-catholic church plant. But evangelical churches do grow faster than catholic ones, on the whole. Holy Trinity, Brompton has, among its other plants, St Barnabas's, Kensington and St Mark's, Battersea Rise. 'The church on the rise', says the brochure, with the words going steeply uphill.

'They've opened a new Holy Trinity Brompton church in Battersea,' is a similar statement to, 'They've opened a new Gateway Superstore in Battersea'. Chain churches, like chain stores, don't mean to poach, but success breeds success and emptiness breeds emptiness. It is lovely seeing churches full, but not lovely if one kind of worship succeeds only by suffocating another.

Niceness and Goodness

T he great saints were often horrible. This is a source of
consolation to selfish and prickly Anglicans. Jesus himself
was not exactly *nice*: he snapped at his Apostles and made
them squirm. But he was goodness itself. It is hard to assess,
when encountering modern Anglicans, to what extent they are
better people than agnostics. Anglicans go to church on Sunday
morning and come back feeling virtuous and hungry; agnostics
read the papers, lay the table and cook the lunch. Who is better?
Who will inherit the kingdom of heaven, if it exists? It will be
interesting to find out. The dead, in their coffins and urns, know.
In my experience, whether people are good or not has nothing to
do with whether they are Christians. Some people just *are* good.
Some churchgoers just *are* horrible. If someone offers to carry my
suitcase I would rather they did it out of innate kindness than out
of a commandment-obeying habit.

In my Church of England year I have come across a great
deal of goodness, and a great deal of niceness. They need to be
distinguished. Sometimes the goodness is hidden behind off-putting
elements such as coldness and bad temper. My heroes (and I have
been collecting them) generally have something unattractive about
them. Months before his arrest and resignation for performing
what the police called 'an act of gross indecency' on a postulant

monk, I used to lie awake wondering, Is the Bishop of Gloucester good or bad? Now he is the ex-Bishop of Gloucester, and the bench of bishops, though safer, is poorer.

The good in him could be weighed against the bad. Here were the good things. He got up at twenty to five every morning to pray on his knees for an hour and a half. The cushion he knelt on was not thick enough. Sometimes he hoovered his own palatial house, in a spirit of meditation. His face was Gospel-steeped, and his smile was enchanting. He was a mesmerising preacher. He said surprising, Jesus-like things, such as that we must live out the paradox of the Gospel, both being as fun-seeking and party-loving as Jesus and giving everything to the poor. He used to run a monastic scheme which invited people to give a year to Christ. They did it, and slept on straw beds, and wore habits, and prayed together, and fell about laughing at the Divine craziness of the created world. Bishop Peter was introduced to me, by one of his ex-novices, as the holiest man in England.

Here were the bad things. He had a strange obsession with celibacy. When he was suffragan Bishop of Lewes he used to go around visiting young single priests and inciting them to take a vow of chastity. They usually didn't want to. When a young clergyman or ordinand was about to get married, he strongly advised them against it. I met a timid young ordinand and his wife who had nearly taken his advice. Two years later, married and less timid, they detested him. I met quite a few people who hated the Bishop of Gloucester. A whole family in Wiltshire – aunts, uncles, cousins – hated him for his unpastoral handling of the funeral of a clergyman in the family. The Church of England was dangerously ill, they felt, if a man like that could be made a diocesan bishop.

Twice I went to see him, once in Sussex, where we talked in the drawing-room while an eager young male Christian cooked courgettes in the kitchen, and once at Bishopscourt in Gloucester, where we put our coffee cups on mitre-shaped mats and looked up at the pale tower of the cathedral. He said deeply felt things and I scribbled them down, riveted. 'I love the giddy old C of E. I love it for its vulnerability. It's infuriating, it's maddening, but it has the spirit of the Gospel about it, more than any other Church.

It's incredibly vulnerable, but Jesus had a tremendous vulnerability. We don't *want* a strong Church, we want a weak Church. We keep our vulnerability by our nuttiness, our openness, our exposedness. I think it takes a God to devise the idea of conquering sin by weakness.'

'Do you think the Church of England tries to be too friendly?' I asked. 'All those family services, everyone welcome, orange squash for the children?'

He nodded a deep nod. 'The Church of England has got into familyism. It's not the Gospel. Jesus said, you must leave your family and come with me. God is saying, I want to take your creative energies and use them differently. Western Europe is built on celibacy.'

'Built on celibacy? What do you mean?'

'All the great art and the great learning, it all comes out of the monasteries. Even the best liqueur does.'

'The best liqueur?'

'Chartreuse.'

I drove back to the family in Wiltshire and told them that the Bishop had said that Western Europe was built on celibacy. The mother of the family was speechless with rage. The man was dangerous.

Goodness in the clergy is not easy to gauge. The Bishop of Durham makes faith-shattering statements about the central doctrines of the Creed, and this, say some Anglicans, makes him bad; but the clergy in his diocese adore him and won't hear a word against him. He takes a genuine interest in them, as a bishop should. Bishop David Sheppard of Liverpool, evangelical, ecumenical and popular with the public, is not loved by his clergy nearly as much. To them he is a lofty figure to whom you speak once or twice in a formal interview. He stiffly asks what poets you like reading. Martin Israel, the vicar of Holy Trinity, Prince Consort Road, in South Kensington, is a hero, but he is not an outwardly friendly man. He knows about goodness, though, and he preaches about it movingly, every Sunday. He is old and frail and sees the skull beneath the skin. He reminds you that if you are pretty you won't be for long, and that if you are showily religious it won't impress

God. He speaks without notes so you really feel that he is a channel of God's grace. But after the service he is not comfortable at the coffee and tea session. He takes a long time to disrobe, so the coffee and tea session is nearly over by the time he appears. He is in his element at silent retreats, where chatting is forbidden.

Canons give sandwiches to tramps. Is this goodness? If you visit Canon Christopher Hill, the Precentor of St Paul's Cathedral, in his house in Amen Court, you usually find yourself standing at the door with a red-faced man in a smelly coat. The canon opens the door, brisk and ready. He spreads a white-bread sandwich, puts it on a plate and gives it to the tramp. It goes on happening all morning. Sometimes the demand is not for a sandwich but for an aspirin.

How wonderful, I thought. The Church *does* something. Canons are in touch; they reach out and help the poor. But then, of course, the doomful argument creeps up on you: what the canon should do is not live in his enormous Georgian house at all, but in a cardboard box. The Georgian house should be turned into a hostel, ten beds to a room. That would be a more Christ-like gesture than spreading a sandwich.

'The Church of England looks after *itself* very well,' scorners say. It is true. The clergy often live in lovely houses, with gardens and garage parking. However generous they are, they exercise their goodness from the safe haven of a centrally-heated world. The doomful argument gnaws away at you. Can it be right that a God-imitating institution should live so comfortably? Should a church raise £200,000 for a new organ while the homeless beg for sandwiches on the doorstep? It is an unanswerable argument and it never goes away. But I find it, in the end, a dull and impoverishing argument. Communism doesn't work, and a canon in a cardboard box would be something like Communism. A canon in a lovely house can read freshly written theological books and think subtle thoughts about how to make his cathedral even more uplifting than it is already. He can add to the beauty of the world. What matters is that he does it in a spirit of magnanimity rather than of greed. It is impossible to be generous if you have nothing to give. In theory, it makes sense for a canon to divest himself of all his possessions and share them out – toast-rack to him, carriage-clock to her. But in practice it probably wouldn't do much long-term good. 'The Church: society for saints or school for sinners?' is the kind of question you are asked in exams on the Early Church. If you have done your revision properly you can name the moments in the third and fourth centuries when it changed from the first to the second. Human beings realised that they couldn't do miracles and be Jesus-like, or even Apostle-like. They were sinners, and the Church was a compromise. But, rich as it is, the established Church has a nourishing presence. It radiates a sense of permanence: there will always be more sandwiches where that one came from.

Guilt none the less racks the clergy. Every week they have to tackle another bit of the Gospel in which Jesus makes some disarming or uncomfortable remark. 'Verily, verily I say unto you . . .' What is it this time? 'It is easier for a camel to enter the eye of a needle than for a rich man to enter the kingdom of heaven.' That is one to wrestle with. Luckily historians have discovered that He might not have meant the eye of a *sewing* needle. There is a gate into Damascus called the Eye of the Needle and a camel can get through that without too much difficulty.

Showing God to people is the clergy's job, and it is a hard one. They are constantly aware of falling short. I have noticed that the Church of England thrives on first aid. Nearly all the ordained people I have met love doing funerals. They don't say, 'I *love* doing funerals' because that would sound flippant, but they say, 'I find funerals very satisfying', or, in a casual tone of voice, 'I took three funerals yesterday'. 'God! You must be exhausted.' 'No. It was good, actually. I don't mind doing funerals.' Funerals are finite. You meet parishioners whom you have never seen before and it is a chance to show God to them, to reassure them that the person in the huge combustible coffin has not ceased to exist altogether. Baptisms are not so popular. Young, spiky-haired godparents are not as open to profound moments of sudden belief as the recently bereaved.

The Bishop of Newcastle, when I asked him what the Church of England actually did, said, 'The congregations and clergy *turned up trumps* during the riots last year. You know, a vicar and a Methodist minister and some mothers saw a group of youths who were about to join in with the riots. They said to the youths, "Why

don't you go home?" and, you know, they did.' When the
IRA bombed the City, the staff and hangers-on at St Helen's,
Bishopsgate, were on the scene all night, helping, counselling and
giving tea. The clergy yearn to be on the spot, at the scene, at
the right time. A vicar called Chris Oxley, who lives in the leafy
outskirts of Leicester, also gives sandwiches to tramps at his door,
although he calls them 'gentlemen of the road'. I asked him how
hard he had to work and he said that sometimes a crisis takes over.
One just had: he had given up three whole days to minister to a
family who had had a stillborn baby. This kind of thing was the
heart of his job and there was no question of minding.

Definable good works alleviate guilt: we all feel this a bit. The
longing to go and work in a Crisis at Christmas bus depot, cleaning
up sick, is a common one. At least you would be *doing* something
for others, rather than just thinking about them, or at the most
praying for them. This yearning to be at the place of need is
felt particularly strongly by priests and deacons. If you have
a parish of your own you love it with a deep, shepherd-like
love. You want everything to be all right in it: the divorcees
consoled, the widows visited, the ill looked after, the people
on the housing estate given some sense that the church is there
waiting for them if only they would use it. It is impossible,
of course, to make everything all right in your parish. You
can only scratch the surface. If you manage to get one family
from the council estate to come to church once, it is a feat.
Much of your work is not finite and physical but indefinable
and vague – it is simply being around. Vicars spend a great
deal of their working lives feeling not needed, out of touch,
self-conscious, *de trop*. A vicar visits a woman in hospital, and
she is either asleep or surrounded by grape-eating relatives. His
voice sounds parsonical and booming in the quiet ward. He doesn't
stay for long.

So when the vicarage doorbell does ring at midnight, and it is a
miserable parishioner who has got involved in the occult and feels
frightened, it makes the vicar's life feel worthwhile. He is needed,
and all his held-in goodness and his finely honed niceness can at
last come into their own.

*   *   *

Niceness is rife in the Church of England. It is a growing phenomenon. There are far fewer sour old clergymen than there used to be: the young, smiling generation is coming up to replace them. Why should this be?

The main reason, I think, is the longing to be liked that the members of any institution feel when it is endangered and said to be shrinking. Radio 3 is an obvious comparison. It used to be a stern channel. Presenters with deep, aloof voices announced the next record with little embellishment and no chumminess. Then panic set in: there were not enough listeners; the young must be reached. Now *Morning Concert* is called *On Air*. Presenters chat, and tell you about the westbound carriageway between junctions eight and nine. Sonatas in the morning are short and sweet.

The parish magazine of the Grantham team ministry used to be called *The Spire*. This came up at the team meeting I went to. 'Could the name be changed?' an incumbent asked. (Not all the churches in the team parish have spires.) 'I feel very strongly that Earlsfield and Harrowby aren't included in that definition.'

'What could it be changed to?' the rector asked.

'I thought of *Team Spirit*, actually.'

There's niceness. The Church of England loves to include rather than exclude, and it goes to great lengths to do so. It longs to shed its reputation for pomposity and loftiness. People must be brought in, welcomed, gathered. The result, in the Grantham case, is that a clear concrete noun is replaced with a friendly punning abstract. The successor to the Book of Common Prayer is the Alternative Service Book, 1980: again, a painstakingly accurate description of what it is, but an unbeautiful collection of words. Instead of talking about Hell vicars tend to talk about 'absence from God', which sounds less frightening and less hot.

They are only trying to make us turn to Christ, and to persuade us that God is not a frowning Victorian father-figure any more. If you are a vicar trying to show God to people, and find it hard, one thing you can do is to be as nice as possible. You love your parish, you long for your parishioners to come to church, yet ninety-five per cent of them don't. The obvious course of action is to walk down the high street on weekday mornings, being friendly.

When people say, 'I'm allergic to clergymen', what they are allergic to is usually precisely this friendliness. Three middle-aged Old Etonians I have talked to have made a 'please don't come anywhere near me' face when I described recent encounters with clerics. 'I can't bear going into a church', said one, 'because I know I'm going to be tapped on the shoulder.' 'One glimpse of the missionary smile', said another, 'and I smell poison.'

Etonians particularly hate being patronised; so, to differing extents, do we all, and one of the dangers of clergy niceness is that it can be patronising. I have tried, while living and breathing the Church of England, to distinguish annoying niceness from unannoying niceness. I have found that it is annoying in the following circumstances.

1) When it is spoken in a Cockney accent by a clergyman who went to a public school. This only happens during banter, in places like hospital wards, high streets and church schools. What is happening is that the Church of England is desperately trying to be classless. Several clergy I have met speak differently in their study from in the street. Richard Christian, a vicar and hospital chaplain in Cowley, near Uxbridge, is an example. Alone with me, he spoke in a taut, highly intelligent way about what it is like being a hospital chaplain with a bleeper – how worrying it is, how satisfying, how important to do it well. But the moment we met any nurses he broke into Cockney banter. 'I'm in trouble wiv you, ain't I?' 'You better wotch it!' That kind of thing. '*Vachement* annoying,' I wrote in my notebook (breaking, just as annoyingly, into French). At the church school he was the same: fascinating to the children, keen to show what Jesus meant when he said, 'Feed my lambs', but, in the staffroom, jokey in a different accent. 'I'm all for the ordination of women but I don't want anyone taking moy job yet!'

2) When it gets in the way. The lectionary at Salisbury & Wells Theological College is written all over in biro. Wherever the words 'mankind', 'man' or 'men' appears it has been crossed out and replaced, in chubby student's handwriting, with 'humankind', 'people' or 'creation'. This makes women feel better and we have

to sympathise with them. It can be terrible being a woman in a man's world, and the Church of England still is one. A woman deacon in the London diocese found that she was working for a vicar who refused to shake hands with her, let alone allow her into the sanctuary, in case she was menstruating and thus polluted. The nastiness of that outweighs the niceness of crossing out male words; but the niceness does get in the way. It makes you think not about the Lord Jesus Christ but about women's righteous anger, and this is distracting.

3) When it is competitive. Niceness competitions are exhausting, and they bring out the worst in people who are trying to show their best. Ordinands in the Church of England are trained in niceness. They are encouraged to love their fellow ordinands in a Christian way. One of the most popular theologians in Oxford, Alistair McGrath, gave an expositary sermon about a passage of Philippians 2 at college mattins at Wycliffe Hall. Gruff ordinands in sweet-smelling jerseys filled the chapel. 'What Paul is saying is, Look for what is good in your neighbour. You should ask, "Why did Christ die for the person sitting next to me?"'

In a hot-house atmosphere like a theological college, niceness can be measured and this can have absurd results. When a member of staff at Cuddesdon was ill in hospital every single student made a point of going to visit him. There had to be a rota on the wall. The man was swamped.

I have been in one or two lay niceness competitions, and they usually involve the washing-up. Evangelicals together are great washers-up. You have hardly finished your cornflakes before your bowl is whisked away and passed from washer-up to drier-up to cupboard. One of the most testing half-hours was when a niceness competition was combined with a know-your-Bible competition, round a crowded kitchen sink.

'O.K. Birds in the Bible.'
'Swallow. A nest where she may lay down her young.'
'I am like an owl that is in the desert.'
'The voice of the turtle is heard in our land.'
'Have you got a special drawer for whisks?'
'The people asked, and He brought quails.'

4) When it is boring for grown-ups. Niceness to children is one of the most striking recent changes in the Sunday life of the Church of England. There is usually a good reason for niceness; it just goes a bit far sometimes. The Church of England badly needed to creep out of its icy age when children had to sit stiffly in silence for hours and were, by a small dose in childhood, inoculated for life. But now you find whole services conducted in Sunday-school language. Sermons take ages if they are addressed to children because everything has to be acted out. I have learned more about sheep in my church year than I could have learned at any other institution except, perhaps, Cirencester Agricultural College. I have seen a little boy on all fours with a sheepskin rug over him, I have listened to convincing arguments from pulpits about how sheep in the Old Testament days used to follow the shepherd rather than the other way round; I have seen a vicar hook a shepherd's crook round a little boy's leg and hoik him back to the flock.

'Children must be persuaded that being a Christian is fun,' a Franciscan friar said at the General Synod, and people made agreeing noises.

5) When it evades uncomfortable truths. Jesus said there would be wailing and gnashing of teeth at the Day of Judgment. If this is true, shouldn't we be reminded of it? We hear the word 'Heaven' used far more than the word 'Hell'. School and college chaplains commended us for every tiny act of goodness and did not condemn us for enormous deeds of wickedness. The general teaching of the Church of England seems to be, 'Who are we to judge?' There is a sense that everyone is Heaven-worthy: even Saddam Hussein will go to Heaven, if he loves his mother. An ounce of love is enough.

This is comforting, and prevents us from being a repressed, guilt-ridden race. Our consciences are clear even if we live in beautiful houses, sleep together in pre-marriage beds and buy Marks & Spencer chicken Kiev while the millions starve. We are heartily sorry and repent of all our sins, and we know we are forgiven. Can it be as easy as this?

The wailing and gnashing of teeth clause has been carefully dealt with by theologians. They have decided that Jesus might not have said it after all; that the Evangelist might have put it in to frighten people.

It all seems too good to be true sometimes.

6) When it helps to sell a book. This book, you will have noticed, is one without a foreword. It will be one of the very few books in Faith House and Church House bookshops that doesn't say, on the cover, 'With a foreword by' someone holy and famous. 'I commend this book . . .' the foreword usually ends, signed Ebor, Cantuar, Oxon or another cathedral city. A foreword does help to sell a book. It endorses it. It is very Christian to endorse your fellow Christian's book. But the shocking fact is that a foreword signed by an archbishop has rarely been written by him. He has asked someone else to write it, and just changed a few words here and there. It is a lazy kind of back-scratching.

7) When it is euphemistic. 'Be rude,' I sometimes long to say to vicars who are searching for words to describe someone they don't like. 'Just say, "He's ghastly."' But they won't. They usually plump for, 'He's a sick man.' I have heard that very expression used of a verger in Wells, a rural vicar in Leicestershire and a sad vicar in south London. Sometimes, even more euphemistically, they say, 'He's not a well man.' They are kind but missing the point.

8) When it makes you feel as if you are getting off an aeroplane. There are ways and ways of saying goodbye. At Dublin Airport you are not offended when an air hostess stands by the door and says 250 brisk and unmeant farewells; but at the door of a cathedral it is upsetting when a canon says, 'Goodbye. Goodbye. Thank you. You too. Come again. Goodbye', with an air-stewardess's lack of genuine attention.

Canons have an excuse. They have said goodbye so many times to non-English-speaking visitors that they simply can't put the emotion into their words that they used to put when they were young curates.

Niceness is unannoying in the following circumstances.

1) When you know that the person who is being nice has the *potential* for wickedness. This makes the niceness convincing. It is worrying but true that my favourite Anglicans are the ones who, sometimes, talk behind other people's backs. They know they shouldn't but they do. They are not malicious, just honestly critical and usually funny. When you are talking to them you feel it is worth listening hard: you won't just be given goody-goody

talk, and you might suddenly realise that they are being rude to you.

This taste for potential nastiness in the clergy is a disturbing trait of mine; it could be seen as a kind of perversion – not sado-masochism but nice-o-horridism. It has been a relief to discover that other people feel the same. The most popular clergy are the ones who are the opposite of bland. 'We love our new vicar,' people say. 'He really talks to you. He's not one of those *smiling* vicars.' I have been sent, in my year, to meet people in the Church of England who are renowned as saints. 'Roger Job, Vice-Dean of Winchester. Saint. 8 The Close' my piece of paper said, given to me by the father of an ex-chorister. I rang up the Vice-Dean and hated him within three minutes.

'I certainly can't see you this week. It's Holy Week.'

This was the fourth holy person in a row who had said they couldn't see me because it was Holy Week.

'What is it about Holy Week?' I asked. 'What do you all *do* during Holy Week that makes you so busy?'

'Don't you know what Holy Week is?' he asked.

'Well, I do, of course, it's the week running up to – '

'If you don't know what Holy Week is, I suggest you go and sit in Westminster Abbey for five days. That'll teach you what it is.'

After Easter I sullenly went to see him at 8 The Close and he became a risen villain, to take the place of my fallen idols. He was funny, humble, honest, hospitable, genuinely interested in what I said, and rude about microphones, the Left Wing in the Church of England and the Movement for the Ordination of Women. I saw what people meant about his saintliness.

Another saintly rude person is John Sentamu, the Ugandan vicar in Tulse Hill. He speaks so fast at the General Synod that you can't understand what he is saying, but it feels like pure Gospel. He was horrid when I first went to have lunch with him at a pub on the South Circular Road. He said I was not a Christian at all, just a Christian journalist. He asked me where I worshipped, and I chose Westminster Abbey. 'I think God doesn't take any notice of what goes on in Westminster Abbey,' he said. 'That place is a shrine.' He laughed and, by his rudeness, put me at my ease. His parishioners adore him.

2) When it is banter between equals. This is harmless, and quite different from patronising banter. Here is an example.

'Your parish in good heart?'

'Fine. Lincoln surviving?'

It is two clergymen sharing a Kit-Kat in the tea-room at the General Synod, and they are asking the ecclesiastical equivalent of, 'How's business down your way?'

3) When it is unselfconsciously humble. Self-conscious humility is cringe-making, and we have all heard it in sermons. The preacher's inability to sing in tune, bake a cake, do his daughter's maths prep or understand a video manual is flaunted from pulpits all over the country. Really nice vicars are ones who can boast about their achievements, but who can also, with no ulterior motive, admit their vulnerability. I have discovered a syndrome and named it the 'one or two' syndrome. It is when clergy bravely admit the narrowness of their sphere of influence. 'How many people have you personally converted to the Christian faith?' I asked the Bishop of Lincoln. 'One or two,' he said. 'You never really know. I think I've genuinely brought one or two people to Jesus Christ.' 'How many people have rung you up in response to that banner on the wall of your church which says "Save this church: ring 081–876 0937"?' I asked Ken Bowler, the vicar of All Saints, Fulham. 'One or two.' If you ask vicars how many families now come regularly to their church as a result of having a child baptised there, the answer varies from 'one or two' to 'I can't think of any'.

Bruce Ruddock, the vicar of St Michael's, Barnes, admits his insecurities rather than being silently hung-up about them, and this is one of the things that makes his niceness unannoying. He is genuinely not sure whether he is doing things right, and asks for advice. Jack Nicholls, the Bishop of Lancaster, cheers up sad curates and priests when they come to see him by reminding them, 'There's more danger of your strengths getting in the way as a priest, than your weaknesses.' 'You're beautiful,' he tells them, even if they aren't.

4) When like sticks up for like. 'The dwarves are for the dwarves.' That cry from C. S. Lewis's *The Last Battle* constantly comes to mind in the Church of England. The archdeacons are for the archdeacons. At Question Time at the General Synod, when an

archdeacon asks a question about the livelihood of archdeacons, all the other archdeacons clap. The vergers are for the vergers. There is a National Guild of Vergers and they meet for an annual carvery meal in a restaurant near the Tower of London. Organists stick up for organists and go to an organists' convention once a year, held in 'some mosque or other' (that is an organist's word for 'cathedral'). Bishops converge regularly to encourage and pray with each other. The bishops of Leicester, Derby, Southwell and Lincoln meet twice a year for what the Bishop of Lincoln calls a 'pow-wow'. He also has a 'cell' of bishops who meet twice a year, once at Fairacres, the Anglican convent in Oxford. 'We set an agenda together,' the Bishop explained. 'We might talk about multifaith worship, or discipline, or a difficult pastoral problem. One of us chairs it, and we don't take notes. Then we go to vespers and have supper, and after that we'll have a leg-pull. Someone'll bring a wine-box or something.'

5) When it actually helps people. Niceness that would be sickly on a high street is perfectly apt at a funeral, where people are feeling bewildered and desolate. Evangelicals, we are led to believe, divide people between the saved and the unsaved. But I have seen a curate from St Mark's, Gillingham, a church where they speak in tongues, give a heartening address at an atheist's funeral in London. This was niceness: breaking your rule where you think fit. You might be against the remarriage of divorced people in church in general; real niceness breaks out if you focus on an individual couple and have compassion: surely *their* marriage is blessed by God and deserves to take place in a church rather than an office. By not laying down rules about such things the Church of England allows individual generosity to shine out.

The pressure to be the professional good chap around the place drives some priests to exhaustion, despair and therapy. Richard Christian, the vicar with two accents in Uxbridge, is not ashamed to admit that he is 'in therapy', being treated for stress. The descent of highly intelligent priests into small talk is painful to watch. Niceness spread thinly is hardly niceness at all. But it is better than nastiness.

A craving for popularity is an understandable clergy urge: the thinking is that if we like His ministers we might like Jesus as well. The fear of unpopularity leads to insecurity, and that can be dealt with in a healthy or an unhealthy way. The healthy way is to admit it, pray about it and laugh about it. The unhealthy way is to repress it and let it show in strange, obsessive mannerisms and topics of conversation.

There are few ordained villains in the Church of England. If I try to think of any, my mind alights on one particular bishop in London, who has a poisonous relationship with women at all levels, and won't allow them into the sanctuary; a sad and disastrous rector of seven parishes in Leicestershire, who has nearly emptied his churches and alienated his parishioners; another bishop, now retired, who filled his diocese with what are known as 'the scented clergy' – ones in the best black clothes, who use the most expensive incense and are, like him, pathologically opposed to women priests; and a suffragan bishop in the north, known as 'Basher' by the younger clergy in his diocese, who seems to lack all the pastoral skills required of a bishop.

But I have heard people stick up for all of these men, and explain the wonderful things they have done to help individual sufferers at individual moments. They might be horrid most of the time, but you do not think, 'This person is the Devil incarnate'. Watching a power-crazed American Christian healer on television, inciting people to cast their wheelchairs to the ground, that is precisely what you do think. Pity rather than fear is the emotion that unpleasant Anglicans inspire.

There is one particular niceness-sullying flaw that I have come across so often that it has gained the status of another Church of England syndrome. Even the heroes have this flaw – the ones who ooze hospitality, goodness and focused liking. It is the inability to be nice about the person who was in the job before them. 'My predecessor' is how the person is referred to; never by name. That maintains an icy distance, just as when a divorced mother says of a daughter, 'She's spending half-term with her father'.

The reasons are confused. It is partly the longing to make the parish look forward and be carried along by the present incumbent; it is also, probably, because the previous incumbent did some terrible thing, such as neglect the vicarage garden for eight years, or wreck the vestments by hanging them on wire hangers. But it is not a nice trait.

Human beings annoy each other. Christians annoy each other all the more because they feel so strongly about what is right and what is wrong: every action raises a theological question. Prayer is an outlet for bad temper but it doesn't get rid of it all, and it certainly doesn't solve the problem of violent personal dislike. Poisonous relationships between canons do develop. Curates despise their vicars, vicars disdain their bishops, the Mass-lover is rude about the mattins-lover in the neighbouring parish. They are all trying to fulfil their vocations and to advance the Kingdom of God. They just do it in different ways, which clash.

3

Worldliness

Evangelicals refer you to 'the text'. Church Commissioners refer you to 'the literature'.

It is a strangely grand word. Bumf has been elevated. Church Commissioners' literature is bright and glossy. It has graphs, tables, cake diagrams, paragraphs called '15.2', and question-and-answer sections to make things quite clear to the dim reader. The message it drives home hardest is this one. The Church of England used to be able to live on its endowments from benefactors of the past, but it can't any more. Church members must give more money. An extra fifty pence a week each would raise an extra £30 million a year. An extra one pound a week would transform the Church's financial position, and make everything all right.

This is a chapter about how the Church of England looks after itself. It is about money, Christian meanness and Christian generosity; and about ambition, perks and the clergy career ladder.

Money first. The public, for some reason, doesn't give a pound a week extra to the Church, however hard the message is driven home from pulpits and parish magazines. The public won't learn, rather as it won't learn to use dental floss, however much dental hygienists beg, cajole and warn. We don't *want* to spend five minutes a day fumbling with our back teeth; and we don't *want* to put a whole extra pound on to a brass collection plate, because we don't believe that those pounds are really necessary.

If you read the literature you soon understand why the Church does need our money. 'BECAUSE,' says one particular bit of literature (printed on 100 per cent recycled paper; the '100' in that statement always looks to me like 'loo', perhaps because it is so near 'paper'), 'the Church Commissioners' investment income will be flat over the next few years as a result of the recession. BECAUSE there will be increasing calls on it for 10,000 clergy pensions. BECAUSE this will leave less money from the Commissioners for clergy pay. BECAUSE this difference can only be made up by your extra giving SO THAT THE NATIONWIDE PAROCHIAL MINISTRY CAN BE MAINTAINED.'

There is desperation in the tone; written words can have decibels and those ones do. The Church is far less embarrassed to be loud in its begging for money than it used to be. Whole sermons are devoted to the subject. Machines are put in motion: dioceses have stewardship advisers, who help to run stewardship campaigns ('stewardship' is a Christian euphemism for 'giving money'; we are *stewards* of our Church). The Bishop speaks into a tape, and copies are sent to every parish to be played during the service for all to hear. Give more, is the message; give in faith. 'Store up for yourselves treasures in Heaven where moth and rust do not destroy, and where thieves do not break in and steal. For where your treasure is, there will your heart be also.' Side A ends and a sidesman turns the tape over.

There are two schools of the art of persuasion. The first is the down-to-earth school. 'We need your money. Three pounds a week is not enough. It must be four pounds.' The second is the theological school, which talks about the power of Christ's Resurrection and quotes St Paul telling the wealthy Corinthians to be as generous as the poor Macedonians. Which method is used depends on the scruples of the orator. Sometimes they are combined: a gentle, theological beginning works towards a shouting and simple climax.

The single aim is to get a pound a week extra from each of us; and we won't give it. We might for a week or two, just as we might floss for a week or two. But we fall back. The tipping mentality is rooted deeply within the British churchgoing public. We put about the same amount of money into the collection as we might leave on the saucer at a restaurant where service is not included. The Church of England, we know, is rich. We were brought up to believe that it was one of the richest institutions in the country, after the Queen and Trinity College, Cambridge. And it is Established. That makes it sound as if it must be funded by the State. How can it need more than three pounds from us on Sundays? Photographs of skeletal children stare out of newspaper pages, and lay people are more likely to give money to help *them* than to raise their weekly giving in church.

The literature fights against this tipping mentality by bombarding the reader with disturbing but true facts. Here are some. The Church Commissioners' contribution to clergy pay and housing is falling by £5 million a year, which means £500 a year less for each minister. The Church of England's historic assets are worth £3 billion, and they produce an income of about £150 million a year. But the Church costs £600 million a year to run. There are 11,300 serving clergy in the Church of England, and 10,300 retired clergymen and clergy widows. The retired ones get pensions and help with a retirement house, and the Church Commissioners pay for nearly all that. (This is church niceness: look after the elderly and the bereaved, and let the young and sprightly look after themselves. The sickly acronym for the Church's Assistance for the Retired Ministry is CHARM.) The maintenance of church buildings costs half a million pounds a day. What are we supposed to do when faced with these facts? Respond generously, and with a glad heart.

Some do. My average weekly giving to the church is one pound, which means that someone must be giving five pounds to bolster the national average. Regular churchgoing families are, on the whole, generous and efficient in their giving. They do it by deed of covenant (the literature, of course, reminds you that one pound given by deed of covenant is actually worth £1.33). The trend seems to be that more is being given by fewer. The regular C of E people pay for the casual C *and* E (Christmas and Easter) people, who would be horrified if their church weren't there any more but don't do much to support it. Tough vicars are starting to raise their wedding fees, just to show once-in-a-lifetime Anglicans that churches don't grow on trees. The total amount given by churchgoers in a year is about £50 million, and that pays for about a third of the cost of clergy stipends. The more retired clergy there are that don't die, the more the Church's money has to be spent on them.

'There are too many of us healthy old things,' said Norry McCurry, a charming old clergyman (b. 1919) at St James's, Piccadilly, who counsels the sad and goes around holding a small long-haired dog. Godly, righteous and sober lives go on for a long time. The country is saturated with retired clergymen. They congregate on the South Coast, and cluster round cathedral cities. They are quite useful to non-retired clergy who need to go on holiday, and to undertakers who call on them to take funerals. At consecrations of new bishops in Westminster Abbey, crowds of retired bishops appear to lay on hands. They get a good lunch afterwards. (You can never see much at consecrations. Unless you are very grand you are put in row P in the south transept. All you can see during the procession are fifty mitres going past. They look a bit sinister, like open jaws.) After lunch the retired bishops go back to their warm retirement homes.

The kind Church of England looks after all these people: they get a package deal. Clergymen used not to have to retire at all, and some old ones still don't because they have been in the same job since before the time when the retirement age of sixty-five was laid down. But most clergymen over sixty-five now absorb the Church's money, living frugally and safely from one year to the next.

At parish level (that is a beginning-of-paragraph expression frequently used in Church of England surveys, documents, leaflets and hand-outs), women make marmalade. The Church of England is an institution where money is raised in a thousand tiny ways. Its character is moulded by this. Every single parish, every member of every parish, can do something or not do something to help. Christians make marmalade; atheists might easily buy it, dragging their children to the church fête. On one Saturday in every September, the English countryside is thick with Christians on bicycles – loud bicycles, shoppers, single-gear bicycles, thick-wheeled Raleighs not pumped up enough – who are raising money for the churches in their dioceses by cycling to as many as possible in a day. At each church a parishioner is waiting in the porch with a biro to fill in your form, and a jug of orange squash covered with a tea-towel. It is a joyful day. The churches called 'the Muddy Saints' in north Suffolk are close together on low land and you can clock up nine in an hour if you do the five in Bungay first. Everyone says hello.

The Deity is inspiring the laity. This, say the most persuasive parters-of-lay-people-from-their-money, is how Christian giving ought to be: it should come naturally out of the joy of faith in the living Christ. His presence is with us: the roof of his house should not have a hole in it. Money is not ours, anyway; we are only stewards of it, and of his own do we give him.

Most human beings are happy to give, but we like to be thanked. If you send £200 to your old school, you get a nice letter from the headmaster. If you make a patchwork cushion for your best friend, she thinks of you whenever she sits on it. What is off-putting about Church giving is that your money disappears into a pool. No one thanks you except, perhaps, the Deity himself in his own mysterious way.

Some Anglicans are delighted to give without being thanked by a fleshly being. Evangelical churches are envied by their catholic neighbours for their astounding ability to extract money from their members. At All Souls, Langham Place, when the brass plates are carried up the nave, they are heaped with ten-pound notes. Only at greyhound racing in Wimbledon have I ever seen so many used notes change hands. I went there one Sunday and heard the Revd Richard Bewes, in his booming voice, rouse the congregation to a pitch of generosity. He had invented a day: 'Thanksgiving and Gift Day'. It was the following Sunday, and its aim was to raise £50,000 to develop Church House (the parish office). 'Now, Helen's going to come to the front and tell us why we need this money.' Helen, in a smart dress, took the microphone and explained that they needed extra offices for some of the Ministry Team, a better environment for the Admin Team, rooms for one-to-one counselling, and several kitchenettes. 'And how can we prepare for that, Helen?' 'It's critical for us to pray a lot this week.' Yes, it was, agreed Richard Bewes, so that we could improve our effectiveness for the Lord Jesus Christ in London. A man behind me said 'Amen' in an American accent so that it rhymed with 'laymen'.

All Souls has a car-borne congregation. It is 'eclectic', 'gathered', in other words, it tends to come in by car from West Kent and Surrey. The affluence of this kind of church has been one of the surprises of my research. I thought, because evangelicals didn't like silver candlesticks or jewel-studded vestments, that they were simple folk in old Triumph Heralds, who wore second-hand cardigans. Actually many have far-down-the-alphabet-registration cars and are dressed at Next. Anglo-catholic congregations, who revel in gorgeous liturgical sights and smells, are generally the ones who walk to church and are dressed in old cardies. But evangelicals give. 'Tithing' is the clever word that pricks the conscience of the giver. It is a biblical word, so if you do it you feel you are taking part in a holy and ancient tradition. Parishioners are required to sit down and work out exactly how much a tenth of their disposable income is. Sometimes it is rather a lot. So the realistic Synod has changed the suggested amount to a twentieth and put it in calculator language: 'five per cent of your net income'. A father who gets a pay-cheque of £1,400 a month after tax would be expected to covenant about seventy pounds a month to his church. His children could then put the normal pocket-money amount on to the plate and no one would mind.

The kind of conversion that happens when you are Born Again in a dramatic way seems to be the kind that makes you willing to give away your money. It is admirable and good, though slightly reminiscent of the ecstatic and mad giving that used to happen in the cult in America where the man in charge kept fifty Rolls Royces. Most parish churches in England have not yet succumbed to the booming art of demanding money. Sensitive, old-fashioned vicars find money a vulgar subject, and try to stay off it. One of the reasons why clergy choose to be chaplains rather than parish priests is that chaplains don't have to spend their lives running appeals.

The Diocesan Quota[1] hangs over parishes. Each parish is

---

[1] Its real name is the Parish Share but it is always called the Quota. 'The Parish Share or Quota' is what accurate people say, as newsreaders are taught to say 'the Community Charge or Poll Tax' and 'Jihad or holy war'.

supposed to give a certain amount a year to the diocese, and the amount always seems cruelly large. Small, cold, ill-attended churches have to pay about £3,500 a year; large, full ones, £45,000 and more. 'How is your Quota assessed?' I asked vicars. 'Oh, the Fairer Shares people come round.' (They would have a name like 'Fairer Shares'.) They sniff about, count the people on your electoral roll, find out if you have any private sources of income and charge you accordingly. The Quota is not obligatory, and some evangelical parishes refuse, on principle, to pay it, because they think the money should be spent on international evangelism, 'There's no immediate sanction if you don't pay,' said Martin Elengorn, smiling and comfortable in his office at the Church Commissioners' headquarters. 'But, in time, events will catch up with you. You might find that, if the living falls vacant, no clergyman is sent to fill it. There might be threats of amalgamation.' There are stories of vicars who don't pay their Quota finding that the diocese no longer comes to clear their drains or seal their draughty windows. It is a passive but effective form of punishment.

The shares are not always fair. Some parishes find it easy to pay their Quota. All Saints, Haggerston, in the East End of London, hires out its old church hall to the Borough Council and pays its Quota from the rent. Others struggle almost to a point of collapse. At a sad, blackened church near Seven Sisters underground station, Holy Trinity, Tottenham, I talked to Elaine Jones, the gentle and hard-worked curate. 'We have about sixty adults who come to church on Sunday. The church is desperate for money to restore its brickwork. I wasn't ordained to think about brickwork. The congregation have got hearts of gold. If they could rip their heart out and put that on a plate, they would. We're beating them with a stick.'

'Church tax is the answer,' said the sturdy and zestful organ designer Matthew Copley in his works in Surbiton. Sweden has a church tax that everyone has to pay, and you should see the organs there, he said: shining, restored, bright-sounding. But most people I talked to thought church tax would be a very bad idea. If churches were State-supported they would have a dead feeling about them: no good ladies of the village fussing about, no sense that the church belongs to and is supported by its own marmalade-making parish. As soon as you make giving obligatory you change it out of all recognition. At St Paul's Cathedral you now have to pay £2.50 for admission. This, say the people who work behind the desks, has transformed the character of the cathedral. It is now more museum-like than ever. Coachloads of French schoolchildren still come in; single girls feeling prayerful in their lunch-hour no longer do. There is a free side-chapel reserved for private prayer, but you have to pay if you want the heights and vistas of the full building.

Yet if begging doesn't work, force is the only option. The Dean and Chapter of St Paul's claim to be delighted with the charging system: it has saved their cathedral. Perhaps it is more honest and simpler to *make* people pay than to descend to the depths of cajoling that other cathedrals have had to stoop to. Transparent money-boxes that look like incubators assail visitors at cathedral doors. The art of making giving your money away seem fun is finely developed in the Church of England. Numbers with noughts on the end – £75,000 to restore the organ, for example – are written in attractive red writing on noticeboards and surrounded by a squiggly cloud done in felt pen. Vicars go on sponsored walks along ridges of English hills and are photographed, beaming and stiff, for the *Church Times*. Kind women give prizes to the church fête: it is heartening that in this supermarket age you can still come across the sight of a middle-aged Anglican woman at a hoop-la stall, aiming for a single bottle of salad cream and clasping it to her bosom in victory.

The Church of England is an inch away from financial rescue and an inch away from financial doom. High-up, far-sighted clergymen have spoken to me with childlike simplicity about money: 'If the £7.50 note were invented, it would all be all right.' 'The £2 coin will do the trick.'

I don't believe that. I think, if we all gave an extra pound, they would then ask for another pound. The trust that we ought to feel for the Church of England's handling of its wealth has been eaten away by watching the way it has sold off its old vicarages and built faceless Lego replacements. If that was meant to rescue the Church of England's finances, but didn't, how can our pound make any difference?

It will, it will, Church Commissioners' literature insists. And if we don't give it – well, terrible things might happen. It might mean an end to the parochial system.

That is a threat worth worrying about. The sense that a real end is in sight to the Church-of-England-as-we-know-it saps the confidence of rural vicars. Andrew Way, the vicar of Duxford in Cambridgeshire, sat in his garden, squinting at the housing over the wall, and said, 'I have the feeling that I'm at the end of something. The Church Commissioners' money is still a good chunk, but it's reducing; people's money is coming in but I'm not convinced that it will in the next generation. I imagine non-stipendiary ministry taking over; incumbents will have to have another job to support themselves.'

At the moment he is hanging on, running three churches and three Parochial Church Councils. He told me that indigenous Duxford people live in new housing; rich, new Duxford people live in the pretty old houses. 'The Bishop sat in our lounge and asked, "What does your parish need most?" "Renewal," I said.' There has been a bit of a renewal lately. 'We have a donkey procession on Palm Sunday from the river. We don't have foot-washing, but we always have a bowl with a towel as a visual reminder. We light the Easter fire; and this year for the first time we had an Easter vigil from 10.30 p.m. till dawn. Each person had their own Church Urban Fund candle lit in front of them. There was a dawn service to greet the Easter morning and then breakfast – Dutch Easter bread. There were thirteen people at the beginning and thirteen at the end.' The church hug has been revived: it is an old local custom. Everyone stands round the church, holding hands in a huge circle and passing a message along: 'God bless our church.' The garlands have been revived as well: little girls make garlands and are judged by the proprietor of the Duxford Lodge Hotel. And Duxford has re-started its Sunday school.

The paid clergyman presides over all this. He devotes his life to it, and his vicarage is the focal point. He is the official paid person in the crowd of voluntary helpers. 'We're very fortunate in Jennifer Gatland,' he said. She runs the Sunday school; and the country, thankfully, is full of Jennifer Gatlands in whom we are fortunate. His other helpers are a lay reader, a retired priest, five churchwardens and his wife Barbara who is the non-stipendiary parish deacon, and is also pastoral tutor for the East Anglia Ministerial Training Course.

In the future (if we don't pay our extra pound) there will be no paid person at the centre of all this. Everyone will be a voluntary helper.

I can't, however hard I try, come to the conclusion that non-stipendiary ministers are the saviours of the Church of England. There are reasons for my prejudices, and I had better admit them.

1) They are NSMs and have been trained on the SDMTS. They are assistants to the DDO. Abbreviations, in other words, line their way.

2) 'SDMTS' stands for 'Southern Dioceses Ministerial Training Scheme'. I can't believe that you get a rounded training on one of those schemes. You go to lectures, do all the essays, and you come into a theological college for five residential weekends a year. You get lots of pastoral practice: you can tick all these off on a list of necessary ingredients. But there is nothing to compare with the corporate residential life of a theological college, where you pray in silence together at seven o'clock every morning and are steeped in the lectionary from season to season.

3) The slight disdain that boarders feel for daygirls I feel for non-stipendiaries. They can go home when they want.

4) The point of NSMs was that they were meant to be 'worker priests', wearing dog-collars on the factory floor and thus bringing Christ into industry. This is a necessary and good thing. But, more and more, people who choose to be non-stipendiaries are not workers in factories and offices but well-off people looking for something to do in retirement. They settle down in a village with a pretty church and get in the way. If they have been the chairman of a firm they sometimes try to bring chairmen's qualities to the church council, sending annoying memos to everyone.

5) Their position is vague. The Church of England is vague enough as it is. This fringe of ordained but unpaid priests and deacons blurs the already blurred edges.

Some NSMs, of course, are the salt of the earth. They work seven days a week for nothing. There is no doubt that the Church needs all the help it can get.

Archdeacons speak harshly. They pooh-pooh marmalade. 'It's no good making marmalade or selling pencils with the church's name on it to raise the kind of money the Church of England needs,' said Timothy Raphael, the Archdeacon of Middlesex. He uses the dietary term 'slimming down' a great deal. His task is to slim down the number of parishes in his episcopal area. 'We were about one hundred. We've got ninety-five now, and there are a few more to go – we should get it down to ninety, which'll be slim enough to manage.' He longs to get rid of all those cheap red-brick churches put up in the 1890s for £4,000 and 'long past their shelf-life'. He hates the conservationist climate which makes it almost impossible to knock churches down.

Does the Ven. Timothy Raphael slim down his own archdeaconry? No, he doesn't. It is an enormous, jolly Victorian house in Holland Park. Now it is time to analyse the perks of the clergy existence, and the different ways in which the clergy look after themselves.

They are a bit mean with stamps. 'I send letters to vicars by first-class post and they reply by second-class,' I wrote in my notebook, fed up after Holy Week when eighteen-pence letters were trickling in, days after their franking date. The clergy live a fascinating mixture between the good life and the bad life. In some ways, they are a bit poor. The cheapest option is often the one the shopping parish priest will take: the Tesco's option. 'Five Penguins for the price of four. I'd better take those.' 'Two first-class stamps and twenty second-class, please.' 'Has the biography of Billy Graham come out in paperback yet?' There is a sense that the belt is being tightened. Holidays are frequently spent in the British Isles, enjoying the geography and teaching the children about the time, long ago, when Britain was a dense forest. (British holidays also provide fuel for liturgical debates. 'When I was on holiday with my family in Cornwall,' you hear at the Synod, 'we went into the local church on Sunday morning and were *lost*. The service was formless. In Book of Common Prayer days, you could go into any church and *know where you were*.') The horrible Family

Assortment tin, in which the biscuits all taste slightly of each other, is something you still find in vicarage kitchens. It seemed a bargain in the shop.

In some things, on the other hand, vicars are extravagant and well off. The ache of remorse that a secular person feels after a long-distance telephone call made from home in the morning is something that a clergyman does not suffer. He only feels a third of the ache: two-thirds of his telephone bill is paid by the parish. Curates agonise with their mothers for hours at peak time about whether they ought to accept the job they have been offered or wait for a better one.

'It's on the cathedral,' said Canon Christopher Smith of Sheffield Cathedral, when he took me out to lunch at the pub opposite. Canons, like journalists, can't help basking in expenses. (That was a cheap lunch, actually, because the canon was baptising the girl-behind-the-bar's baby, so she gave us a discount.)

Parish priests are cashless but perkful. That is the thing. In shops they must skimp. But their cars are new and shiny. Clergy can get an interest-free loan for a car, and it has to be a new or young car. That new-car smell is now something I associate with keen and busy young priests. And, of course, you get a house to live in. This is wonderful if you like houses and have the gift of making a room look nice with a lamp, a table, a vase and a picture. But I have seen new young parish priests cower in their free houses. Vicarages are meant to be family homes, and 'celibates' (another term often used euphemistically) float about in them, hopelessly trying to spread their few belongings fairly among the spare bedrooms. Gardens can be a sad sight. The diocese pays for vital repairs: it will send someone along to put new PVC window frames in, or to whitewash the pebbledash. But it won't do cosmetic work like clear away eight years' growth of brambles and nettles. Neglect breeds neglect.

Fr Andrew Piper, a team vicar in Lewes, comes to mind. He is young and lives in a celibate way in his vicarage which is one of the prettiest houses in Lewes. His garden is bare and the spare bedrooms barer. On each spare bed he keeps, in readiness for guests, a neat heap of blankets, and on the heap a toothbrush in a packet, a razor and a sachet of shampoo.

It is a bit sad and tidy. Money might be more useful to such a person than square-feet of vicarage. 'There's a tension in the lifestyle,' Fr Andrew admitted. 'These are houses designed for amateurish gentlemen. Something I've never resolved is how far I should live for myself, and how far for others.'

'I suppose Jesus understands what it's like to be human,' I said.

'Yes. It's the only thing that keeps us going. But it's quite difficult to translate *His* ministry, which lasted three years, into something ten times that length.'

Ambition is built into the human condition. For very good people, the desire to get to the top can be explained purely as the desire to do your best for God. But in most people this pure desire is made murky by motives like the need to be praised and the desire for money to spend on luxury goods. The clergy pay scale goes like this:[2]

Curates and assistant staff	£11,425–11,940
Incumbents & clergy of similar status	£12,830 (average)
Residential canons	£15,870
Archdeacons	£18,300–19,300
Suffragan bishops, deans & provosts	£19,410
Diocesan bishops	£23,610
Bishop of Durham	£31,380
Bishop of London	£35,560
Archbishop of York	£38,150
Archbishop of Canterbury	£43,550

Telephonists at the Church Commissioners get £12,000. The Deputy Secretary gets £60,000. The clergy are rewarded with less money but more pomp. They can rise from shabby flat to palace, from stole to mitre, from 'Mr' to 'the Most Reverend', from stall to throne. The ladder exists: they must decide whether to climb it. 'Is ambition a wicked thing?' I asked the Clergy Appointments Adviser, Canon Ian Hardaker (he is occasionally known as

---

[2]The table is an 'as at' table. It comes from the Church Commissioners' Annual Report and Accounts, 1991, and refers to the years 1992–3.

Canon Hard-On because he once gave a post-ordination-training lecture called 'Examining Our Equipment'. He is a pukka and clean-minded man; *he* would never invent a wicked nickname like that.)

'That's a difficult question,' he said, and laughed a pukka laugh. 'A *very* difficult question. Ambition is always suspect. It tends to be ambition for status. It's also suspect because we know clergy whose ambition has not been fulfilled, and who have turned into disillusioned people. The Georgian church in the eighteenth century was full of place-seeking clergy, and I think this is in our corporate memory: we still feel suspicious of that cast of mind. But it isn't a bad thing if people want to be better servants of the Gospel, to develop their ministry, to be ambitious for the *Gospel*. Lack of ambition is sometimes due to fear of rejection – cowardice, really.'

He is a one-man job-centre. About 400 job-seekers come to see him each year. He sends them a fortnightly vacancy list, and sends bishops and patrons a list of their names. This list is not shown to the job-seekers, so rumours of what it is like fly about. There are asterisks, I had heard, next to the names of unsuitable clergy.

'Is it true that there are asterisks next to the names of unsuitable clergy?' I asked.

'Absolutely not. There are no hidden signs on the list. That would be *most* improper. There is information about each person, and words from their bishops. No hidden signs.'

If you have worked for Marks & Spencer or ICI, or on the shop floor at British Aerospace, and get a calling to be ordained, you come fresh from the world of assessment sheets on which the person above you can write whether you are excellent, very good, good or have difficulties with inter-departmental relationships. The Church of England comes as a shock. It is a mess by comparison. No one assesses you except your judgmental congregation. And how you are meant to get on to the next rung of the career ladder it is impossible to know. Luck plays a large part, and knowing the right person. It is interesting, in clergy drawing-rooms, to look at the blown-up photograph on the wall or on top of the television. It is usually of the person with someone famous and grand. For young clergy or beginners, it is the person with the ordaining or

instituting bishop. For grander clergy, it is the person with one of
the Archbishops. For very grand clergy, it is the person shaking
hands with the Queen.

The system of job-finding, Canon Hardaker admitted, is 'a mess.
But I think there's a certain beauty in the mess.' Parish priests
have eight kinds of patronage from which to choose. Canon
Hardaker rootled about in his drawer and found the statistics
about patrons. Thirty-one per cent are bishops, nineteen per cent
private patrons, twelve per cent Oxford and Cambridge colleges,
six per cent the Crown and Lord Chancellor, six per cent Deans
and Chapters, and three per cent diocesan boards of patronage.
So if none of the bishops likes you, there is still a chance that a
ruddy-faced landowner might see the point in you and give you a
jolly living. It does mean that eccentrics, homosexuals, collectors
of barrel-organs, people in touch with God but out of touch with
the Alternative Service Book – flawed heroes, as the Bishop of
Edinburgh called them – can have a chance of finding a job.

It really happens, this ruddy-faced landowner business. I followed Humphrey Southern in his search for a new job, and he
told me that a landowning friend of his family's had rung him up
and asked whether he wanted a living in the country. 'And you're
not against blood sports, are you?'

Humphrey wasn't, but he didn't really want a country living.
Young clergy generally prefer the town life. Humphrey was doing
his second curacy in Walton in Liverpool, where he lived in a
small, damp curate's house next to a flyover. He loved the parish
but couldn't help yearning for the south. ('Go north, young
man!' is still what people in their early years after Cuddesdon
are encouraged to do. In the abbreviated Crockford biographies
of people who are now canons, deans and bishops you frequently
discover that they started off as 'C' (curate) in some northern and
underprivileged place. They are for ever proud of it: it was their
finest hour, to work in a rainy, dark and needy place with high
unemployment.) Humphrey put himself on Canon Hardaker's list,
and also went to see the Crown Patronage people at Downing
Street, who only seemed to have two or three unexciting livings on
offer. Livings dangled before his eyes: Portsmouth! (The Provost
was taking an interest.) Sheffield! (A needy church needed him.)

He could belong to a team in Kidderminster! He might be chaplain of an Oxford college! Humphrey prayed about it a lot. God seemed to be having a calming influence: 'There's a sense', Humphrey said, 'that whatever I choose will be *right*.' Then the man who was his Principal at Cuddesdon and is now the Bishop of Dorking rang him up and told him there was a job going in Farnham. Humphrey drove down to Surrey, saw the Bishop of Guildford, was scrutinised by the churchwardens, looked at the two churches and the vicarage and after a few confusing weeks was offered the job and accepted it.

The element of choice in the Anglican clergy's career-path is something that puzzles students at the English College in Rome. Roman Catholic seminarians prepare themselves for a life of puppethood. I sat with a few of them in a café in Rome once, after their oral exam in Italian on Christology and Mariology, and one of them said he couldn't believe it when an Anglican ordinand he had met said, 'My vocation is to work in middle-class parishes'. Middle-class parishes! How choosy and snobby could you get? The *Catholic Herald* does advertise jobs in its classified section, but they are all things like 'Head cook', 'Head teacher' and 'Assistant warden': lay jobs for Roman Catholic readers. In the *Church Times*, real vicars' jobs are advertised. 'Vicar', 'Incumbent', 'Team Rector', the advertisements say, attracting the skimming eye. 'A strong, lively suburban church seeks a new Vicar – an experienced man of prayer and leadership – who will further develop our spiritual gifts for the full ministry of all members.' 'Vicar ready for vigorous imaginative leadership and work with young families. Catholic tradition. Modern vicarage.'

'The jobs advertised in the *Church Times* aren't the ones you want,' Fr Andrew Piper told me. It is just like the 'Creative and Media' pages of the *Guardian* that young girls who want to get into publishing are told to read on Mondays: the jobs are in unheard-of places at unheard-of firms. The Church of England is getting better at advertising its more sought-after jobs. 'Advertising used to be a last resort – a sign of desperation,' Canon Hardaker said. But fairness is creeping in. Christ Church, Oxford, for example, now has a policy of advertising its livings. It has nearly one hundred, and they are quite cushy because they come with a delicious extra:

money from the Southey Bequest. Robert Southey left land to the college in the seventeenth century and said that a proportion of its income could only be spent on vicars in college livings. 'It produces an enormous amount of money each year,' Canon John Fenton at Christ Church told me. 'We dish out money for cars, dishwashers, sabbaticals, lawnmowers, school holidays. We send them all *large* book tokens at Christmas. Plus we have them for a conference here every second year. It lasts from Monday to Thursday: there are lectures and food and drink, and we take them to the theatre at Cheltenham. There's no justice. Life isn't fair. It's just a historical accident. People who have jobs in our parishes get financially hooked.'

Nearly everyone on the clergy career ladder has a dream job in mind – a dream rung. 'What is your desert-island job?' I often asked people. 'St George's, Hanover Square, strangely enough.' 'I'd love St Stephen's, Gloucester Road.' 'I'd like to be a member of the team at Holy Trinity, Brompton.' 'Dean of Windsor. No doubt about it.' None of them said, 'I want to be a bishop'; that would have been tempting Providence as well as showing off.

Parish priests on the make are an unattractive breed. The symptoms are the following: gossiping with the Bishop for hours when he comes to preach; being a member of and slightly in love with the General Synod; getting slightly *tired* of doing funerals and baptisms; being away from your parish a great deal, at conferences. Behind your back, you are scorned: 'It's archdeacon or bust for him.'

It is at precisely this stage in your clergy career that you have to stop applying for jobs and wait to be head-hunted. This relieves you of the guilt of having to be actively ambitious. It also means that brilliant people are overlooked. You only have to mention Canon Peter Pilkington and the person you are talking to says, 'He should have been made a dean.' The hopeless and weedy Church of England overlooked him, the canon headmaster with one of the best ecclesiastical minds in England. 'He was headmaster of King's, Canterbury, wasn't he, and then of St Paul's, and now what is he?' people say. 'Chairman of the Broadcasting Complaints Commission, or something? A dreadful waste.' His successor at King's, Canterbury, Canon Anthony Phillips, is another not-quite-dean.

'I got a letter from the Prime Minister,' he said, 'saying she was going to recommend me to be Dean of X. But I didn't want to be Dean of X, and I said so. I got black marks for that.'

Black marks hamper your career. You can come within a whisker of being Dean of Windsor, but if the Queen doesn't take an instant liking to you that is the end of the matter.

Where does power *lie* in the Church of England? I often wonder. With God, the Queen, the Prime Minister, the Archbishop of Canterbury, the General Synod, the Bench of Bishops, or none of these? Who chooses whom? Who makes the important decisions? Power is so dissipated that you have to squint to look at it. God's will is impossible to discern unanimously. The Queen gives final approval to the name of a bishop presented to her, and she usually politely agrees to the choice. That can hardly be called power. I have rarely heard the present Prime Minister mentioned in any explanation about how the Church of England is governed. The Archbishop of Canterbury voices his opinions and they are printed in the papers: his power is to articulate the thoughts of a Christian nation through a microphone. But he can't change the way things are done.

Power shows itself suddenly and vigorously, in unexpected quarters. This affects the career paths of the called. The enormous question of whether women should or should not be ordained to the priesthood depended, in the end, on whether five members of the House of Laity were willing to change their minds. Democracy is silly in this way. Here are some more examples of eccentric power: a diocesan bishop chooses his own suffragans. It is the diocesan bishop's treat: he can choose his friends. The churchwardens and Parochial Church Council have more power now than they used to: following the new Patronage Measure of 1989, they can say to the bishop, 'We don't want that person to be our vicar,' and the bishop has to agree. The beneficed clergyman himself is fairly powerful: he can't be thrown out of his freehold living unless he has caused either a grave scandal or irretrievable pastoral breakdown. Being a bad vicar is not enough.

Committees and councils tend to make boring decisions because everyone is trying not to offend everyone else. The tyranny of the PCC in the choosing of incumbents is a worrying trend, because *of course* PCCs will always prefer a married clergyman with a pretty wife and two children to a 'celibate' with a high-pitched voice. They might be choosing the safe but dull person over the devout but flawed genius.

So perhaps it is a good thing that the element of whim survives in the choosing of suffragan and assistant bishops.

The Crown Appointments Commission meets for twenty-four hours in utmost secrecy to choose diocesan bishops. No one knows when they meet, and no one knows where. It is in a holy place – a monastery, convent or retreat house – but precisely which is a hidden fact. The two archbishops are present, plus four clergy from the bishop-seeking diocese and six other people elected by the Synod to be on the Crown Appointments Commission. The secret meetings start and end with prayer, and prayers happen in the middle. By midnight, the shortlist has been whittled down to three or four. The next morning someone says, 'Shall we pray some more?' and they do. They want to give God as much of a say as possible.

It is all great fun, and quite smug-making for the people invited, who vanish for the night like spies, leaving no address.

The Archbishop of Canterbury was chosen in much the same secretive and prayerful way, though it took more than twenty-four hours. How, after days and nights of intensive prayer and informed discussion, Dr George Carey came to be chosen as Archbishop is one of the most debated questions in clergy circles. I have seen, late at night, two drunk clergymen trying to reconstruct the scene in the way that *Crimewatch* does; imagining the Crown Appointments Commission in conclave, re-enacting the discussion and trying to work out *how* it could have happened that someone said, 'What about the Bishop of Bath and Wells?' and someone else said, '*That's* a good idea. Let's have him. *He'd* make a good archbishop.' Was it the bravest decision, or the most cowardly decision, that the Church of England could possibly have made?

The mysterious system of clergy career paths in the Church of England has given the Anglican Communion a leader as nice as John Major; an archbishop whom nobody had heard of before, with a face which is strangely annoying because of the gap between the front teeth, who seeks to revitalise the Church and spread the Gospel, and whose wife, lugging carrier bags into the lift at Lambeth Palace, I mistook for the palace cleaning lady. I always think she is called Norma, but she is actually called Eileen.

4

Busyness

There is a certain kind of 'tum-tum-tum' sound that clergy make when they are looking through their diaries for a free hour in which to see you. I have grown to loathe this noise.

'What about this week?'

'Just looking at the diary. The next two weeks are a bit frantic. Tum-tum-tum. Then I'm going to Devon for a week. Back on the thirteenth. Can't see you *that* week. But I'm free for an hour at eleven o'clock on the twentieth. Come then. You'd better give me your number in case something comes up.'

What do they *do* all day?

I have done a bit of craning-of-the-neck in my year, and have noticed that the grander you are the longer the arrows of continuation get in your clergy diary. Curates are busy for two hours at a time, hospital visiting or down at the crem. Once a week they do a beautiful diagonal arrow from top left to bottom right: the day off. Parish priests sometimes have an arrow which lasts from Monday to Thursday: they are at a conference. The longest arrow of all lasts for three months, page after page slashed. That is for ageing and learned clergy, who have earned their sabbatical.

It was a news item in the *Church Times* when the bishops said they were going to 'write three days out of their diaries' after an important Synod debate on the priesting of women. Their general unavailability was for a brief moment transformed into availability for 'hurt' people. ('Hurt' is the adjective always used to describe the losers in this debate.) Why can't bishops always be as available as that? the reader wondered.

Fear of being under-occupied leads to making yourself over-occupied. This is especially true of the clergy, who are aware that the world is in a desperate state and that part of their vocation is to do something about it. The corporate memory which remembers eighteenth-century place-seekers also remembers absentee parish priests, living comfortably while their curates slaved and got ill. The thought of being caught at home on a weekday afternoon, doing nothing except reading the sports pages and eating a macaroon, is too much for modern clergy to bear. It is not so much, 'What will the neighbours think?' but, 'How could I live with myself if I behaved like that?' The conscience is what peers through the net curtains.

'What did you do yesterday?' I asked the Bishop of Lincoln, who came to tea in my garden a few days after his sabbatical. (We had banana sandwiches. He stared at the compost heap while talking. I wished he would stare at the pretty flowers.)

'Well, I got up at five thirty, had a shower and a shave, said me prayers – '

'Where?'

'In a little room in my house which I use as a chapel. I dictated letters into my machine thing, and then the Archdeacon came at nine for a meeting. At nine forty-five I went over to the diocesan office and chaired the Bishop's Council till twelve twenty. Then I opened a new bit of the diocesan office. Then I had lunch – a sandwichy lunch – and a bit of a rest. I took my mother to Sainsbury's and had to fill up with petrol. Then, till six thirty, I did more admin and post, and then had some supper and drove my mother over to Wakefield.'

From this we learn, more than anything else, that the Bishop of Lincoln is an honest man. We also see a few of the elements common to the clergy day: the early rise, the prayers before breakfast, the letters to write, the ability to remember precise times of day (twelve twenty, he said, not twelve thirty; he has become a time-spotter), the meeting, the ungluttonous lunch, the kind deed for the relative, the clocking-up of car miles. 'It's a particularly Anglican thing,' he said, 'to take ordinary things and consecrate them to God. There's that Keble hymn, isn't there?

> The trivial round, the common task,
> Would furnish all we ought to ask.'

Tuesday 2 June was a random day in the working life of Bruce Ruddock, the vicar of St Michael and All Angels, Barnes, in the diocese of Southwark. I joined him at ten o'clock, by which time he had said his prayers, had breakfast and shaved. He was wearing vestments because it was time for one of the weekday Masses. The day went like this:

10.00. Mass in the side chapel. Five in the congregation and two dogs. The church was cosy and cut off from the noise of weekday traffic.

10.30. Long intercessions led by Bruce. He started us off on subjects to pray about then gave us several minutes of silence. This was wonderful. It made us concentrate. A lot of praying was for the parish. 'We pray for Vera Grey House.' I thought that was someone with a double-barrelled surname but it turned out to be an old people's home which was being opened that afternoon, named after a beloved parishioner from the next-door parish.

11.00. Home (large white vicarage) to check the answering machine. A man sent by the diocese was painting the outside walls and splashing the flowers. Bruce was in a joyful frame of mind. To the Montessori school in the church hall (a source of rent), where beautiful well-brought-up children in gingham overalls fell on 'Father Bruce' and showed him their tadpoles.

11.40. Walk to the high street through alleys. 'They're *shining* with God, those children,' he said. In the high street he talked to the woman in the jersey shop and then to the under-taker and his daughter. Bruce was marrying the daughter soon (marrying in the clergy sense of doing it to two people). The undertaker's wife was ill and Bruce asked which ward she was in. He crossed the road and talked to the girl in the hair-dresser's, whom he had also just married, and to the man in the dry-cleaner's. Women shaking tins asked us for money. Vicars always oblige.

12.30. To seedy riverside pub for a cheddar ploughman's. Bruce knew the people in the pub: he hangs out with his parishioners.

1.15. Home for coffee to take away the taste of onions. Answering machine again. Four new messages.

1.30. To the parish primary school for after-lunch assembly. Not a good time for assembly. Children were crammed on the floor, full-up and sleepy. 'Sit up!' the headmistress kept having to say. Bruce played some storm-calming music on the tape-recorder and talked about God wanting peace in the world. 'And what should we be doing to help bring peace to the world?' A few hands were raised. 'Recycling.' 'Picking up Coca-Cola cans.' It was hard, Bruce found, to bring the subject back to God.

2.30. Hospital visiting. To the private hospital in Putney first, along hot corridors, to visit someone who was already being visited. Then to the National Health hospital. 'Holy Mary, full of Grace, please find us a parking space. Look! She always does!' It was the undertaker's wife who was ill this time, and she was very friendly and chatty.

3.30. To the opening of Vera Grey House. Very smart, with a fountain in the courtyard. Words from the Bishop of Kingston. Good tea. Bruce chatted to the other vicars and to some of the old people already in residence. Three old women from the old people's home next door sat crossly on a bench outside the front door, furious not to have been invited.

4.30. Home. Answering machine.

4.45. Army-type man appeared at the vicarage door. 'You the vicar?'

'Yes, I am.'

'I'm looking for Sunday morning mattins with the Cranmer Prayer Book and the King James Bible. Just moved to Barnes.'

'You've got me there,' said Bruce. 'Hmm. I don't know of one near here. You'll sometimes find mattins at St Mary's. But if you want it every week you'll really have to drive to one of the cathedrals.'

'You're Anglo-catholic, aren't you? Smells and bells. Came here once.'

'I *hope* Anglo-catholic with a human face.'

The army-type man said thank you and marched off.

5.15. Evening Prayer in St Mary's, Barnes. Four of us there, two ordained, two lay. Long reading about Balaam's Ass. Late-afternoon noises from the street (tired traffic, tired children).

6.00. To see a family about a baptism. This is Bruce's chance to meet the parishioners who never come to church. A blonde woman and a black man with huge bare toes; smooth-skinned, dusky twins. White piano, white violin on the wall, Mozart medley on CD, turned down low. 'There's one thing we want to get straight,' said the woman. 'What's the difference between a baptism and a christening?' Bruce was the model of the explaining vicar. He said the normal practice was to have the baptism as part of the Communion service on Sunday morning, so that babies could be welcomed (gathering arm-movement) into the family of the Church. The couple said they would prefer to have a separate service in the afternoon because their relatives had to come a long way. Bruce's policy is not to refuse this request; just to plant in people's minds that it is not the ideal way.

6.45. Home, hoarse. Answering machine.

I crawled away and slept deeply. Parishioners rang Bruce all evening. The urge to crawl under something is one that he feels quite often. After Christmas, especially, he is so exhausted that the crawling urge almost takes over. The only way in which he and his wife Vivien can get a proper rest is by vanishing to a cottage in Wiltshire and not giving their telephone number away.

'We all of us ought to have an eye on Heaven,' the Bishop of Lincoln said. 'This is something that has been lost in the C of E. Busyness absorbs people.' There are good and bad kinds of busyness. Bruce Ruddock's is good because it contains daylight: the walk down the high street wasn't planned in his diary; he had an hour to spare. He didn't *have* to go and visit the children at the Montessori school, but he wanted to. 'One of nature's parish priests' is an expression I have often heard used; and a property of one of those is the ability to be available, some of the time, to the casual passer-by. John Inge, the vicar of St Luke's, Wallsend, in Newcastle, rides round his parish on a bicycle being called 'Father' by little boys who are trying to make him fall off. He loves his work; he, too, is one of nature's parish priests. They do exist. They are intimately familiar with, and constantly praying for, the obscurest streets in their parish.

Bad busyness is the fidgety kind which suffocates the diary with small meetings. I always find it a bit worrying when I walk into a room in the morning and find a crowd of vicars on sofas. They shouldn't all be together in a room: they should be out and about, with their flocks. The General Synod is quite a shock in this way: hundreds of shepherds have deserted their sheep to come and sit in a cosy circle. Team parishes have team meetings once a week and this soaks up a morning: the diary arrow can be half a day long. Loneliness is assuaged by meetings and vicars need this: they are potentially very lonely indeed and they are made to feel needed by sitting in the team rector's[1] drawing-room with an agenda which begins 'Apologies' and ends with 'AOB'. Meetings, soporific though they often are, boost the morale of the people at them.

The Grantham team meeting started at '0900', but there was Holy Communion in the crypt at eight thirty. Seven members of the team came. Only the day before they had each been laying up for Eucharist in their own churches; now, here it all was again: the wafers counted, the starched white board on the chalice, the mood of holy humility. A bit soon after Sunday, I thought. Then, back to the rectory for coffee and the agenda. There were thirteen items and the first was the remarriages of divorced people in church. Case numbers 97, 110, 112, 113 and 114 were discussed confidentially (no visitors allowed) and permission or non-permission agreed. 'One hundred and fourteen's an interesting one, to put it mildly,' said Bob Reiss, the team rector, but he didn't say any more. Second item: the parish magazine. 'I'm always desperate for material,' said Sue Stagg, who puts it together. Colin said, 'Do you want me

---

[1] The word 'rector' is a word you never quite dare to use, just in case it is meant to be 'vicar'. One of the good things about teams is that they have given the word 'rector' a fresh injection of meaning. The man in charge of a team is *always* the team rector. Everyone else is a team vicar or a team curate. You don't have to worry about whether or not 'the tithes are impropriate', as you do when you are trying to distinguish historic rectors from historic vicars. (It is infuriating when people patronisingly try to explain this historic difference: 'A vicar does it vi-cariously,' they say, dividing the word slowly into two. It doesn't help.)

to write a short article about redundancy in the Forces?' Third item: *Noyes Fludde*. We skipped it. Fourth: Deanery Synod: New Times, New Ways. This was deeply serious, to do with the whole crippled state of the Church of England's resources. 'New Times, New Ways' was a euphemism for 'some of you may have to be amalgamated'. And so on. 'Five have Filofaxes, four have beards,' I wrote in my notebook. Agreeing a date for anything took ten minutes while everyone flicked from page to page. AOB, the miscellany at the end, lasted a long time too. How should they publicise the Quiet Day at Launde Abbey? Did anybody take photographs at the barn dance? A girl has asked for financial support to go on an exchange to the diocese of West Malaysia. Can the barn dance support her?

'Can the barn dance support her?' is a strangely beautiful collection of words. It is the kind of thing Anglicans say, and it stuck in my mind for days. It was good to think of these professionals with Filofaxes and agendas asking such a sweet and galumphing question.

The adjective 'busy', when used of bees, is supposed to be flattering. It means contentedly absorbed in a single worthy task, deaf to distraction. When used of a human institution, however, the word is pronounced in an emphatic and disapproving tone of voice. 'It's a very *busy* little church, the C of E,' gloomy lay people say.

It seems an apposite remark. If you shut your eyes and think 'Church of England', what do you see? I see the following: the red and white flag on St George's Day fluttering from the top of a glinting Norman tower. A large woman in stretchy leggings holding her arms in the air and singing with her eyes shut. A tiny vicar in his car driving along a narrow lane from one of his seven churches to another. A coach full of grey-haired parishioners on their parish outing to York. A photocopying machine saying 'Add toner'. A thermometer sign showing how much money there still is to raise. A woman doing the church flowers and talking to another woman about whether it is better to bite the stems, stamp on them or try to slit them with your secateurs.

Most of these are images of busyness. It is the most prominent feature of the Church of England. The image of a row of devout people in ashen clothes, sunk in silent prayer, is not one that comes to mind. Nor is the image of a Mother Teresa figure, holding ill babies and ladling out soup. The praying is usually not as monkly as that, and the busyness not as heroic and photogenic. The Church of England consists mainly of fairly happy people ministering to other fairly happy people. The vast mass of the unchurched – the millions of unemployed twenty-year-olds watching television at home, their millions of dejected parents – is a world which vicars long to reach, but which, in general, they don't, unless one of the dejected parents dies. The Church of England is not the knocking-on-doors organisation it used to be. It hasn't got enough time. In the 1950s, curates were sent on weekday afternoons to knock on the doors of every single person on the civil electoral roll. They said, 'How do you do?' and 'Would you like to come to our harvest supper?' Now there are far fewer curates and their parish visiting has to be more focused. This is a relief for the twenty-year-olds, who prefer to be left alone anyway.

Bereavement visiting is quite a thing these days. Good parishioners, lay and ordained, go on a rota and visit bereaved people for a month or so after the funeral. This is niceness, goodness and busyness combined. It helps to change a few people from unchurched to churched. But the people who get ministered to most are the regular churchgoers. I asked Kevin Hunt, the Anglo-catholic priest in Sunderland, whether he was actively trying to raise the numbers in his church, and he said, 'I see my job as to minister to the *congregation*. I hope that if I nourish them they will tell others and bring them in.'

So the regular churchgoers get Mass three times a week, and tea, outings and long chats. The non-churchgoers don't get anything until they make the decision to step through the church porch.

I spent a weekday with Humphrey Southern when he was a team curate in Walton, Liverpool, during an interregnum, before he became a beneficed vicar in Surrey. This was his curate's day.

Morning Prayer at eight fifteen in the church. Three people there. A whole chapter of Ecclesiastes. (The readings have to be crammed in towards the end of the lectionary year.) Back, under the ring road, for breakfast. To the church primary school for morning assembly, where a hundred cross-legged children chanted, 'Good

68

morning, Mr Sou-thern, good morning, everyone!' Humphrey told them the story of the Good Samaritan. He asked the question at the end and hands shot up. 'The Samaritan!' 'Yes. Very good.'

To the parish office, frequently broken into, to talk to the parish secretary who was putting letters into envelopes.

To the church for the comprehensive school's harvest festival. Not a single fresh vegetable or piece of fruit in sight. Bigga Marrowfat Processed Peas in tins. Humphrey preached to them about happiness, meals and gratitude. They sang '*Kum ba yah*'.

Lunch in Humphrey's freezing little house. Gas fires on full.

Humphrey took Holy Communion in an old people's residential home. They were up and dressed and in a village-hall-like room, all outside walls. He could only stay for half an hour because he had to take a funeral down at the crem. It was of a large and much-loved old man. Humphrey preached beautifully, causing people to weep in a healing, cathartic way. He went to the party afterwards for a few minutes.

We took his dog for a walk on one of those huge, bare bits of hilly green land you get in Liverpool. Back home for telephone calls. Evening prayer in the church and, in the evening, a school governors' meeting in a classroom.

Humphrey didn't leave the parish all day. The hours passed in a series of short, crammed visits to crowded rooms, connected by cold journeys of a quarter of a mile each.

Humphrey smokes a lot. He needs to. Holy Week is one of the most exhausting times of all, he said, because there are so many extra services to prepare. 'I managed to give up smoking for nearly all of Lent last year, but I couldn't keep it up in Holy Week.'

Clergy stress is one of those conditions, like dyslexia, anorexia and repetitive strain injury, which has existed for centuries but has only recently, in this compassionate and descriptive age, been given a name. The vertical frown line on the brow of a busy Anglican deepens earlier than it naturally should. Why should this be? In Terry Waite's and Lord Runcie's cases, the furrows are understandable. But why should the condition appear in nature's young parish priests and nature's curates?

Their job is infinite and their capacity for work finite. To adjust to this fact takes some clergy years. They tend to work too hard.

Rebecca Watts, my favourite curate of all, has one evening a week free; in the others, she gives Bible classes, goes to meetings, takes services. She is a curate on one of the largest housing estates in Western Europe[2] in a suburb of Woking, where people drive round for ages trying to find her house because all the streets look the same. She seems to be the only single person in a world of married couples with push-chairs. Her sermons are diligently and lovingly prepared, for ten or eleven hours each. Her working day never finishes earlier than ten thirty at night.

Grenville Gibbins is a curate in Market Harborough. He married Liz a few years ago and their honeymoon consisted of a take-away salad in Leicester. They are a realistic and happy couple, fat and talkative. Grenville used to work in a hosiery firm which supplied Marks & Spencer, so he is very good on standards of efficiency. Marks & Spencer used to lay down the kind of light-bulbs you had to use in the factories; the diocese wouldn't even come and change the Gibbinses' dangerous split-level kitchen into a single-level one. But the Gibbinses are delighted with their new, non-factory life, and grateful to the C of E for providing the security which makes it possible for Liz to be a non-working mother. Here are the Gibbinses on busyness:

'I have to defend his free time. We hear so many tales about clergy marriages. Your job trespasses into your private life. It's different, even from when we were working shifts. At some point during every day there was that cut-off: it was *our time*. We could do anything and go anywhere. Here you can effectively be on call twenty-four hours a day. People come and say, "It'll only take five minutes". But it's five minutes and five minutes and five minutes. You find you're solving everyone's problems but your own. We got twenty phone calls on Monday. The undertaker rang with five funerals. It was a sixteen-hour day. And you live in a goldfish bowl. People notice everything. You can't even buy a *gâteau* without being noticed.'

Sudden and macabre tasks – such as calming down a teenage

---

[2]'Everyone is a curate on the largest *something* in Western Europe,' Humphrey Southern told me. 'I did my first curacy at Rainham which has the largest commuter station in Western Europe. And now, in Surrey, I work near the largest roundabout in Western Europe.'

parishioner who is convinced that he is possessed by the Devil – are mixed, in the clergy life, with soothing jobs like counting out the wafers. On Saturday night in the magnificent parish church of Grantham, Bob Reiss counted out one lot of thirty wafers, two lots of 100, and two non-gluten wafers for the two non-wheat-eating communicants. 'Two non-gluten wafers to be put next to priest's wafer,' said the checklist. A Roman Catholic order of nuns in Liverpool make these particular wafers, he said. The two non-wheat-eaters both go to the eight o'clock Communion and they have made friends through this similarity in wafer needs. Then Bob Reiss had to slide the numbers into the hymn board. 'I sometimes wonder,' he said, 'what would happen if we ran out of numbers – if the organist chose 777, 77, 37, 127 and 7.' There are other small but satisfying tasks: locking up, for example (you have to know three or four padlock-code numbers by heart), and laying out the vestments beautifully so that they read 'IHS', or 'AΩ' if there is no maniple. All this could be seen as annoying and fidgety busyness. But it oils the wheels.

The need for diversion from life inside the square mile of the parish is strongly felt, and some parish priests become freebie victims. 'I'm going on holiday – er, a study group – to Israel for a week,' I heard one priest say to another in the General Synod lunch-hour. You hear of coachloads of clergy being taken off to Scandinavia for an ecclesiastical convention and coming back converted to the smorgasbord. *Oecuménisme* is the excuse some have to vanish off to Belgium.

Congregations like travelling as well. 'Anyone else who would like to come on the pilgrimage to Assisi, please sign on the noticeboard before you leave the church,' Fr Freddie Jackson said in St Michael's, Brighton, in a housemasterly tone of voice. He takes his congregation to Assisi more often than they strictly need. Bruce Ruddock and the Franciscan friar Brother Angelo went to Assisi *once* with the congregation of St Michael's, Barnes, and it had such an effect on people that a year later Bruce was still picking up the pieces. But the Brighton congregation has come to expect its regular pilgrimage. Evangelical congregations are taken off to Butlins for Spring Harvest, where they sing and pray for days in a huge tent. Self-catering out-houses around

Minehead are full to the last bunk-bed with exhausted and happy believers.

'What would you say your job *is*?' I asked Neil Collings, the rector of St Nicholas's, Harpenden.

'At the heart of it all is prayer and God, and the way God works through people,' he said. 'I think busyness is a fantasy. It's the only job I've ever done – I was ordained at twenty-three, I'm forty-six now – so I can't talk from any other perspective. That's very unfashionable now. You're meant to have been a coalminer. It's difficult to say, "What is a priest *for*?" I get very irritated when clergy say, "I'm bogged down by admin." Another fantasy is buildings. I don't think clergy should be weighed down by buildings. You should work out your priorities.'

Neil Collings is calm and single. After lunch every day he listens to *The Archers*, and he reads a book a day during meals. He sees his spiritual director, the Dean of Westminster, twice a year and reads the lessons for the day to himself in New Testament Greek. He doesn't go to all the parish meetings. 'And', he said, 'I have a very low opinion of the telephone.' His parish thrives; his relaxed attitude spreads out among the non-stipendiaries. The parish magazine is more full of groups and their coming events than any journal I have ever read: scout troops, old choristers, mothers, single people, couples, silent Julian-of-Norwich-inspired worshippers, young wives, all have a venue. At the centre of all this is the serene and prayerful rector, strolling about on the commuting-village green.

Church of England nerve centres are a bit of a disappointment. There is hush where you expect bustle. One of the iciest and dreariest reception desks in England is at the headquarters of the Church Army. It is in Blackheath. The building is red-brick Victorian Gothic and it stands sentinel over the railway tracks. The woman at the desk is quiet and prickly. A timid person called Joy comes down slowly from upstairs and brings you leaflets. Inside the leaflets, all is action: a double-decker bus drives evangelistically round the diocese of Carlisle, converting little boys; 'People at Street Level' are given counselling and beds; the Church Army College of Evangelism goes from strength to strength in Sheffield; senior citizens get cake and custard in Bournemouth.

Why the hush at the centre of things? There is a certain *type* of overworked-Anglican-at-the-nerve-centre and I think it must be something to do with being underpaid and working for an institution which is not run as well as Marks & Spencer. Anglican bookshops are often a bit hopeless and sad, weighed down by the constant necessity of saying, 'I'm afraid we're out of it' and 'I haven't heard of that one'. If you peer through the window of the Church Urban Fund headquarters behind Dean's Yard in Westminster, you see a gloomy, ill-lit room, milk cartons with no refrigerator to live in, and a frowning person typing. My first brush with Church House, the nerve centre of the whole Church of England machine, was an anticlimax. I plumped for the Advisory Board for Redundant Churches. What did they do? Which converted churches were they particularly pleased with? Jeffrey West, the Secretary, was the man to see, in Fielden House, which is an annexe of Church House. His office looks out on to a huddled Westminster roofscape and it was almost empty. His desk was bare except for two brown files.

'I'm in a sort of post-meeting everything-all-over-the-place mode,' he said, when I asked him the first question. 'What *is* that new measure called? The Care of Churches and Ecclesiastical Jurisdiction Measure. That's it.' He told me about extracting monies, then explained, 'The measure which controls redundant churches was the Pastoral Measure of 1983. Section 41 sets out what this body does and we can do no more and no less than that.'

'How many cases do you have on at the moment?'

'All those filing cabinets out there are full of them. It's just that I won a battle to get rid of filing cabinets and that's why I don't have any in here.' He fetched a blue booklet. 'You should also take note of the Skelmersdale Agreement of October 1986, *re* non-statutory public inquiries. By this time your readers will have gone to sleep, but never mind.'

He suggested that I read the Wilding Review, and dictated the long ISBN number of a book called *Churches in Retirement*. 'A church in use can sometimes be less well looked after than a redundant one, which receives public funds. It's certainly something we are sensitive of and sensible to, or vice-versa.'

Half an hour into the conversation, and in spite of my prompting he had still not mentioned a single actual church. But he was wearing a tatty jersey and this gave me hope. He must explore crypts and belfries in this jersey, and read tombstones.

'Are you passionate about churches?' I asked.

'I don't know about that. "Passionate" is after all a fairly loose term, isn't it? I mean, I don't know. Why people work here is not a question I feel entitled to answer. I'm a medievalist. There are only a few places where I *can* work. The job has its administrative *longueurs*, there's no doubt about that. The Council for the Care of Churches, now you might say *that's* more exciting, dealing with treasures. It would be naïve to think that all the churches out there are Beverley Minster or something.'

I tried a know-your-own-neighbourhood test, in a last effort to make him name a church. 'What about Westminster? Are there any churches around here you are dealing with at the moment?'

'Westminster? Without looking in the files I don't think I can tell you. We *have* got one and a half four-drawer cabinets. That's not to say all the churches are redundant. They are cases which have come up.'

Rainy Westminster lunch-time was approaching, and Jeffrey West showed me out. 'This is my secretary. We end up with the ridiculous situation of having a Secretary's secretary, but there you are.'

5

The Brain

S ome disappointing sermons, and why they were bad:
   Michael Till, Archdeacon of Canterbury, compline, Canterbury Cathedral, 12 January 1992. I had high hopes. We
had said the compline psalms, and the crypt was glowing in the
winter darkness. The Ven. Michael Till, handsome and reverent,
spoke softly but audibly for twenty-five minutes about trying to
understand what 'Behold the Lamb of God' meant. I tried to take
notes but couldn't, because nothing was graspable. 'Look at the
crucified Christ and you will see the child of God that has been shut
away in you by the very forces that put Christ there.' Images wafted
in and out of my head: nails and dripping blood; a frightened child
imprisoned under my skin; a mob in Jerusalem. The juxtaposition
of the mighty with the mousy is meant to wake you up, but in this
case it had a soporific effect.

> They screw you up, your parents do,
> they may not mean to, but they do.

The bowdlerised version of the Larkin poem came later in the
sermon.
   Faults: infatuation with paradox; ruining a good poem for the
sake of cleanness.

75

Nicky Gumbel, Holy Trinity, Brompton, 5 April 1992. Forty minutes. 'There are many reasons why individual Christians need to be interested in politics, and I'm going to mention just three of them.' A three-point sermon, listened to by 600 bright young Christians back from their weekend away. The quoting started within minutes. 'Martin Luther said this . . . William Temple said this . . . John Stott put it like this . . . K.S. Latourette sums it up like this . . . John Selwyn Gummer speaks of . . . St Thomas Aquinas said this . . . Owen Chadwick wrote of Shaftesbury . . . J.R. Lucas said that . . . Abraham Lincoln said that . . . Lenin himself said . . . Harold Wilson wrote . . . Let me read you something by Martin Luther King . . .'

'P' words were also used to glue the sermon together: Prayer, Proclamation, Prophetic role, Pressure groups, Participation, Party Politics, Potential, Policies, the Person.

Suddenly there were forty rhetorical questions in a row, each starting 'Whadabout?'

Faults: flaunting of shallow knowledge by endless quoting of famous people. Gimmicky and patronising use of 'P' words, as if a congregation needed them in order to remember anything. Slowness: rhetoric takes ages if you have to say 'Whadabout . . .?' forty times.

Graham Cray, St Michael-le-Belfry, York, 24 May 1992. A thousand listening. 'Christ is if you like a key to the Scriptures. It's a book about Jesus.' Then he played bits on a tape-recorder, first a Van Morrison song called 'When Will I Ever Learn?', then a Bruce Cockburn song which said 'the Bible is nothing but a burning light', then an extract from a black preacher's sermon a long time ago, taped off the radio by a man who used to be in the Talking Heads. Moral: it is wrong to pick 'n' mix.

Fault: utterly confusing, the whole thing. The taped bits of song didn't explain anything. The preacher latched on to the Woolworth's expression 'pick 'n' mix'; he used it four times, vehemently, and said we shouldn't do it.

Anthony Harvey, Sub-Dean of Westminster, Westminster Abbey, 17 November 1991. He is well-known and clever so again I went full of hope. But again I could hardly bring myself to take notes. He spoke in a parsonical voice, looking across at a distant column, about God disclosing himself, and growth being a preparation for death, and death, in this dimension, being irrelevant.

'What, then, is this eternal life?'

That question came slowly after a longish gap which I mistook for the end. Not a single illustration from real life was used.

Faults: lack of excitement. Draughty style. Too many grand-sounding generalities. Confusing about body, mind and spirit. My bewildered notes read: 'Body (decay); mind (enriched until sudden death); *spirit*'.

John McQuarrie, Canon of Christ Church, Oxford, at St Mary's, Bourne Street, on the Feast of the Assumption, 16 August 1992. He is known to be one of the few really clever theologians left, so I expected fresh and bracing thought. He spoke about the oldness of the idea of corporal assumption: Elijah was taken up to Heaven by a whirlwind, and Moses went up a mountain to see the Promised Land and never came back. Canon McQuarrie said the Feast of the Assumption was one of the most humanistic festivals in the Christian calendar. The Assumption was a glorious event in the Blessed Virgin's glorious biography, but it was also a transcending event for the human race. What he didn't mention was that the Assumption of the Virgin is not mentioned in the Bible at all; it can be traced back as far as the sixth century, and it was declared a dogma of the Roman Catholic church by Pope Pius XII in 1950.

Fault: not coming clean.

'It's the Devil getting inside you,' a concerned evangelical said to me when I complained of sleepiness and daydreaming during Church of England sermons. 'He's stopping the message from getting through.'

Perhaps the Devil has got something to do with it. Some force, certainly, is preventing enlightenened modern Anglican thought from reaching the ears of the worshipping public. It is astonishing how many sermons are less good than you hoped. The sermons mentioned above were preached not by obscure clergy in remote pulpits but by famous churchmen of our day. It is easy to pick holes in sermons and perhaps I have been unfair. Each sermon did leave the congregation with *something* to take home, even if only an odd fact about Elijah or a memorable nugget from the writings of William Temple. But we expected more than that. We expected fresh air, fire, light; we wanted to be given new insight into Jesus, fresh from the mind of someone immersed and inspired.

Some good sermons now. Dr Martin Israel is consistently riveting. He preaches, on Sunday after Sunday in his gloomy church in South Kensington, fluently, without notes. It is only when he is reading aloud that he stutters and stumbles. He is intimate with the Old and New Testaments and draws on them all the time, so you learn quite a few stories and facts; but he also convinces you that what you do really matters and is noticed. He seems to be in touch with God, and he never drones on. Canon Brian Brindley, preaching at All Saints, Margaret Street, on the Feast of the Epiphany, and dressed like a cardinal, spoke honestly about how unlikely the whole Wise-Men-of-the-East story was. He said he was 'stripping the tinsel away'. This was refreshing. He also admitted that he had preached the very same sermon the day before. George Lings, the charismatic blond vicar of St George's, Deal, sustained a good analogy between the Holy Spirit and a word-processor. His wife movingly described her first experience of speaking in tongues.

Simple teaching sermons can be good in their way. John Stott at All Souls, Langham Place, gives you a practical criticism of a chunk of the New Testament. He examines the precise orthopaedic condition of the cripple in the parable, and talks about the fascination 'Dr Luke' had with the medical condition of limbs. You come away enriched with biblical knowledge if with nothing else. The life of a saint, on his or her Day, can make good material for a sermon: at least you learn something.

It is disturbing when someone asks you on Monday, 'What did he preach about yesterday?' and you can't even remember. I went to Hexham Abbey, for example, and sat passively in the large congregation listening to a charming retired vicar in the pulpit. What on earth was he talking about? It was the day the clocks changed, so he said more than once, 'As the dark evenings draw near . . .' and told us about the light. I vaguely agreed – yes, light in the darkness, the darkness comprehending it not – but, again, there was nothing worth writing down. Our expectations of sermons are now so low that we applaud silently to each other if a sermon manages merely to be concise and honest. The biography of St Dominic, simpy told, gets more points than it deserves.

The man in Hexham Abbey also mentioned concentration camps, and this is a Church of England sermon syndrome. In over fifteen of the sixty or so sermons I heard in my year we had a bit about Dachau or Belsen or the man saying, 'Where is God now?' and the other man saying, 'He is hanging on that scaffold'. Concentration camps make compelling listening, of course. The comfortable congregation at the Edington Festival, there in order to listen to perfectly sung Anglican music, were woken up and shaken by a concentration-camp sermon on the Thursday morning. But it is a trumping subject, and too easy to preach about. The use of extreme examples is one of the things that makes Anglican sermons wash over you. We are told to love our enemies: it would be much more memorable if we were told to be slightly nicer to our best friend whom we are subtly competing against.

If you have been to a single sermon in your life in which the tinsel has been stripped away from a biblical event your eyes are opened and it becomes impossible to listen with your childhood ears to sermons which take everything in the Bible literally. The brain of the Church of England is split between those who discover that more and more incidents in the Bible didn't really happen and those who continue to scour every verse of the New Testament for minute detail and atmosphere.

The intellect is a powerful weapon and it can slash its way through the life of Jesus, killing the idea that he was born at Bethlehem of a virgin with cattle lowing over his manger, killing the idea that he came out of his tomb and gloriously ascended a few weeks later. He did it metaphorically but not literally, say liberal Christians; what matters is the Reality that these metaphors point to. He didn't even do it metaphorically, say non-believing theologians. A. N. Wilson demonstrates what happens when you probe the New Testament to its factual depths, not allowing yourself to *want* Jesus to be the Son of God just because it is such good news for modern man. All that you get, if you so probe, are chinks of authenticity hidden in a mass of fulfilling-of-the-Scriptures, every verse echoing a prophecy in the Old Testament.

Lay Christians, when faced with all this, have to decide either to give it all up or to cling to their faith by other means. We want it to be true. We have decided to give it the benefit of the doubt. If Jesus really did bear our sins in his own body on the tree there is hope for us, and God loves the world. So we allow woolly but overpowering feelings to come along and swamp even the powerful intellect. The feelings might be something like these: think of George Herbert: *he* was a Christian, and what a man! He knew. Think of all those monks and nuns who have shut themselves away, so firmly do they believe. They are praying for me at this very moment, probably. Why has Christianity lasted this long if it isn't true? Think of those Chadwicks, Owen and Henry: they are two of the cleverest men alive and *they* believe. We are told to have a childlike faith, anyway. The Apostles were simple fishermen. C. S. Lewis said that Jesus was our friend and that we had to stick with him through thick and thin, as we would with our best fleshly friend. Think of Bach's Passions: could all that music have been set to nonsense prose, and be sad for nothing?

Woolliness, in other words, can be put to good use. It keeps faith alive where rigorous factual probing of the Gospels might kill it. Christianity *might* be true, so let's believe that it is, until definitively proved not to be. If we go to Heaven we will know that it is; if we go to oblivion we won't know that it isn't because we won't know anything.

Christian thought, as imparted to the laity from the pulpit, ignores one enormous possibility: that Christianity might be 2,000 years of wishful thinking. The very foundation of Christian thought is the leap of faith which leaves the ice-cold intellect behind. So the hand-out at Oak Hill Theological College called 'How do we prepare an expository sermon?' goes:

(1) Pray!
(2) Select your text.
(3) Read and analyse the text.
    Do exegesis not eisegesis.
    Look at context and content.
    Consult commentaries for clarification.

Praying has an instant de-intellectualising effect, putting the sermon-preparer into the realms of faith and trust. The thinking comes in section (3) and is of a different kind: it is long Greek words which look alike but mean opposites (exegesis means bringing meaning out of a text; eisegesis means bringing dogma into a text). It is hard enough, in other words, to learn long Greek words and to learn how to break a text down into its parts, without questioning the overriding truth of Christianity and discussing whether it is all a figment of St Paul's imagination.

I spent a day at Oak Hill and watched the brain of future clergy in the making. What I noticed was that learning to be nice and good, and to interrelate with your fellow human beings, are as important in the college as learning to be clever. Before lunch there was a 'Communication I' class given by the delightful and accessible Principal, Canon Gordon Bridger, who stood in front of a whiteboard with a squeaky pen. The subject of the class was house groups — small weekday evening meetings of members of the congregation for chatting and Bible study — and why they are a good idea. What Canon Bridger did not do was tell us what to think. He asked us to split up into pairs and decide between ourselves what reasons we would give a PCC to convince it that there should be house groups in the parish.

Paul, an inspired skinhead, was my pair.

'Well,' I said, 'I suppose it's good to be able to discuss last Sunday's sermon and decide how to act on it.'

'It's good for understanding,' said Paul. 'And that leads to prayer.'

He wrote '1. Understanding → prayer' in his notepad. We ploughed on, imagining with all our powers of imagination this necessary house group — the open Bibles, the biscuits, the calm, the homely sofas in the evening. The classroom was in a din of discussion. 'All right!' said Canon Bridger, 'Let's hear what conclusions you've come to.'

'It's good for lay people to meet each other and care for each other,' said a woman by the window.

'Yes,' said Canon Bridger. 'It affirms the ministry of the laity.'

He wrote 'Ministry of l. affirmed' on the whiteboard. Fifteen minutes later the whiteboard looked like this:

Ministry of l. affirmed
Pastoral care
Good for Bible study/Application
Evangelism/learning/worship
Prayer – confidentiality
Relationship and worship
Leadership skills
Unity and mission
N.T. models. Acts 2:46

'As usual, you've worked it all out for yourselves,' Canon Bridger said. 'Here's a hand-out for you to keep.' The hand-out was called 'Communicating in small groups'. (Small groups is their correct name because sometimes they are not in houses, and the ones that aren't don't want to feel left out.) Here, in perfected and typed-out form, was what we had all just discussed. It was categorised into five sections and twenty-two sub-sections. There are, for example, four kinds of group: the family group, the small group, the congregation and the celebration group. (N.B. Jesus related to each of these different-sized groups: the three, the twelve, the seventy, the crowds.) There are ten biblical texts which show that the small group has an honourable history. The small group meets human needs. It meets:

1) The need to *communicate* with others
2) The need to make *social contact* with others
3) The need for *mutual support*
4) The need for *solidarity* with others
5) The need for *group identification*
6) The need for *social status*
7) The need to be with people who share a common *purpose* or *interest*.

Church buildings have the following limitations:

1) Immobility
2) Inflexibility

3) Unfriendliness
4) Pride
5) Class

The small group, on the other hand, is 'flexible, culturally adapted, informal, personal and friendly, giving identity, security and fellowship'.

We came out of the class for lunch, our heads spinning with abstract nouns. Most of the facts on the hand-out were pretty obvious: you don't need a hand-out to tell you that some groups are larger than others. We had not battled with arguments. What we had learned was to listen to what other people had to say – to *build* a hand-out together.

The urge to categorise is a strong one in the evangelical wing of the Church of England, and hand-outs like that can perhaps be blamed for nurturing the urge. The home of the three-point sermon is St Helen's, Bishopsgate, in the City of London, where the rector Dick Lucas has inspired hundreds of young clergy to preach in the way he does: by going through the text from verse to verse and discussing the three main points we learn from it. He let me read his copy of *Preaching and Preachers* by Dr Lloyd-Jones in his drawing-room, and I noticed that he had gone through a chapter writing one, two, three in the margin, dividing it into point-sized chunks. 'Amen!' he had also written up the side of one paragraph. He is a brilliant man, keen to preach the Bible and not to leave out the frightening bits such as Jesus saying there would be wailing and gnashing of teeth. 'A wonderful preacher doesn't mean a wonderful orator or a wonderful after-dinner speaker,' he said. 'A preacher isn't a preacher unless he preaches the Bible. You've got to have something to preach that isn't your own. Liberalism doesn't produce great preachers because in a sense it doesn't have anything to preach.'

I asked both Dick Lucas and John Stott, the two best-known evangelical preachers in England, whether there were any brilliant young preachers coming up the career ladder. They conferred, and said that they couldn't think of any. This was depressing. 'Why is preaching getting worse?' I asked Dick Lucas.

'I imagine that the great Victorian preachers had a clear

morning, don't you?' he said. 'I don't think you have a clear morning now.'

The busyness of the modern sermon-preparer leads to formulaic sermons because they are easier and quicker: rather than being faced with huge questions (Why does pain exist? If Jesus knew he was going to rise again, was the Crucifixion really as awful as all that? Do bad people go to Hell? What percentage of the time does prayer bring the prayed-for result?), you can find three particular points from a finite text and talk about them. Categories sound good, but sometimes they are a substitute for thought.

The word 'ordinand' used to bring to my mind the image of a single pale young man in a study frowning over a bit of Hebrew. Now, after days spent in some of the theological colleges of England, the image has changed to a bearded and much older man, or a plump and married woman, laughing and sitting on the grass with other married people, and their children running around in circles as at a wedding reception. At Salisbury & Wells Theological College, in particular, the marriedness of the ordinands hits you. At lunch, you see not rows of single and hungry essay-writers but family groups. Sometimes the mother is the ordinand, sometimes the father. They give their children soup and Christian salad. Notices say 'Children welcome' and 'Do bring your spouse'. 'Spouse' was the word I heard used more often than any other in my day at the college. It covers both husband and wife, in the same clever way that 'parsonage' covers both vicarage and rectory. The place is overrun with spouses. The eight members of the tutorial staff alone have twenty children between them. If I were a single student I would feel utterly miserable and would pray and pray for a spouse of my own.

Families together provide good practice for niceness. Any recent ex-ordinand from Salisbury & Wells is well trained in the art of getting on with other people's children. I found it impossible to guess whose father was whose, so much did children transfer from man to man for new games. But all this interrelating does mean that students have less time and energy for silent poring over books.

A growing trend in theological training is to spend more time on parish placements (getting practice in real parishes) and less time doing academic study. This seems odd to me. As you are going to be doing nothing *but* parish placements all your life wouldn't it be better to spend your theological college years preparing the ground intellectually, steeping yourself in the Early Church, the Caroline Divines, the Victorian Church Parts I and II? Wouldn't this feed your sermons for years, and teach you how to think? Won't you go to enough hostels for the homeless in later life? Do you have to go to them now in order to learn your theology?

I encouraged people to agree with me about this, using the 'Don't you think . . .?' construction. Generally, middle-aged ex-Cuddesdon men of the 1950s agreed, ordinands of the 1990s disagreed. 'You learn far more by actually going *out there* and trying to put your dry theology into practice,' a woman at Salisbury & Wells said to me. Here are some extracts written by a first-year student called Viv Young, describing a typical day at the college. It is part of the bumf that prospective students are given.

8.30: Morning Prayer. This week's worship group focusing on a mosaic, some of the pieces askew, some missing. It filled my mind with images through the fifteen minutes' silence.

9.40: Second day of New Testament unit on 1 Corinthians; spent some time with Dave, Peter and Jenny sorting out the significance of body (!) before we reported back to the whole group. Course notes handy, but as usual it was the discussion that really got the ideas going.

11.15: Last session on 1 Corinthians. The discussion went on so long I only just managed to get to . . .

12.40: Midday Eucharist. My group's worship week. I had to read the Epistle. Guess what? A bit of 1 Corinthians.

2.15: Weekly visit to Sarum Centre for training mentally handicapped adults. John, nineteen, remembered how to write his address from last week – big grin, everyone grinned back – great. Julie very withdrawn in a corner – tried quietly to get her to talk, didn't want to push it. Trouble at home, perhaps. Eventually we carried on with a jigsaw between us. A wrench to leave her.

4.45: Back at college, a review of last week's group handling of

the worship. Constructive comments from staff and students
. . . on the whole.

6.00: Home. Daughter cooked tea; ingredients unidentifiable,
appearance amazing. Made suitably appreciative noises and
ate. Tasty. K and J. dropped in from college for a drink.
Between us, we mended my typewriter. Now only five letters
inoperative.

Except for the fifteen minutes' silence at the beginning, the day
is spent talking, laughing, helping, and being *out there*. Raw
academic study plays no part in the day. The Epistle to the
Corinthians comes alive not through lectures but through the
interrelating of Viv with Dave, Pete and Jenny.

Exams still happen. You can't be ordained without, at some
point in your training life, sitting in a silent row and answering
Three Questions Only. It is comforting to know that every curate
and vicar (like every doctor and lawyer) has had to pass exams.
Bad theology does make its way to the chancel ('Lord, we welcome
you to this church!' I heard a minister at All Souls, Langham Place,
say. Whose house does he think this is? I wondered) but not often:
usually the fault is weakness and woolliness rather than getting it
wrong.

One of the things I liked about St Stephen's House was that if
you knocked on someone's door in the middle of the afternoon
they were generally there. 'Come in.' The sight was pleasing. An
ordinand, a desk, open books, a fountain pen with its lid off, a
crucifix, choral music on CD, a potted plant. Here, I felt, people
did spend time on their own, grappling with ideas.

A third of the students are married and that, for nowadays, is
a small fraction. They all have to be resident, even on Sundays,
and the married people live in a married annexe across the lawn.
They are constantly scuttling backwards and forwards for services
and meals: attendance is obligatory. At seven in the morning every
ordinand is up and sitting in silence in the chapel in an allocated
and non-transferable pew. Morning Prayer follows, then Mass.
Life is quite monastic. Students have jobs: guest master, bar tender,
almoner, sacristan. The staff wear clerical dress. The ordinands
wear polished shoes.

The words on the whiteboard at the Ethics lecture I went to were harder than the ones at the House Groups class at Oak Hill. They were:

Teleological
Epicureans
speciesist
deontology.

The lecturer said the word 'utilitarianism'. But he didn't then say, 'And you know what that is, don't you? The greatest happiness of the greatest number.' This was marvellous. Lecturers normally can't resist saying 'the greatest happiness of the greatest number' when talking about utilitarianism, and it is *not necessary*. We learned about it when we were fourteen. The lecture was generally not patronising. We learned about Rule Utilitarianism and Act Utilitarianism, and we were given a hand-out to take away. There were essay titles on the hand-out and each student would have to do four in the year. Examples:

Are the grounds of goodness firmly rooted in the Godhead, or are they somehow independent of God?
What is the significance of Old Testament law for Christian Ethics?
Is loving an enemy ever morally suspect?

Essay questions ought to be daunting, and those are. And because everyone had been to Morning Prayer at dawn the lecturer could say, 'That's what the reading from Deuteronomy this morning said,' and get a nod.

The ordinand who showed me round was a charming man called Mark Oakley, a theology graduate doing his M Phil at St Stephen's House. His subject is a contemporary American theologian who is now at Harvard, and the questions which haunt Mark are ones like, In a relativist age, how can theology make absolutist statements?

Of course I had hoped to meet outrageously camp gay men (St Stephen's House is said to be full of them), calling each other Rachel and Janet. Mark showed no signs of being someone like that. I tried to guess who was. You really never know, unless you are gay yourself. A single gay man would have a horrible time at the kind of theological college where everyone was married. But at St Stephen's House he can become fully human (that is one of the things you are always being told to do in sermons). 'If you are a single gay man,' said Teehan Page, an essay-writing married ordinand in his room, 'this is a safe place to learn a good trade. Chichester and Mirfield are the only two other theological colleges where homosexuals are not (a) patronised to death or (b) hounded to death.'

Fr Edwin Barnes, the Principal, has to go to 'The Concept of Residence' conferences, fighting his cause that residential training is a good thing because it instils in people a discipline of prayer, study and corporate silence. He also pleads that ordinands in their early twenties are often preferable to forty-year-olds. This is an unfashionable view. Far more people think that older ordinands must be better because they have seen the world a bit. Fr Edwin suggests to committees that younger ordinands are more willing than older ones to expand their horizons, to be moulded, to think life-changing new thoughts. The Director of Studies agrees: 'Give me the youngsters any day!' he said at elevenses. 'It's a load of *bunkum* that you ought to be experienced. The young are much more flexible. The worst of all is the forty-year-old middle management executive who wants a change of life, and whose wife hates the idea anyway.'

The ideals of residence and youthfulness reach their apogee at a wonderful institution in Durham called the Society of the Sacred Mission. It is the closest the Church of England gets to a junior seminary, and I was impressed with the kinds of brain I saw being formed there. Boys aged between eighteen and twenty-one who suddenly feel they have a vocation to be priests, but have no A-levels because they left school at sixteen, can go there and live a strict corporate life presided over by a monk called Fr Jonathan. They do their RE and one or two other A-levels at the sixth-form college across the road, and they go back to the house for all meals, and for daily Mass, Morning Prayer, the Midday Office, evensong and compline sung in a polygonal chapel.

Corporate gardening was going on when I arrived on a hot

Tuesday afternoon.[1] Fr Jonathan was presiding and working harder than anyone else, as good monks do. 'If there's one thing these lads have in common,' he told me, 'it's a conversion experience at the age of about seventeen.'

The rigorous life suits these boys. One called Mark was joining together two bits of netting to put over a flower-bed. He had been told to. He was wearing a pink T-shirt with a brooch on it in the form of Christ hanging on a cross except that there was no cross – it was an arty brooch – and he said 'sort of' four times a sentence. He was humble, kind and dedicated – just the sort of person you hope will lose his shyness, pass his exams and succeed. He had spent the years after school selling windows by telephone.

Timothy, who comes from Stillington in north Yorkshire, was making a fishpond with five other clever, T-shirt-wearing boys from the north. He showed me his room in the back cottage: tidy, with a prayer desk and a television he is not allowed to watch. 'I think of it as my penance,' he said. The boys are, in general, keen on penance. Getting teased for wearing Christian sandals is something they also consider a penance. So are the house duties: 'I'm on Grub Department.' 'I'm on domestics.'

'Happy St Barnabas's Day!' they said to each other after early-morning Solemn Mass the next day. They meant it: on feast days, talking is allowed at breakfast. The acts of St Barnabas are never forgotten if your day at the age of nineteen has been altered because of him. Fr Jonathan, instead of reading his Iris Murdoch novel in breakfast silence, talks, reads out some of his letters, and explains about Arius and Origen to panicking boys before their exam.

They will probably not be PhD students, these boys; but calibre is not the only quality important in a religious brain. Not showing off is just as important; thinking rather than cribbing; reading books on your own; praying in a clear-minded rather than a woolly way.

*   *   *

---

[1] The garden needs it. The Society of the Sacred Mission lives in the house which used to be the vicarage of St Nicholas's, Durham, but was sold by the Church Commissioners. The last vicar and his wife to live here were Dr and Mrs George Carey. They were not horticulturalists.

When I asked the Bishop of Newcastle questions he spoke first to his dog and then to me.

'Are there fewer really *clever* theologians now than there used to be?' I asked. 'I get the impression that clergy are more interested in being pastoral now than in being thinkers.'

He looked at the dog. 'What makes her think *that*? What shall we tell her? Hmm. *What* a question!'

He looked at me. He is small, old and polite and we were drinking sherry. 'I would not say that was true. Paul Avis, a country vicar in Devon, writes prolifically. John Clark, the vicar of Longframlington, has defined the canon of Walter Hilton's works. The rector of St Stephen's, Hackington, in the diocese of Canterbury, wrote a learned work on J. P. Liddon. It is an *enormous* reinforcement to the Church of England that the Regius Professor of Divinity at Cambridge is now the Bishop of Ely.'

That shut me up. The Bishop of Newcastle is himself one of the brains of the Church of England. He is so steeped in the sixteenth and seventeenth centuries that some of the clergy in his diocese believe that he would quite *like* to have his head chopped off by a monarch for a reason no one understands. His drawing-room is book-lined. He reached for Luther's primary works to show me, in the essay called 'The Babylonish Captivity of the Church', how Luther was drunk on St Paul. The Bishop was not comfortable talking about homosexuality: 'It is difficult to know how you deal with it – as you know, some of the problems are *medical*.' But as soon as I asked him whether the writings of Lancelot Andrewes and Hooker were still affecting the Church today, he floated into bliss. 'Ah! There you are! The documents of ARCIC are breathing the whole spirit of Caroline Anglicanism.' This is his real interest. In this subject, he basks.

There are pockets of intellectual excellence still to be found in the Church of England. *What* a loss to the brain of the Church of England Rowan Williams was, people say. He is one of the brains but he has changed from being Lady Margaret Professor of Divinity at Oxford to being the Bishop of Monmouth. A pastoral urge swept over him, and off he went. Bishops hardly have time to be academics. Most cathedrals have one canon theologian who is allowed to spend less time than the others at meetings and more time hidden away behind books. But it is getting harder to do that: administration seems to take more and more time, and one Diocesan Board seems to create another. The Canons of Westminster Abbey are still overwhelmed with gratitude towards Queen Elizabeth I, for laying down in 1560 the rule that three of them must have exactly half of their time free to devote to 'the wider church in the wider world'. 'She was brilliant. Absolutely brilliant,' said Colin Semper, the Canon Treasurer. 'The three are me, Canon Harvey and Canon Bates. I broadcast, Canon Harvey writes books and Canon Bates is a teacher and trainer. In today's Church of England the number of jobs where that specification is given is very small.'

For the mass of overworked clergy other ways have to be found to keep the brain oiled. It can go rusty all too easily. Clergy have little time for reading. Archbishop Ramsey used to go into vicars' houses and notice when the books stopped: none post-1940, for example. Nearly all the clergy I have spoken to are highly aware that they ought to read more than they do, and some really try. Richard Ames-Lewis, the vicar of St Mary's, Barnes, goes on retreats to Bede House in Kent and takes a pile of improving theological books. Bruce Ruddock, his neighbour, tries to spend a Wednesday a month in Sion College Library on the Embankment, rich with theological books and periodicals and pitifully under-used. Neil Collings in Harpenden has started three New Testament Greek classes, which his parishioners adore.

There is a danger, if you read a lot, of being unable to resist quoting others rather than thinking for yourself. It is remarkable how many of the Archbishop of Canterbury's lectures start with somebody else's words: 'It was H. L. Mencken, the American humorist, who once said . . .' 'Voltaire thought . . .' In a shortish lecture at the University of Kent he managed to quote Gore Vidal, Nietzsche, Gertrude Himmelfarb, E. M. Forster, Matthew Arnold, Basil Mitchell, Sir Peter Strawson, Iris Murdoch, Bertrand Russell, Jonathan Sacks, William Temple and Hans Kung.

Knowing how to use knowledge is as useful as knowledge. Sometimes, in the Church of England, knowledge is flaunted. This is excusable in young curates, fresh from theological college, who can't help rebuffing your comments by saying, 'That's a really

Kantian and Back-to-the-Enlightenment idea'. But I have heard grown-up vicars use Greek words where the English one would do just as well because they both sound alike anyway. 'These are phy-sical phe-no-me-na, but they have a theo-lo-gical significance,' said John Stott, very slowly, in his sermon. 'Healing is a sem-aion: a sign.' 'It is the li-turgia,' I have also been told. 'We are all la-os – laity.' 'We are part of the e-ccles-ia.'

Neil Collings, on the other hand, said interesting facts about Greek – facts that his Harpenden parishioners had just learned in their class and were pondering. 'D'you know, the Greek word for forgiveness comes from the starting line at a racecourse. It suggests lifting and releasing, horses galloping off. Isn't that wonderful? And God *encamped* with us. That's much better than "dwelt", isn't it? It suggests impermanence, travelling.'

Brains are nourished by untampered-with morsels of information like those.

6

The Sense of Humour

Sometimes you can't help wishing that the Apostles had written more down. It would be fascinating, for example, to know whether Jesus ever laughed. He does not laugh once in the Bible; he weeps. And if you look in Cruden's *Concordance* to see if he ever even smiled, you find that the index goes straight from 'Smelling' to 'Smite'. No one smiles in the Bible, and most of the laughing is laughing to scorn.

But modern Anglicans like to talk about Jesus's wit. Finding themselves being funny, they justify their behaviour by clinging to the thought that Jesus himself was funny. He turned water into wine at a wedding; he told everyone to consider lilies; he hung out, Prince Hal-like, with drinkers; he said that you had to go back into your mother's womb; and he spoke in a shocking and compelling way with what Gospel psychoanalysts hope was a twinkle in his eye. The advice in the Sermon on the Mount, given by someone else, could have sounded dreary and confusing and the great multitudes of people from Galilee and from beyond Jordan would have gone away. That first sermon, and countless sermons ever since it, needed wit.

Was there laughter in the Garden of Eden? I worry that there wasn't. What would there have been to laugh about? Nothing was wrong. Something has to be a bit out of place for there to be

93

any reason for laughter. The closest I have come to a Garden of Eden-type joke was in the beautiful walled garden of West Malling Abbey in Kent, on a Sunday afternoon, when Sister Mary Paul was taking the guests for a walk to the Cistercian barn.

'Oh, look!' said Sister Mary Paul.

A hollyhock was growing, on its own, among the Brussels sprouts.

'It *wants* to be there,' said a guest.

We laughed.

It was not very funny. The only reason it was at all funny was that the poor hollyhock was not where it was supposed to be. In pre-Fall days there would have been no such thing as a 'wrong place' for a hollyhock to grow, so there would have been nothing to laugh at at all.

And are they all laughing at the heavenly banquet? Laughter is so wonderful that you can scarcely imagine Heaven without it. But, again, what could they be laughing about? Not about us on earth, struggling away with our illnesses and overdrafts: *that* wouldn't be very heavenly behaviour. Not about the funny food you get at the heavenly banquet: *that* would be a bit ungrateful. Where everything is delicious and perfect, nothing is funny.

The Pale Copy theory is one that helps to solve this problem. The theory is popular among imaginative Anglicans because it is so intriguing and gives you something to strive for. It is the theory that perfection exists, but not on this fallen earth. The banana you are eating is a pale copy of a Garden-of-Eden banana. The Brandenburg Concerto you are listening to is scratchy and out of tune compared with the one you might one day hear at the heavenly banquet. There, no cat-gut or horsehair will be needed to make the sound. Laughter, similarly, exists in Heaven in a perfect, non-cruel form. On earth, our sense of humour is tainted by the Fall. Just because *we* happen to find something funny it doesn't mean God does. Our laughter might just be the voice of the Devil working in us, inciting us to belittle our noble thoughts.

The God Puts Bad Things to Good Use theory helps to solve the problem of why laughter plays such a large part in Anglican life. Human laughter is nearly always at someone's or something's expense. But laughing relaxes people. If a speaker is funny you like him more, and you will listen to him. You might be fooled into laughing at yourself, and we all know that there is no better medicine than that. The uncomfortable fact about earthly humour is that it has got to be a little bit cruel to be really funny. Hollyhock humour is all very well, but it is a bit unsatisfying (to the same degree that it is unsatisfying when someone washes your hair and tries to be gentle. 'Harder, harder,' you say. You want it to hurt.) I have read theories in Christian books that the best humour is when you are laughing *with* rather than laughing *at*. I'm sure it is the best humour, but it is not the funniest.

Anglicans specialise in sweet humour. The fear of blasphemy is a powerful emotion, and so is the fear of being hurtful to other human beings. In the middle of the spectrum of humour, which ranges from the hardly-funny-at-all to the creasingly funny, the Church of England is mostly to be found in the long band in between – the *quite* funny. *Church Times* cartoons make you happy. They are about vicars and microphones, or vicars and organs, or vicars and the collection; there are churchyard jokes, bat-in-the-belfry jokes, Harvest Festival jokes. Human nature is teased, and the vicar is always addressed as 'Vicar'. Before Guy Fawkes night, two little boys to passing man in dog-collar: 'Thanks, Vicar – er – actually, "penny" was more a figure of speech.' It is touching, and telling about the poverty of the clergy; but, as I was taught to write in essays on Molière, it does not produce a belly laugh. The *Church Times* diary, written by a different person each week, is similarly witty and charming, brimming with affection for fonts, autumn leaves, children, country lanes and hymn tunes. But, for guffaws, the browser at the news-stand would go for *Private Eye*. 'Three billion Archangels axed as recession bites, by our Celestial Staff. On other pages: Never a crossword up here, p. 24. Unfunny cartoon by Leonardo, p. 94.' That really is funny and you cut it out and keep it. But it verges on the blasphemous.

The fact that exclamation marks make things less funny rather than more funny is something that many Anglicans have not grasped; and use or non-use of exclamation marks is a useful sign to distinguish people who are trying to be funny and not succeeding from people who are. Round-robin letters sent by

Christians abroad to all their friends at home are usually riddled with exclamation marks. From one photocopied letter, here are the exclamation-marked phrases:

One ostrich had just laid an egg – a huge egg!
Some visitors may object!
It provides us with a deadline to get things done by!
all sorts of animals including *all sorts* of people!
(quite harmless!)
(perish the thought!)
they seem to squawk *all* night long!
It is amazing how noisy the countryside is!
noisy neighbours (!)
Phew!
I shall need some refresher courses!!

'Perish the thought!' and 'Phew!' are interjections, so the exclamation marks are justified. The others would be better not there. They are meant to cheer the reader along, but all they do is exhaust you, forcing you to read the sentences in an exclamation-marky tone of voice. Really funny writers don't need them. The *Church Times* is mercifully free of them, and that is one of its strengths. Harry Williams hardly uses them and he is one of the funniest writers in the Church of England. He is a Mirfield monk now, doggedly praying and being quite antisocial with the other Fathers. The gooey title of his autobiography, *Some Day I'll Find You*, does not prepare you for the delicious wit of the book, or for the movingness. He describes his transformation from a zipped-up young Anglo-catholic, worshipping a monster God, via a terrible depression, to a freed and fully human man, able at last to pray. He is honest, and doesn't use any Christian guff. One of his friends taught him the useful lesson that if you are offering to share your umbrella, always offer to share it with two people, so you can hold it in between them and keep dry.

That is *not* behaviour that the saint who tore his cloak in half would approve of. But it is honest about what human beings are like. It is funny about human nastiness. The honesty makes me like him more than I would like the saintly cloak-tearer.

The Church of England laughs at itself, and this is healthy. It is a truism that Anglo-catholics laugh at themselves more than evangelicals do, because evangelicals are frightened that making fun of anything to do with Jesus is blasphemy. You will find Anglican catholics having long and hilarious conversations about priceless vestments; you will see them sniffing incense in packets in shops and saying 'Mmmm!' with sensual breath. The St Stephen's House ordinands were unimpressed that the evangelical Wycliffe Hall ordinands down the road refused to buy raffle tickets for their good cause, because it counted as gambling. 'Oak Hill came here to play soccer,' said the Bursar of Salisbury & Wells Theological College, 'and one of our students censed the touchline and the goal. The Oak Hill chap in the prayers afterwards made it clear that he was *not* amused.' Anglo-catholics have lots of toys to worship with and they play with them.

Even so, the truism needs modification. Anglo-catholics talk about humour a lot, and they can be hilarious in the vestry, drooling over the cope chest. But Anglo-catholic services can be utterly humourless, and cause girls to get the giggles until they almost burst in the po-faced atmosphere. Servers just *don't* smile. Concelebrants wear expressions as rigid as the expressions on the faces of icons. Processions are formal and the people in them hardly ever catch your eye and smile at you. Fr Gerard Irvine smiled at me once from a procession at St Cuthbert's, Philbeach Gardens, and that was marvellous. It was human, and punctured the pomp. Evangelicals may not make wicked jokes about sex and jewels, but fun and laughter play a huge part in their worshipping life. Their sermons are illustrated with humorous squiggly drawings done in felt-pen on squares of transparent plastic and placed on the overhead projector. Notices are casually delivered. Members of the congregation put their hands up in the sermon, when asked questions. On the walls, where you would find the Stations of the Cross in a high church, there are posters saying, 'Are you coming on the parish weekend?' The hot-water urn wheezes during the Third Eucharistic Prayer.

It provides lots of scope for laughter, and thus little need for getting the giggles. It is almost impossible to be a believer and have no sense of humour at all, because faith requires a sense of the incongruity between human beings with bodily functions and God the perfect and all-powerful. It is funny merely to think of the godly Bishop of Lincoln taking his mother to Sainsbury's.

The clergy recognise this source of humour and use it for converting purposes. The funniest humour is humour without any ulterior motive. But often humour is used in sermons as a way of luring you in: it is a sweetener. At St Paul's, Onslow Square, the visiting preacher in a swirly waistcoat started with three anecdotes, one about witnessing sexual intercourse on a train to Margate, and we all thought, 'What an accessible man!' The jokes suddenly dried up and the Christian message was driven home. It was a bit of a trick. The British public is sophisticated and we are not really taken in by this sort of thing. We can tell the difference between humour glued on to the beginning of a sermon and real wit which suffuses it all. Preachers are so desperate to be liked, and to rid themselves of the image of being Victorian father-figures, that they sometimes try too hard to be funny.

I actively liked about ninety per cent of the Anglicans I interviewed, and one of the things I liked was that they were funny. The Bishop of Grantham was jokey about the cross before his name, which had recently been mistaken for a kiss. John Sentamu, the vicar in Tulse Hill, said, 'The Church of England has the engine of a lawnmower and the brakes of a juggernaut.' Rebecca Watts played pop music on her CD player in her housing-estate curate's house, and we talked animatedly about buying trendy poloneck jumpers from John Smedley. Humphrey Southern, describing a vague old man, said, 'He doesn't know whether it's Christmas or Easter.' I was intrigued to compare the level of humour at Humphrey Southern's dinner party (ex-Cuddesdon clergy, in Liverpool) and Kevin Hunt's dinner party (ex-St Stephen's House clergy, in Sunderland). The ex-Cuddesdon people were much funnier because they were more scurrilous. They imitated bishops, they were rude about goody-goodies, and they had running jokes, such as that Roman Catholics were Romanies and spent their time doing gypsy things like stealing the washing. 'What was Peter Cornwell [RC] doing at Church House?' somebody asked. 'He should have been saying his rosary or stealing babies or making clothes-pegs.' Delight in the eccentricity of others formed the basis of conversation. Humphrey, when introducing a new person to talk about, said, 'He's a man of *immense* barkingness.'

The topics of conversation at the Sunderland dinner party were less gripping, although they still made the priestly listeners fall about. There was a long story about a hamster. (Stories about rodents have to be *very* well told in order to be funny.) Fr Mark told the story of the time when he rang the college bell for Morning Prayer at six fifty-five rather than seven fifteen. They talked about washing machines and how you had to spread the clothes *round* the drum so that they didn't make a bashing noise.

The clergy have to let off steam in the privacy of their own homes and preferably with each other. Parishioners are highly offendable: the gentlest tease can be taken as a terrible insult. The parishioner's strongest weapon is non-attendance at church, and it always hurts. So you see clergy being safely and feebly funny on the high street, keen not to hurt anyone and thus not daring to say anything rude. In private, hilarity breaks out.

I have noticed that male clergy are generally funnier than female clergy. This is not the natural state; it is just that the women I saw were more downtrodden in their jobs than the men, especially in the months before the vote in the General Synod. They were in no mood for clubbish humour. The nearest to being funny that the Revds Pam Wise and Jane Wilson could get, for example, was to compare the insults women had received at the altar (people refusing to accept the chalice from them), and to compare what they were allowed and not allowed to do in the service. Sucking humour out of the glorious eccentricities of others, relishing it, imitating out-of-touch old men but not wanting them any other way – these are the pursuits of confident people. The dreary life of the middle-aged female curate, drowned in parish work and sending prayerful letters to other downtrodden female campaigners, did not produce evenings of relaxed mirth.

Bitter humour makes sour little appearances at Synod debates, and causes a cross titter. 'What is the difference between a liturgist and a terrorist? You can negotiate with a terrorist.' Anglicans make jokes about what they are afraid of. (So do Roman Catholics. The clergy at Westminster Cathedral used to have a Portuguese cleaning lady called Concepción. They referred to her as 'Contracepción'.)

Female clowns make people laugh. It is well known that clowns are the saddest figures of all, and there is now a national organisation called Holy Fools which consists of clowns who bring people closer to God by being hilarious, wise and as vulnerable as Christ. It is part of the movement to make Christianity more palatable than it is when it comes straight from the Epistles of St Paul. It has caught on. Fêtes all over the country have Holy Fools events, and children cluster round. I went to Raynes Park to have coffee with a married American clown called Sandra Pollerman.

She justified her clowning by saying, 'In the actions of the clown, others see themselves reflected as in a mirror. And the ripple and sometimes even the explosion of laughter which follows releases the tight hold we have on our own self-importance. Such a letting-go makes space for God to dust us off and set us back on the Godward path which will lead us to our deepest and best selves. I invite people to fall in love, all over again, with Christ the Clown, who calls us all to come and play in his kingdom.'

'Ugh!' sceptics say, wincing. But the effect Sandra Pollerman has on English audiences is remarkable. 'We've got this holy clown coming to the school tonight,' three St Mary's Calne sixth-formers told me when they showed me round the school for a *Tatler* article I was writing. They sounded a bit fed up. 'How did it go at St Mary's Calne?' I asked Sandra Pollerman a few days later. 'It was wonderful,' she said. 'The girls gave so much. One of the girls played Jesus, and you could see all that love coming from her.' There are few people as embarrassable as female sixth-formers in front of their housemistress; it is impressive that Sandra Pollerman had such a converting effect on them.

She does her clowning in front of nuns as well. At Bede House, the enclosed Anglican community in Staplehurst, she performed in front of the Sisters of the Love of God and they adored it. 'There was a resonance. I explained to them how clowns cover their whole skin so that the personality of God shines through, and the sisters pointed out that this was exactly what happens when you wear a habit. Sister Helen Columba, the Superior, she just laughed. "Well, have I got something for *you*," she said. She went and got her wimple and I put it on. Now I wear it all the time for clowning. Many of my students have gone on to wear a wimple too.'

There is what Sandra Pollerman calls 'vocal opposition' to holy clowns – it means rude letters and telephone calls from people who think it is irreverent to behave in this way. But there is also vocal support. The Bible made palatable is something for which the laity have a huge appetite. The Christian review *Rolling in the Aisles*, put on by the Riding Lights Theatre Company of York, was sold out in Rickmansworth when I tried to go. I had to go to see it in Cambridge instead. This was one of the sketches:

'Hello. It's Myrna from Cana Catering. John, I've got some *great* material for you, for Chapter 2. *He's* here. He's been chatting to Lebanon Lil for the last half an hour. She's as common as dirt but it doesn't seem to worry him. And the funny thing is, he's so *normal!*'

And then, of course, they ran out of wine and the miracle happened. The cast was vigorously Christian: they prayed backstage for twenty minutes before every show on the four-month tour. 'David who does the lights wasn't a Christian before the show started,' one of the actresses told me, 'but he is a Christian now.'

Humour used for converting purposes tends to be laboured. It didn't make us roll in the aisles, but it was moving to see these actors sweating away, changing out of bloody rags into angels' sheets, all in order to win our souls for Christ.

I asked Lord Runcie about the Anglican sense of humour, over Dundee cake at St Luke's Hospital for the Clergy. 'There's no laughter at the innermost recesses of our faith,' he said. 'Tragedies are dealt with by a cross. But on the outskirts of our faith humour is the best safeguard against fantastical nonsense.'

Then he gave a speech, to the doctors and nurses, accepting on behalf of St Luke's Hospital an ophthalmic microscope from the Corporation of the Sons of the Clergy. His eyes sparkled with merriment on either side of the deep furrow down his brow. He was funny about his own retina and the doctors and nurses laughed. His gratitude was steeped in natural wit.

7

Modern Anglican Usage

Abbreviation. The Church of England insists on abbreviating its inventions. The Alternative Service Book quickly became the ASB, and from then on the Book of Common Prayer was known as the BCP. The Movement for the Ordination of Women quickly became MOW, though the Cost of Conscience never became COC because it would have sounded silly. Abbreviating is a possessive urge. Once you have abbreviated something it becomes graspable and familiar. You avoid having to define it every time you say it. It is shorter, of course: this is the excuse abbreviators will give. It is meant to attract people by being easy and fun to say. The effect it has is to make people who know what it stands for feel proud and fond, and people who don't feel left out. Outsiders are far from attracted by clusters of capital letters.

Archaic slang. Safe and unblasphemous Americanisms of the 1940s to 1960s still abound in Church of England speech. From a recent sermon in south London: *You look at the splendour of creation and think, 'Wow'. Jaws hit the floor.* A vicar with a diminishing congregation: *It's a case of, as the Americans say, hanging in there.*

Atypical. A word used by Anglican clergy to explain that this Sunday is different from most Sundays. *The service today is* *atypical. It's Remembrance Sunday.* Or: *It's half-term, so you've come on an atypical day: half the congregation's away.* More Sundays seem to be atypical than typical.

Biblical language, use of in ordinary speech. A contagious habit, easy to catch. The Bishop of Guildford, introducing a Synod motion: *We must be ready to cast our bread upon the waters.* David Leal starting his Christian Ethics lecture at St Stephen's House: *Right. Here beginneth.* Good churchwardens are *the salt of the earth.* You often hear someone say, *Greater love hath no man,* when one friend does a small chore for another.

Blither and blather and bluther. Sometimes just 'blither and blather', but the 'bluther' is added at moments of extreme anger. It is the old, Prayer-Book-loving layman's expression for all the *nonsense* they have put in the new order of service for Holy Communion, between the consecration and the moment when you are allowed to come up to the altar. *I don't want all this blither and blather coming between me and my Lord.*

Bridge-building. *One of the key things I think is leadership. Leadership is about bridge-building.* (David Uffindell in Surbiton, describing his job.) An over-used Church of England word, grand, vague and nice, implying the urge to comfort the alienated and bring a community closer to God. Perhaps the churchy use of this word comes from 'Pontifex', the head of the college of priests in Rome; but it is more likely that it simply appeals to the Anglican taste for parable-like images.

Bunfight. The help-yourself meal in the church hall after a parish event. You feel you ought to go to it.

Car crash. The name for the scrappy and messy supper you get on Sunday evenings at Cuddesdon. It looks like one.

Catholic with a small 'c'. A proviso put in after sentences like, *I have catholic tastes in music.* Quakers, in the same way, say, *He's a friend with a small 'f'.*

Commitment. Just the kind of word that puts non-churchgoers off the whole idea of going to church. The word is all too easy to use, and clergy resort to it in an effort to wake up the complacent laity. They even talk of Jesus's commitment: *Costly commitment is at the heart of His faith,* says a Duxford parish magazine. Bishops *reaffirm the church's commitment to the Decade of*

Evangelism. (News release from Lambeth Palace.) The Victorian virtue words like 'fortitude', 'verity', 'prudence' and 'constance', beautiful enough to be used as Christian names, have been replaced by modern virtue words like 'commitment', 'effectiveness' and 'action'.

Dear. Some quite young Christian spouses still call each other this.

Definite article, non-use of. Nouns must attain a high degree of familiarity to become articleless. These are the ones that have. A vicar on the telephone: *Diary's rather crammed at the moment.* At West Malling Abbey: *Please stand when Community comes into the sanctuary.* At Church House: *There is one thing I must still tell Synod.* In a tent at a Christian camp on the Norfolk coast: *This is something that you will discover at Camp.*

Evangelisation. Catholic Anglicans like to say *Decade of Evangelisation* rather than *Decade of Evangelism.* The suffix '–isation' frees the word from its overtones of missionaries winning souls for Christ which '–ism' delights in.

Flak. *Can you take the flak?* is, at PCC meetings, the most-used way of saying, 'Can you bear it if people are rude to you about this?' *Can you cope?* is a similar parish question. Frayed nerves and overwork give birth to expressions like these.

Football imagery. Used as bait for the unchurched, e.g. on the noticeboard at Christchurch, Fulham: *Jesus Christ is a permanent fixture.* Also used as an instant man-to-man metaphor. The Bishop of Lincoln tells his clergy, *What matters is not where you get in the Church, but what division you're in.* The Archbishop of Canterbury, talking about the priesting of women, said to a group of peers and MPs that it would not be a good idea *to kick this issue into touch.* No doubt some of the peers hadn't played rugger for so long that they had forgotten what touch was. David Uffindell, a forward-looking musical vicar in Surbiton, said, *The old people would feel deeply alienated if we kicked the organ into touch.*

Foreign languages. Modern Anglicans positively like singing in them. It is a bit of a snub to the easy diction of the songs in *Mission Praise,* which say things like

> Thank you, Lord, for clothes to wear,
> Thank you, Lord, for clothes to wear,
> Thank you, Lord, for clothes to wear,
> Right where we are.

Taizé chants are often in Latin and they are becoming increasingly popular among the young. They are simple (e.g. *Jubilate Deo, Alleluia*) but the dead language they are in preserves a sense of mystery. The gentle and unending song *Thuma Mina* is popular among ordinands, who also like to talk about the *shalom* of God.

Grasping the nettle. Doing something we don't particularly want to do, and doing it now. The expression is much used in persuading debates, and it is as English as stinging nettles.

Humble Crumble. The nickname for the grovelly prayer in the Eucharist which goes 'We are not worthy so much as to gather up the crumbs under thy table . . .'

Inclusive language. Language which, whenever possible, exchanges the word 'men' for 'people' in order to be fair to women. But if it comes in a line that has to scan, the only possible harmless word to use is 'we'. So verse 3 of the Sussex Carol, as printed in the new *Popular Carol Book*, now goes:

> Angels and we with joy may sing,
> All for to see the new-born king.

The opposite of inclusive language is gender-specific language.

Little Puddlecombe. The stock English village (imaginary) used in Church of England argument and description. Dame Betty Ridley on the subject of freehold livings: *'Those dear old boys who sat in Little Puddlecombe for forty years, they're not so common now.'* The other stock English parish is Great Snoring, and that really exists, in north Norfolk.

Madre. Organists' expression for the gay parish priest who runs the church that they play the organ in. *Ask the Madre for the key to the vestry.*

Meeting needs across the board. What a good Anglican at work is doing.

Meeting people where they are. The longing to reach the unchurched causes expressions like this one to be used. *We must meet people where they are* means 'we mustn't make them sing Victorian hymns or expect them to know all about the way of the Cross'. Jesus met people where they were.

Mispronunciation. When Anglican pronunciation is out of step with secular pronunciation, the reason is not unintelligence or deafness on the part of the speaker but a desire to be dissociated from the word because it is new, foreign or wicked. *Would you like another slice of pittzer?* a monk at Mirfield asked me. *I think he's a ho-mo-sexual,* an evangelical said, using long 'o's and therefore making the word last a full three seconds. The Archbishop of Canterbury said, *We are now going to sing the 'Veeny Creator'.*

Mock-Tudor. The adjective that is used to describe Rite B in the Alternative Service Book. The language is all 'thee' and 'thou' and 'meet and right so to do'; but the order of the service is 1980s revival, with the *Gloria* near the beginning and the uplifting words *Christ has died, Christ is risen, Christ will come again,* which were not there in the Book of Common Prayer.

Numbers game, the. *What's the average size of your congregation?* clergy can't resist asking each other. If it is small, the answer is sometimes accompanied with, *But I don't play the numbers game.* Evangelicals with bursting churches love playing the numbers game. They justify themselves with an apposite biblical text. Paul Weston at Oak Hill: *St Luke at Pentecost counted: 3,000 came to faith.*

Old. *It's a funny old organisation, the C of E.* 'Old' is the adjective used more than any other before 'Church of England'. *Are you Roman Catholic? No, just good old C of E.* When you compare the ages of the two Churches, this seems an extraordinary thing to say. But, of course, 'old' here implies 'I am fond of it even though it can be infuriating sometimes'.

Paradox. Christianity is founded on the paradox of a servant king, God becoming man and dying to save us all. *Whose service is perfect freedom.* Part of the soothingness of prayers is this joining of opposites. So steeped are the clergy in holy paradox that they use it a great deal in speech. *You must suffer to grow. Doubt is an essential part of faith. You're not letting the baby in the manger*

become the man on the cross. The way to find peace is to look for war. We need increased flexibility within an ordered framework.
Plus, used as a noun. Sloppy, and fairly common. A non-stipendiary priest is *another pair of hands to say Mass. That's a plus.* (Fr Piper in Lewes.) *Christian Music* magazine is full of nounal pluses and minuses about new hymn books.
Pom For All the Saints. Popular title of a hymn.
Prayer Book catholic. An Anglican catholic who does not use the Roman missal.
Prepositions, emphasising of. Shy vicars do this. It is a habit, and they are unconscious of it. *I'd like the godparents to come up TO the font.* Emphasising the unimportant is a way of making the important less embarrassing to say. St John sets a bad example at the beginning of his Gospel: *The same was in the beginning WITH God.*
Pretty pairs. On a single page of the appeal leaflet at St Gabriel's, Pimlico, you read that *worship and prayer are a guide and a discipline,* a means of expressing our *joy and thankfulness,* and a comfort to those in *sorrow or in need.* The church has groups for *study and prayer.* The clergy visit the *sick and housebound,* and they organise *outings and pilgrimages,* and regular *concerts and recitals.* Words in pairs soften each other, so the whole tone of the page becomes caressing rather than abrupt. Perhaps this pairing urge derives from a love for the tautological but beautiful expression in the Prayer Book: *It is meet and right so to do.*
Punctuation, power of to change meaning. Choristers like playing with hymns. They switch the comma round in

> My Lord, I love thee, not because
> I hope for heaven thereby.

Puns. Often used for teaching purposes. Zealous Anglicans particularly like puns which illustrate how deceptively similar the truth is to the non-truth: how, by changing a single letter in a word, you can switch from the path of wretchedness to the path of everlasting life. *GOD IS DAD,* a sign outside St Mark's, Kennington, said for months. *Some say, 'God is nowhere'. I say, 'God is now here',* said an RE teacher. It is as if God is speaking to us through the English language.

Queen. 1. Queen of Heaven. *Is it going to be good weather at Walsingham this weekend?* Reply: *It'll be Queen's weather.* 2. The Governor of the Church of England. *O Lord, save the Queen. And mercifully hear us when we call upon thee.* 3. Homosexual. An ordinand at St Stephen's House: *The St Stephen's House queen alarm goes off when someone like that comes to talk to us.*

Quinquennial. Five-yearly. *The Archdeacon's coming round for the quinquennial inspection.* Clergy love saying the word. Few words have 'qu' twice, and the mouth enjoys it.

Resource. A new hymn book or song book is called a resource. *New Songs,* says *Christian Music* magazine, *is a useful resource.* A good bishop *resources* his clergy.

Roman leanings. *We're Rite A with Roman leanings.* (Kevin Hunt in Sunderland). This means that Mass is said in the Roman order, and that they keep the saints and stand for the prayers.

Sheep-stealing. Congregation-poaching. Successful, growing churches do it to dying churches. The only modern use of the word 'sheep' to mean 'people'. 'Flock' is still used to mean 'parishioners'.

Soporific abstracts. If you trace the moment in a sermon at which your mind drifts off, it tends to be when there is a cluster of large, long and abstract nouns. *This synergy, this interrelationship between God and man* is an example from Wycliffe Hall.

Soundalike words. *If there is communion with God there will also be communication.* (André Maries in *Christian Music.*) *The middle word of appraisal is 'praise'.* (Francis Hewitt, the Rural Dean on the North Yorkshire moors, reassuring clergy who are worried about his new clergy appraisal scheme. The etymology of 'appraisal' is, in fact, not 'praise' but 'prize'.) There are many examples of the use of soundalike words in the Anglican art of persuasion. From the Synod: *The aim is no longer to divide, but to decide. We want evolution rather than revolution.* The aim is to be punchy and memorable.

Staggers. The nickname for St Stephen's House in Oxford, used by its own students. It is one of the last surviving examples of the '–er' suffix which swept through Oxford in the 1920s, when Holy Communion was called Hugger-Commugger.

Trespasses. This sibilant word in the Lord's Prayer, pronounced *trespassiss* by children who don't know what it means, is surviving remarkably well in spite of the bad climate for old prayers. In the most forward-looking churches you will suddenly find that the Lord's Prayer is being said in its old language, and that everyone is lost in it, repeating the deeply familiar prayer of childhood rather than reading the strangled version in the Alternative Service Book.

Triplets. Often used in oratory and persuasive prose. There is the plain Climactic Triplet: We must do this so we can become *the praising, rejoicing and serving church we are called to be.* (Newsletter from St Giles's, Durham). And there is the Alliterative Triplet: we must *lift the air of survival, struggle and sectarianism which surrounds too much of our own church.* (Same newsletter.) The Bishops of Durham and Jarrow hope for a future of *ministry, mission and maintenance.* In such triplets, the burden of responsibility to mean something is passed from one word to the other. None of the words speaks as loudly as it would if it was on its own.

Wireless. Traditionalists still call it that. The word 'radio' never passes the former Bishop of Gloucester's lips. Talking about the tameness of Church of England language, he said, *I can cope with Wireless 1, and I can cope with Wireless 3, but the C of E has become like Wireless 2.*

8

The Point of Cathedrals

Very big, very old buildings make you think very big, very old thoughts. Here is an example of a train of thought which starts at the gate of a cathedral close.

'It's in scaffolding. It would be, wouldn't it? But it's beautiful. How did they build it? No cranes. Pulleys, I suppose. Men with horses and carts. Imagine being a medieval peasant with a pig on a string, who has walked miles to see this. I *am* that peasant. I stink and have a medieval toothache. I am struck dumb by this. Noticeboard. Services today. 5.30 p.m. Evensong, said. It would be said rather than sung, wouldn't it? Byrd yesterday, Byrd tomorrow. Entrance. Does it really cost that much a day to run? All this for the glory of God. He exists. This is proof. It's huge. What were the masons like? How many lifetimes did it take to build?'

The thought is all fairly middlebrow. There is a certain lostness-in-thought that only takes place in cathedrals. It is almost beyond belief that these jewels which adorn our land were actually built by human hands rather than winched down straight from Heaven. The gawping visitor at the south door is simultaneously humbled by ignorance and disbelief and uplifted by a sweeping feeling of awe. Simple but powerful thoughts flood into the consciousness: 'Why can't modern architects design buildings like this? What have we lost? Imagine this rising out of a hovelly medieval town. Did the masons believe or were they just doing it for money?'

At some English cathedrals, just when you are most lost in thought, a cathedral guide with a badge on comes up behind you and asks whether you have come a long way. She shows you a picture of the Saxon church which used to be on the site, and points up at the triforium.

She is doing it for nothing. This thought now sweeps over you. The building is full of volunteers. They work here for love.

A new train of cathedral thought which has come to me this year, after conversations with proud Anglican deans, is, 'How much more alive this cathedral is than a French cathedral!' Deans love to talk about this aspect of cathedrals. Trevor Beeson, the Dean of Winchester, said: 'Architecturally, they are of the same standard; but cathedrals are *very* short of life in France. They're still very clergy-centred. They've never developed that wonderful quality brought by lay people.'

On holiday in France you can test this theory, and be gratified. The noticeboard in Laon cathedral says:

Lundi	Messe 11 h
Mardi	Messe 11 h
Mercredi	Messe 11 h
Jeudi	Messe 11 h
Vendredi	Messe 11 h

Winchester Cathedral has about thirty services a week, and they are rich in variety. In Laon, there is no woman in a blue husky coat to say hello to you. There is not even a priest in sight, although there must have been at 11 h. The only people in charge are the people selling the coloured booklet about the cathedral, so you buy one and learn about what happened to the *nef* in the *Ve* and *VIe siècle*. It is a museumy experience.

English cathedrals are always out for your money, and this is wearing. But because they are struggling buildings, relying not on the State for maintenance but on the pound coins of their visitors, their daily existence is exciting. Lay people can make a difference, and they do. 'I dust at ten in the cathedral,' said Sarah Stancliffe, the wife of the Provost of Portsmouth. Lots of lay people dust at ten in cathedrals all over the country, and they dust with joy, for nothing.

Portsmouth Cathedral is young. When you first come upon it, it looks like a toy cathedral. It was only made into a cathedral in 1928 and it still has to pay its Parish Share or Quota. Its Provost, David Stancliffe (soon to be Bishop of Salisbury), is a man of vision. On Shrove Tuesday and Ash Wednesday he allowed me to hover a few feet away from him and glean something about what a provost does. Portsmouth is a good place to learn about the point of cathedrals, because the cathedral itself is still learning. You see it growing out of its parish-churchiness into something grander: a place of beauty and a centre of excellence. But it is still a parish church as well, in a villagey square in Old Portsmouth: baptisms, weddings and funerals of local Portsmouth people take place there all the time.

Shrove Tuesday hovering round David Stancliffe went like this:

7 a.m. Twenty minutes' silence in the cathedral, sitting wherever you like. All four canons are there, lurking behind pillars and lost in thought. You can choose your vista.

7.20. Morning Prayer. The liturgy used is pioneering liturgy from *Celebrating Common Prayer*, which is the Franciscan office book adapted for use by non-friars. David Stancliffe has done much of the adapting. Every Friday is a mini-Good Friday. There are satisfying responses, e.g.:

V: Christ is reigning from the tree.
R: O come, let us worship

7.45. Eucharist. This means that the Provost and canons are in the cathedral for a whole hour and a quarter before breakfast.

8.15. Breakfast in the Provost's House which is six windows long but not icy or prim. Lots of post. At least five letters with real handwriting. A postcard of a French abbey.

9 o'clock. The secretary arrives from the Isle of Wight. She and David sit at a banqueting-table-sized desk covered in green baize and go through the mail. David's diary is slashed to bits

with vertical arrows. He is one of the busiest people in the Church of England, and thinks his job is one of the best in the Church of England. He rings up the Dean of St Paul's and a secretary answers. 'Who's speaking, please?' 'The Provost of Portsmouth.' It works.

10.30. David shows me round the cathedral. I later learn, from ordinands at St Stephen's House, that this tour is known as 'the Stancliffe experience' and is given to many. Presided over by him, a plain and beautiful new west end has been built on to the cathedral. You can go up some steps into a gallery and gaze at the clear new stone space. David gazes at it too and moves his arms in curvy forward motion, explaining how you go on a journey from the Old Testament at the west end, past the font (which represents rebirth), past the lectern (the Word) to the sacrament at the altar and the hanging pyx at the end. He would like eventually to have a garden outside the west end (the Garden of Eden) and hints of paradise (trelliswork, leaves) on the wall at the east end to show that it doesn't all finish at the hanging pyx.

11.30. The County Music Officer comes to talk about the vast numbers of county musicians and how best to use their talents. The organist, Adrian Lucas, joins us, and there is a delicious musical conversation. 'We've had a tremendous response to recruiting this year — so much that we've had to have the choir stalls enlarged.' What the County man needs is someone to train the young voices of the county. It all seems possible.

1 o'clock. Lunch. Sarah Stancliffe is the cookery writer for the *Church Times*. This week she is trying out Lenten vegetarian recipes.

2 o'clock. David takes a parish funeral in the cathedral.

3 o'clock. The great question of the Nuclear Testing Veterans dedication stone. Where will it be laid, and when will its service of dedication be? The veterans come for a meeting with David and the Cathedral Administrator called Brian Jones. The diaries which must coincide are: the veterans', the Cathedral's, the Precentor's, the Administrator's, David's and the Lord Mayor's. The first possible date is two and a half months away. The veterans are always free. 'Yes, the thirteenth is fine.' 'What about the next day?' 'Yeah, that's all right with me.' They have to check that the Lord Mayor will be free. The Lord Mayor isn't. It's the Hampshire

County Council service and the Dunkirk Veterans. They go back a day. 'Yep. We're free,' say the veterans. But the Lord Mayor still isn't. 'The Deputy Mayor might be,' says the Mayor's secretary, 'but we don't yet know who the Deputy Mayor is going to be.'

'I think that's the best date all the same,' says David. '*Excellent*. We'll need an organist.' David makes the veterans feel important. No one else does.

Where will the dedication stone go? The first shock to the veterans is that it will go on the ground, and get trodden on. 'Don't worry,' said David. 'It's a very hard stone. These stones are designed to be walked on. It can go dead centre, at the meeting of the paths.'

'Not *dead* centre,' said Brian Jones, 'because we want to put a piece of sculpture there.'

'It's just the walking-on part that rankles a bit,' said a veteran.

'It could go on the *side*,' said David. 'The nearer the centre it is the more it'll get walked on.'

All this takes a full hour.

4 o'clock. David meets the architect of the new west end, Michael Drury, and Jon Collan whose drawing paper explains that he does 'Stained Glass and Leaded Lights'. He is designing windows which say

H AMP SHIR E CO NSTA BULA RY
SERVI CE TO THE P EOPLE.

5.30. Evensong. The choir wear fetching rust-coloured surplices, the dye designed especially by Watts & Co of London. The canons come back to the Provost's House for gin, before going home to pancakes. One of the canons gives Sarah a wartime vegetarian recipe involving mashed potatoes and beetroot. She tests it the next day and it appears in the *Church Times* a week later.

7 o'clock. Annual General Meeting of the Cathedral Guides. David gives an energetic and grateful speech, telling the guides what good jobs they do showing visitors round. 'I realise that the cathedral you are guiding people round is very different from the cathedral you used to guide people round.' The guides soak up the gratitude then ask questions such as, 'How do

we stop visitors from tripping over the step when they come in?'

The guides themselves go on a guided outing once a year. 'What about Warpington?' More diaries. 'Not the sixteenth because the Cathedral Ladies have got a skittle alley at Wickham.'

8.15. Delicious Stancliffe recipe-testing supper, then a slide show of their pilgrimage on foot to Santiago de Compostela (it was what they did in David's sabbatical). They said the Divine Office every morning and evening, trying out the new Office Book. One of the slides was of a Continental canon playing an electric organ and singing into a microphone.

Some of the point of cathedrals can be gleaned from that Provost's day.

At 11 o'clock, cathedrals are thick with visitors strolling up and down and reading the plaques. But, at crack of dawn, there has been that monkly meeting of the Dean and Chapter and anyone else who wants to come (usually not many) to pray together and sit in silence. Beneath the museum there is always a layer of pure church.

The British appetite for occasion can be gratified. Veterans can have their stone blessed with pomp. This is important to them. Their God is a grand God, and he takes particular notice of *them*.

A man of vision like David Stancliffe can bask in life if he is a provost or dean. He can make his cathedral into a theological experience, and bring his Continental knowledge to bear. He can be charming to volunteer guides and nice to veterans.

The municipal can meet with the ecclesiastical, and do it grandly.

Canons living in proximity can learn from each other and be usefully spiritual together. A good Dean and Chapter is the opposite of ineffectual and pathetic.

Some Deans and Chapters are miserable, of course: in Lincoln it came to light that canons had been saying their prayers together every morning for years, locked in mutual hatred. Christian hatred is powerful because it arises out of deep convictions which really matter to the haters. The collegiate existence can be a glimpse of Heaven or a glimpse of Hell.

Lay people wandering in and out of a cathedral are highly sensitive to its friendliness or unfriendliness. Whether the Canon Treasurer is on speaking terms with the Canon Chancellor is not what determines this. Canons aren't generally around for visitors to talk to at all. They turn up for services, then go away again. The people who do talk to you are the vergers, the stewards, the marshals, the guides and the postcard-sellers. They are front of house, and they have the power to enhance the atmosphere of holiness or to wreck it.

Norwich wins the Cathedral Atmosphere test, and Ripon comes second. Durham comes low down, although it wins the beauty contest. I talked to one or two canons at Durham and they were in a lofty hurry. Evensong, though faultlessly sung, was icy, and no one caught anyone's eye. At Norwich, the Precentor's four children sat in the row in front, sunlight streamed in, the Precentor preached merrily, the woman on my right said hello, and the cathedral vases were full of picked rather than bought flowers. At Ripon the guide seemed delighted that visitors from the south should actually turn off the main road and make the effort to come to look at what Ripon had to boast of.

Quiet cathedrals are easier to keep holy than noisy ones; and the famous ones are noisy. St Paul's has to be run like a machine, with a verger at each aperture telling you not to do this and not to do that. A snooty marshal at Westminster Abbey tells tourists what to do and keeps them quiet with the subtlety of a sergeant-major.[1] The more swarming a cathedral is with coachloads of French schoolchildren the more it has to become a strict and prickly place full of 'Private' signs and hooked velvet ropes. On the front steps of St Paul's vergers in black being brusque with tourists in white are a continuous summer sight. 'We hate them but we know that this is the way our bread is buttered,' said the Canon Treasurer at Westminster Abbey of French tourists. 'We are now funded seventy-seven per cent by tourism and twenty-three per cent by inherited wealth.'

---

[1] 'Westminster Abbey's not a cathedral. It's a Royal Peculiar.' This has been said to me at least ten times by correcting canons and organists. 'Westminster Abbey's different.' I know it is; but, to the wanderer in and out and the dropper-in for evensong, it is indistinguishable from a cathedral. This chapter is where it belongs.

Tourists may not know it, but by casually dropping coins into boxes that look like incubators they are helping to keep the choir going. Cathedrals need tourists, in the way that publishers need bestsellers in order to be able to carry on publishing obscure first novels. And of course God needs tourists as well. However much noise they make, however quickly they head for the shop to buy a cathedral bookmark, the Peace of God which passes all understanding may have touched their inner being, if only for a second. Canons hope this is the case. 'People sit in the nave during evensong,' said Canon Christopher Hill at St Paul's. 'What they're getting God only knows, but they're obviously getting *something*. And lots of visitors light a candle beside "The Light of the World".' A candle-lighting craze has swept through cathedrals in the last ten years. 'Unchurched people love lighting a candle,' said the Revd Neil Collings in Harpenden, who is fascinated by the success of cathedrals in the late twentieth century. 'They'd be too embarrassed to do it in their own parish church.' Perhaps it is simply the hint of pyromania in us all. If you pass a rack of lighted candles in a cathedral it is almost impossible to resist adding to it. The urge may very well be partly God-inspired.

'The number of people coming to cathedrals is larger than at any time,' said the Dean of Winchester, 'although church attendance is in decline. More and more bodies are asking to use it: townsmen's guilds, the British Legion, the County Council. About 10,000 schoolchildren come a year. We have to take enough from visitors to get half our income. The cathedral costs £600,000 a year to run, so £300,000 must come from visitors.'

Some more of the point of cathedrals, as gleaned from Winchester:

A cathedral close is a beautiful enclosed world. When you walk into it, you think, 'The world's all right after all.' This is precisely what some evangelicals hate about cathedrals: the world is *not* all right, and cathedrals are inward-looking clusters of comfort, not going *out there* very much.[2] But people who have been taking their video back to Dixons and trying on a jumper at Jumpers

---

[2] I vowed to write this book without using the sentence 'Theirs is a *reactive* rather than a *proactive* ministry.' It was tempting to use it here.

are nourished and reassured by visiting the cathedral afterwards. Unlike their parish church, it is unlocked. The world might not be all right, but cathedrals make it more all right that it would otherwise be.

Mattins, fifty years ago the staple diet of the Church of England, is rapidly going out of fashion in parish churches, and being replaced by the high-fibre Eucharist. This is sad for old people, who love the *Te Deum* and the *Venite* and feel that Holy Communion ought to be a special treat. At cathedrals, mattins is still served handsomely every Sunday morning. Winchester is the only cathedral where it is still the main service of the day. The good people of Hampshire (many of them retired army officers) flock to it: 'It's so well attended,' said the Dean, 'we'd be very nervous about abolishing it.' The organist, David Hill, wishes they would. 'It can be a pretty drab service. The congregation don't even try during the *Venite*, even though it's supposed to be congregational. But they put a lot into the collection and this matters to the Dean and Chapter.'

'The only place in Hampshire where you can find adult worship is in Winchester Cathedral,' people tell the Vice-Dean. 'The services in our parish are all watered down for children these days.'

A cathedral is a lovely place to have a scone. The restaurant business has taken off at Winchester Cathedral, and at many others. 'Within six weeks of opening the Cathedral Refreshments Room,' said the Dean, 'one thousand people from the diocese had volunteered to come and work in it free. It made £38,000 in its first year and £41,000 in its second.' What is this waitressing urge? I have a bit of it myself. Standing behind a counter of baked cathedral food all day is a satisfying and finite occupation. You talk to the others and eat scones vicariously. At Wells Cathedral you do it in what used to be the cloisters but are now glassed in and heated, so you can savour the sensation of twentieth-century warmth in a place that was once bitterly cold.

Sung evensong on a winter weekday evening is one of the treasures of English life, and cathedrals allow this tradition to flourish. They have choir schools, so boys can go from games to choir practice to evensong to supper to prep without having to walk very far. Scholarships support them. Choral evensong, live on Radio 3 every Wednesday afternoon, is tuned into by solitary listeners in their thousands, who like to know that the service is happening at this very minute in a living quire.

Anonymity is said to be one of the blights of our urban age. One of the few occasions when the word is ever used approvingly is in reference to a cathedral. Deans know that people who don't quite believe in God but are thinking about it can be positively helped towards conversion by *not* being tapped on the shoulder and asked to teach in the Sunday school. Cathedrals allow anonymity. Guides sometimes hinder it but they don't mean to. You can wander in and sit behind a pillar and be left alone.

Canon Christopher Smith in Sheffield has sideburns, smokes a pipe, wears a Roman cassock with red silk buttons and piping and adores his cathedral. It is not tucked away in a close but in the middle of the busy town and opposite a throbbing pub, as parish-church cathedrals often are. He has managed to get the Reserved Sacrament back and proudly unlocks the aumbry to show it off to his friends. There it is, blessed and covered in a handkerchief.[3] 'We use this chapel on Wednesday, and this is the one we use on Saturday.' He is a Franciscan Tertiary: 'I say my prayers. That is the most important thing I do.' He thinks it important to be *around* in the cathedral so people can come off the street and talk to him. One did, while I was there. It was a woman who had stopped taking her anti-depressants because evangelicals had said to her, 'Can't you put your trust in God?' He talked to her in a pew, and suggested that she go back on the anti-depressants.

Brief encounters like that are what cathedral canons specialise in. Being a canon is in a way less demanding than being a parish priest because canons only have to be nice to most people once. It is not difficult to stand benignly at an exit, asking strangers where they come from. '*What* a nice canon!' people will all too

---

[3]Whether or not a cathedral has the Reserved Sacrament in it is, for many high Anglican clergy, its sole defining feature. If it does, it is a holy place. If it doesn't, it is merely a large prayer-box.

easily think. Parish priests have to become familiar with the true discontent of their parishioners, week after week.

'It attracts me and excites me that the whole world passes through,' said Christopher Chessun, a minor canon at St Paul's on a five-year contract. 'I showed Chandra Swami round last year. You *can* minister to people who pass through. I've just been given this watercolour of the Falklands by a grateful mother after the Falklands service last week.'

He took me into the cathedral and showed me how to crack the nut. (I had come to talk of 'cracking the nut' with cathedrals. How did you get through the museum-like, verger-controlled outer layer to the soft kernel?) It is easy when you are with a minor canon. You don't have to pay an entry charge, to begin with. Sister Hilary was saying the prayers on the hour every hour that day, asking everyone to stand still. (This is a good system for bringing tourists up short and reminding them that they are in God's house. Most noisy cathedrals have an hourly prayer now.) She came down from the pulpit and carried on with the rest of her duty, which was to be there for people to talk to. Christopher Chessun also makes a point of wandering round the cathedral with nothing particular to do, making his welcoming presence felt. If you look for humanity, you can find it. A retired headmaster called Maurice Sills works in St Paul's for nothing almost every day, showing round parties of enthralled schoolchildren. The Sills experience is as memorable as the Stancliffe experience. 'There's Daniel up there. Is there a Daniel among you? Is there a Matthew?' Maurice's wife Ellen Sills stamps postcards behind a table.

'I'll put you through to Protocol,' the Westminster Abbey office said when I rang it up to ask about going to a consecration. This was hard-edged. The Abbey is dominated by special occasion. Roger Job used to be Precentor there and he remembers. 'That was my life: getting ready for special occasions. You could see them coming, like the jumps at Aintree.' But, again, if you know where to look you can find the kernel. If you talk to the fey vergers nicely they will talk Christianly back. There is always a pastor on duty if you are desperate.

'It's like living in Medieval Coronation Street,' said the wife of a Vicar Choral at Wells Cathedral. 'The Vicars', as they call themselves, live rent-free in one of the oldest inhabited streets in Western Europe, cobbled and thick with historic chimney-stacks. To the wanderer in and out Vicars Close seems a dream street. The sound of children practising their scales sings out through the later windows. But in a street where everyone knows everyone the inward-looking can be driven mad. Just as there are nature's parish priests and nature's canons there are nature's chatty neighbours and nature's antisocialites.

On Bank Holiday Mondays the best bell-ringers in Hampshire meet at Winchester Cathedral and ring all day. The sound, to visitors, is joyful; but for people living in the Close it is a bore, in the same way that it is for people in Eton classrooms who go deaf to the human voice because of aeroplanes every two minutes. 'You have the screaming ab-dabs by the end of the day,' a canon's wife said.

Apart from the fact that it must obey sixteenth-century statutes that can only be changed by an Act of Parliament, the Dean and Chapter of a cathedral is a powerful little body. The laity has little say in how a non-parish-church cathedral is run. Even the Dean can't do much, except exercise his right of veto, unless he gets the votes from the canons. Cathedrals are slow to change, but they are beginning to now. 'We had a big firm of management consultants down from London last year,' said the Dean of Winchester, 'to reorganise the daily running of the cathedral. They decentralised, and divided the cathedral up into different departments. There was no real line of authority: this they picked up.'

The thought of men in suits descending on men in dog-collars and cleaning up the way they run their institution is a sad one. Not being run as efficiently as the French railways is one of the Church of England's strengths. It allows individuals to succeed or fail in their own way. But since the ugly Lincoln affair cathedrals have started to look at themselves to check that they are not similarly diseased. A Cathedrals Commission has been set up to form an official conclusion about whether cathedrals ought to be more standardised, and to make sure that they can't sell their priceless treasures without permission.

Even if there are signs of rot at the centre, the surface efficiency of cathedrals is striking. Services happen as punctually as hospital meals. On the dot of five thirty the sound of the vestry prayer, muffled by distance, is heard from the quire. The procession starts; the congregation rises to its feet; the organist ends on an A. 'I never worship in the cathedral,' said a troubled ordinand at Salisbury & Wells Theological College (which is fifty yards from the door of Salisbury Cathedral). 'It's like a concert in there. The congregation's so passive.'

It is his loss. Being physically passive to the sound of psalms can cause a frenzy of mental activity, some of it carnal but much of it spiritual. Human anguish and human gratitude are keenly felt, contrasting violently. The world seems precious and rescuable.

9

Going to Church and Not Going to Church

The truth spoken with disarming simplicity appeals to the Anglican taste for aphorism. The Very Revd Ian White-Thompson, who is old and good and used to be the Dean of Canterbury, told me the following when I went to see him in Wye. He spoke in a soft, frail voice which was almost a whisper. 'You know, a Scottish friend said this to me once, and I've never forgotten it. The reason why people don't go to church is because they don't want to. *The reason why people don't go to church is because they don't want to.*' The simple and bleak pronouncement had lodged itself in his memory. He thought about it often, and it seemed to have a ring of profound truth about it.

The Swan at Chappel is a pub at a crossroads in deep Essex. It is a quarter of a mile from two churches, and after going to mattins at one of them, at which the congregation consisted of eight, I conducted a random Going to Church and Not Going to Church survey at the Swan. It was half past twelve and the pub was filling up. Of the twenty-two people I interrupted and interviewed not one of them had been to church that morning. Only one of them ever went except to weddings and funerals. A family of three finishing plaice and chips said, 'No, never any more.' The mother said, 'You can't force it on the children. But I still read the parish magazine. As soon as it comes through the door I make myself a cup of coffee and sit down with it.'

Two men propping up the bar said, 'No. Only funerals.' 'I used to sing in a church choir when I was a lad but I never go now.' 'The last vicar, he used to come in here and have a drink. We never see the new vicar.' 'But would you mind,' I asked, 'if the church wasn't there any more?' 'Oh, yes. It's like the viaduct. Nobody in the village notices it but if it were to go there'd be a huge row.'

Four surly men in the front window said, 'No. They're a bunch of hypocrites, aren't they, Christians? Look at Ireland, the way they all kill each other.' 'But do you celebrate Christmas?' 'Oh, yes.' 'And would you mind if the church closed down?' 'It's got to be maintained, there's no two ways about it.'

A swarthy man having lunch with two lapsed Catholics said, 'I sometimes go in Romford. That's where I come from. I like the Anglican music. I used to be a chorister when I was a lad.'

Four well-dressed younglings said, 'No.' 'What do you do instead?' 'Lay in and read the papers.' 'What puts you off going to church?' One of them was in the construction industry, so work was his excuse. 'Would you go if you weren't in the construction industry?' 'No.' Another said, 'They're so hypocritical, Christians. There was this priest at home who built a huge great extension on to his vicarage. The church roof was still leaking. I wouldn't call that exactly Christian. The church has got to change its image.' 'Well,' I said brightly, 'women priests ought to help do that.' 'Are there going to be women priests? Yeah, that's a start. Could there be a black priest?' 'There already are quite a few, actually. Would you have your children baptised in church?' 'Oh, yeah, I'd have them baptised.'

The conclusions drawn from this short but intense survey were the following:

1) People in pubs are approachable and don't mind being asked this sort of question, as long as you convince them that you are not a Jehovah's Witness.

2) The pronouncement that is lodged in Dean White-Thompson's memory does not go far enough. People don't go to church because

it doesn't even occur to them that they might. It plays no part at all in their weekly life or thoughts.

3) Vicars might get more people into church if they made their presence felt at pubs.

4) If you ask people in pubs whether they believe in God they become embarrassed and shifty. The question is too large. It is best to change the subject.

5) More beer-drinkers than you expect were choristers in their youth. But the experience did not make them into life-long churchgoers.

6) People expect the church to be there and would be horrified if it suddenly weren't. They use it at certain important moments in their life, and it doesn't occur to them to wonder who keeps it going.

The word 'unchurched' is still much-used by the clergy, even though it sounds as Victorian as the word 'masses' which sometimes accompanies it. Some of the people at the Swan were unchurched. The word implies that the church has not reached them at all; that they are ignorant about it. 'A bit over a million people a week' go to Church of England services, Martin Elengorn at the Church Commissioners told me, statistics at his fingertips. That is a fiftieth. If you wander about in a town on a Sunday morning, peering tactfully through windows and across forecourts, you get a good idea of what the majority of the remaining fraction is up to. It is all the things that are listed in sermons about our materialistic age: watching morning television, reading the Sunday papers, tinkering with the car, eating supermarket food, staying in bed with the curtains closed, changing into keep-fit clothes. The fabric of home life is being maintained. But there are grades of non-churchgoer, from the atheist upwards. Many would be insulted to be called 'unchurched'. They would much rather be classed as 'people who don't go to church'.

'I'm afraid I find the idea of organised religion about as attractive as the idea of organised audience participation,' Miles Kington replied to my letter about writing a portrait of the Church of England. He is an example of a person who doesn't go to church. It has got nothing to do with whether he believes in God or not, or whether he is a nice person or not. It is just that he keeps away from church.

The thinking non-churchgoer – the person who has decided, on balance, that he or she would rather not go – is an intriguing figure. I have been collecting types of non-churchgoer and have found that the interesting ones are those who know quite a lot about the Church of England; who did Scripture at school and know the Creed by heart; who like stone carvings and cloisters; who pray at moments of crisis; but who none the less never step inside a church between the hours of 8 a.m. and 7 p.m. on a Sunday.

There is the Lunch-Party Agnostic, who lives in a lovely house in the country and is having friends to Sunday lunch. The table, she notices, has been laid for thirteen: *that* won't do. She lays another place, and imagines, while she is doing it, what they would have had to eat at the Last Supper. She puts the meat into the low oven then goes into the garden to pick flowers. There certainly wouldn't be time to go to church, even if she wanted to. Anyway, she couldn't bear the idea of putting on a church face. Home is where she would much rather be. She stays there.

The Newspaper Reader wants mental stimulation on a Sunday morning. He goes straight to the leader pages, then back to the Focus on Europe page. He doesn't mind the sound of church bells in the distance, but they have no power to draw him. If you ask him why he doesn't go to church, he says, 'How can you justify a church which has the Queen as its head? Look at this article here, about the Prime Minister turning down both names of bishops suggested for Manchester. What does the Prime Minister know about bishops? It's a scandal.'

The Prayer-Book Complainer has refused to go ever since her parish church started using the Alternative Service Book and reading from the New English Bible. '"Through a smudged mirror", that's the worst one,' she says. '"Now you see through a smudged mirror." How *could* they do that to "Now you see through a glass, darkly"? They've taken all the poetry away.' She refuses to say the new Lord's Prayer, and she winces at weddings when the bridegroom says, 'I give you this ring as a token of our marriage'. '"With this ring I THEE WED", it ought to be. *So* much simpler and prettier. They knew how to say things in those days. They knew how to build houses, too.'

The Candle-Lighter loves singing carols at Christmas; she believes in the healing power of singing. She looks at lighted candles and meditates on them, thinking how amazing light is, and how the world needs more of it. She loves Jesus and meditates on him sometimes, but church seems rather narrow and social for all this. At church you have to believe in 'One church, one faith, one Lord'. The Candle-Lighter does not want to be as categorical or jingoistic as that. She believes that everyone has as much right as everyone else to walk in the light.

The Allergic Sixty-Year-Old is still recovering from the ghastly experience, forty-five years ago, of being forced to put up with school religion which made him feel sick in the chapel. He hated 'I vow to thee, my country', which started off as an innocent nationalistic song and then, in the second verse, turned into a religious hymn which was supposed to lead naturally on from it. The thought of it makes him feel sick even now, and the smell of a church reminds him of the long, cold and bitter hours of his uncomfortable youth.

The Priest-Punisher *tried* to get used to the new vicar. 'It was so awful when Eric left, and any vicar would find it hard to step into Eric's shoes. He was loved by everyone – a marvellous man. But the new one! He's worse than you could possibly have expected. The first thing he did was to abolish the barn dance. Then he decided to abolish mattins. The PCC had something to say about *that*. His sermons show that he is *quite* out of touch with what a village needs. I think he must be rather a lonely man. Poor chap. He needs a wife, I suppose.' Instead of going to church the Priest-Punisher stays at home and talks about why she is not going. 'Well, the result of all this is that he's lost a communicant.'

The Embarrassable Father went to church once last year and was horrified when he found that women in front, and women behind, were trying to shake hands with him and say 'Peace b'with you'. He found he just couldn't say it back. That was the last time he was going to let himself in for *that* sort of thing. He can't bear all this gooey niceness that the old Church Militant has gone in for.

The Pevsner Collector carries binoculars around especially so that he can look up at bosses and crockets when visiting cathedrals. He loves churches and is an expert on the magnificent naves of Northamptonshire. But the last thing he would want to do is go to a service in one. Churches are what you stop to have a look at when you happen to be driving past.

These hardened non-churchgoers who have good brains and are not atheists form a large layer of English society. Nearly all of them get, or got, married in church. The bleakness of register offices has been a great help to the Church of England's cause. But the reason can't only be the unpleasantness of register offices. Intelligent and serious marriers need a better reason than that to choose a holy wedding rather than a secular one. My Cambridge contemporaries have been trickling into marriage over the last six years, and many of them are hardened non-churchgoers: but not one of them has got married in a register office. When the moment comes they can bring themselves to say,

> In the name of the Father,
> **In the name of the Father,**
> And of the Son,
> **And of the Son,**
> And of the Holy Ghost,
> **And of the Holy Ghost,**
> Amen,
> **Amen,**

repeating after the vicar in too-short chunks and solemnising the most important decision of their life. It just seems right to do it in church. All the things that go *with* church are so pleasant: hymns, Bach organ music, beautiful language, flowers, bells, the lych-gate. To get married in a register office would be a public declaration of atheism; agnostics get married in church, working on the 'As if' principle. 'It just might be true. Let's behave *as if* it were true.' The parish system in England allows this. You don't have to belong to a congregation. You can just ring up the vicar, who is delighted. He hopes that there might be a grain of real Christian faith hidden in the heap of other reasons for your choice: slavery to tradition, fear of shocking your parents, superstition, the desire to be watched by 300 friends when you make your vows.

This sudden non-allergy to church is short-lived. The allergy comes back with its full force, keeping good, thinking, uncynical English people away week after week. Part of the reason is simply a lack of belief that the death of Christ was the turning-point of history. Non-churchgoers might rustle up enough belief for a wedding and a few baptisms, but they can't sustain it in the long years afterwards. It all seems less and less likely to be true, the more you discover about those maniacs in the first century who were expecting a Messiah and getting ready for the end of the world. It would be a farce to go to church and pretend to worship someone you didn't believe was God.

But, for almost-believers, there are more superficial reasons for keeping away.

If Jesus had been a Dr Johnson figure rather than a Middle Eastern man in sandals he might appeal more directly to the modern English taste. The dislike of hippies is widespread in England, and if you read the Gospels it is easy to think of Jesus as a hippy-type man who said way-out things and spoke in dreamy pictures. Dr Johnson, on the other hand, could express truths without having to tell whole stories about an erratic sower or a woman searching for a coin. He struggled and suffered and believed in God, and spoke in inspired aphorism. The modern fashion for biography has trained us to ask, 'What were people in the olden days *like*?' The way in which Jesus told stories was part of his character. Some people find it gripping; others find it long-winded and annoying.

St Paul-hatred is another reason for keeping away from church. The outrage of having to say,

This is the word of the Lord.
Thanks be to God.

after a reading from Romans is enough to make the St Paul-hater walk out. It *isn't* the word of the Lord. It's the word of St Paul, guilt-ridden and obsessed, preaching unrealistic goody-goodiness to the inhabitants of ancient cities. He was a remarkable man and a wonderful poet and thinker; but the po-faced reverence you are supposed to give him seems out of proportion to what he deserves.

Then there is squeamishness about the Cross. The revolting instrument of torture and death is something that churches force you to stare at. 'Yes, it *is* disgusting,' vicars agree, 'but the killing of Christ was disgusting, and pain is disgusting. Christ suffers with us, and for us.' But is there need for such wallowing in the Cross? You can suddenly be struck with the thought that we might as well be wallowing in an electric chair; and this thought can lead to violent Cross repulsion. At St Gabriel's, Pimlico, during the Duruflé *Requiem* I became lost in thought about the way in which a church can reek of death, if you let it. A cross on the London *A to Z* marks where it is. There are crosses wherever you look: on the walls, on the altar, behind the pulpit, attached to the lid of the font. You can find yourself sitting next to one of the Stations of the Cross – 'Jesus falls for a second time', for example – and reliving a moment of terror and agony in the hours before Christ's crucifixion. The words 'He opened wide his arms for us on the Cross', at the beginning of the Third Eucharistic Prayer, are particularly macabre. He didn't have any *choice* but to open his arms wide on the Cross. To turn this hideous posture into an image of embrace seems in very bad taste. It was done by an Early Father.

One of the smallest congregations I have been part of this year was at All Saints, Haggerston, in the East End, on Tuesday evening in Holy Week. There were four of us; two were the vicar and his wife. We did the Stations of the Cross and had Eucharist. 'Doing' the Stations of the Cross meant walking round the church from one Station to the next and, in front of each, describing it (the words were in a booklet), meditating on it, praying about it, genuflecting and singing a verse of 'My song is love unknown'. There are fourteen Stations of the Cross, each depicting a horrible moment in the Passion. It took nearly an hour and by the end we had sung the whole of 'My song is love unknown' twice.

Pews are hard. Churches are cold. Organs frown down at you. The lighting is harsh and inadequate. Church furniture can suddenly seem to reek of death as well.

Then there is the fear of boredom. The feeling of being captive in a church service can induce panic. If the vicar takes ten minutes to say 'We are now going to light the first Advent candle' there is nothing you can do about it. He explains that next week the second candle will be lit, and the week after that the third candle, and the week after that the fourth candle and on Christmas morning itself the candle in the middle. You can't interrupt him. You just have to sit there until he finishes. Services are long, and getting longer: Eucharist takes longer than mattins because of all the Ministry of the Word business at the beginning, and more and more churches have the Eucharist as the main service on Sunday. There are five hymns, and the habit of omitting verses in the middle seems to be dying out. A single linguistic habit of the celebrant can become so irritating that you decide you would rather stay at home next week than come back from church boiling with frustration and annoyance.

Then there is the pressure to settle down into a parish, which a church can't resist putting on its visitors. You can feel, rightly, that the church wants to get its claws into you, and this causes some people to run a mile. 'Do you worship regularly in a parish?' Philip Venables, the curate of St Mark's, Gillingham, asked me.

'Well, no. I don't like my parish church and I haven't really found the right one.'

'Well, you should.'

Geoffrey Lang, the eloquent vicar of St Peter's, Hammersmith, asked me where I worshipped when I was at Cambridge.

'I went to St John's quite a lot,' I said.

'Ah, St John's, Hills Road. I know it well.'

I couldn't bring myself to admit that I meant St John's *College*. A real Christian goes to a parish church, not to a college chapel to hear a good choir.

This disapproval of flitting is an off-putting force in the Going and Not Going question. An almost-believer might well stay away for fear of being asked to go on a rota or fill in a form saying 'I wish to be visited'.

Being disapproved of by a vicar is an uncomfortable feeling. But in this age it induces you not to mend your ways but to stay away from the vicar. I have found that there are clergy you can relax with and clergy you can't relax with. With the relaxing kind, you can say rude words, drink, smoke, talk about sex, discuss people behind their backs and take your shoes off. With the unrelaxing kind, the air is thick with taboo subjects. All you can say are things like, 'Are you sure I can't do some drying up? Find me a tea-towel,' or 'Was St Paul really a tent-maker, or is it just legend?' You dread being disapproved of and having to justify the self-indulgent things you spend your time doing. The Church of England has shed much of its disapproving character, but some of it remains.

'The man in the pew' is Anglican for 'the man on the Clapham omnibus'. Who is he, and what attracts him to the pew?

He is, more often than not, a woman. If, at the end of a service, you get into conversation with one of the strangers you exchanged the Sign of the Peace with, it might well go like this.

Evangelical church

Visitor: 'What a lot of people! I've never seen so many children running about. Have you been coming here for years?'

Regular: 'We moved here in 1989. My husband's an engineer and he got a job here. This place has been very welcoming to us. I don't know how we'd have managed without it. My husband's over there, actually. He does the sound system.'

Visitor: 'It's a good sound system here, isn't it? As good as a cinema. Has the worship changed much since you've been here?'

Regular: 'It's more geared towards the youngsters than it was. You get a huge age range here, from Marjorie over there who's ninety to the tiny ones. The new vicar, Paul, has done a lot of good. We have lay people leading us in worship more now, and different house groups do the intercessions.'

Visitor: 'It's so lively. So cheerful.'

Regular: 'Paul's written five or six books about his journey of faith. You can buy them at the bookstall at the back. I thoroughly recommend *Truly, Truly.*'

Anglo-catholic church. (A man this time. The conversation does not take place among the hushed pews but in the church hall twenty yards away.)

Visitor: 'It's a fascinating, mad-looking church, isn't it? Wonderful, though. Is it about 1888?'

Regular: 'Three or four of these were put up in the town in the 1870s. This was the first, and the biggest. D'you take milk?'

Visitor: 'A little. Stop. Have you been coming here for years?'

Regular: 'For ten years or so, when I'm here on Sunday. I was brought up in the evangelical tradition, you know. I owe a great deal to it. But this now seems richer, deeper, fuller.'

Visitor: 'Would you ever miss Mass on a Sunday?'

Regular: 'It's our duty and our joy, isn't it? I wouldn't miss it if I could help it. Sometimes, of course, one's stuck in the country without a car. But I don't like to miss it. Fr Jack's a marvellous priest. It's a jolly good little congregation, too. Olivia over there grew up in the evangelical tradition like me. She's had a difficult time. Her husband left her, without any warning. She feels accepted here.'

Après-service, like après-ski, is a world in itself. Conversations like the above happen in their thousands every Sunday. Lively churches have good après-service, and this is an attraction. If, in the coffee-drinking buzz after Sunday Eucharist, you stop and think to yourself, 'How different do I feel now, having come to church rather than not come?' the truth is often that you feel fizzing and exhilarated, rather as if you had just had a bath. You have *done* it. You are here, standing up and mingling with the outside world. You have made the effort, and you feel somehow cleaner. Going to church can become a drug that you need a weekly fix of. It is comfortingly regular and easy to do. You can blend into the congregation and you don't have to try very hard. Just by being there you are adding to the volume of Christian prayer, even if you hardly listen or if you stop saying the Creed half-way through, for lack of energy.

Regular churchgoers find that a Sunday spent without going to church feels bleak and wrong. Habit becomes a reason in itself for habit. Of the forces that drive a churchgoer to church every Sunday habit tends to be the most powerful. But there are others. They are different for different churches.

If you were having toast and marmalade and planning to go, in half an hour's time, to Mass at St Cuthbert's, Philbeach Gardens, near Earl's Court, the forces at work might be these. A sense of obligation, because it is the Feast of the Conversion of St Paul. A hunger to be fed with the body and blood of Jesus Christ who, in a sacramental manner, is present in the bread and wine. A thirst for the beauty of worship in that church: the incense wafting up into the dark heights, the candles, the lovely mouldings and marble pillars, the huge, symbol-rich lectern. A sense that you are needed there: the congregation is small, and by going rather than not going you will be filling the church with a whole extra human being. A desire to see the server.[1]

Cornflakes in Gillingham, and the forces at work would be quite different. What would pull a mother of two to St Mark's? A determination to steep the children in Sunday-school Christian stories from an early age, so they grow up knowing all about Lazarus, Herod, Jesus the helper, and the Feeding of the Five Thousand. A craving for the buzz of the church: the crowds of wide-awake, brightly dressed Christians on Sunday morning, who know each other and hug each other and whose children go to the same school. A craving to praise the Lord in music: it is impossible to know what songs the band-leader will choose, but he just might choose 'Meekness and Majesty'. A craving for a life-changing sermon which will explain how you can unblock the blockage which is stopping the Holy Spirit from flowing as it should.[2] The hope that you might find yourself at last able to speak in tongues.

Scrambled eggs in a farmhouse in Wiltshire, and the forces at work might be these: 'Shall we go to mattins in the village, which will be sweet and beautiful and pure Prayer Book, and where we will be needed to lower the average age of the congregation? But if we do the children will hate it, and will want to talk and play loudly with their toys. So shall we go to the Wantage Christian

---

[1] One of the most endearing traits of the Church of England is its allowing slightly strange and sad people to be servers. I have seen quite a few backward servers in sanctuaries round the country. 'The Mad Cotta' has become the generic nickname. The server at St Cuthbert's is fascinating. He has been serving there at every single solemn Mass since 1962. He is very thin and walks all the way in from Chiswick. I don't think he eats during the week, because if there is a parish lunch in the church hall he hovers round the table and can't stop picking. I tried to ask him about his long and stalwart serving life, but he said, 'I don't talk to strangers. Keep myself to myself', and carried on with his chicken drumstick.
[2] This plumbing image is used quite often in charismatic churches to explain how the Holy Spirit works.

Fellowship instead? There's a crèche. We can relax.' Thus the Church of England option is rejected for the independent-church option, for the sake of convenience and peace of mind.

All Bran at dawn in Gloucestershire, and these are the forces at work in the head of the elderly tea-sipper. The feeling that you ought to go to church and you might as well get it over with. The decision, taken at the same hour every week, to go to the Book of Common Prayer Holy Communion service at eight o'clock. No fuss, no shaking hands, no hideous language, no need to talk to anyone afterwards. All over by nine.

The church responds to these forces. The eight o'clock Holy Communion, not much liked by many clergy (who feel that the Prayer Book communion service concentrates too much on sin and not enough on joy) is none the less kept on year after year. Old people like it. They are called the 'eight o'clockers'. If you get up very early on a Sunday morning in a village and go out before eight to buy the papers, you see the eight o'clockers walking slowly to church with their hats on.

At the other end of the spectrum, and at the other end of the day, you get the 'seven o'clockers'. Vigorous evangelical churches ('vigorous' is the adjective most used to describe a large, happy and growing church) have in many places decided to move their Sunday evening service from six thirty to seven, to allow the young things to come back from wherever they have been all weekend. On summer evenings, relaxed Christians in young London congregations have a sun-tanned, tennis-playing, M4-traffic-jam-enduring look about them.

Crèche life is growing in parish churches. When a church is re-ordered, new space is allotted to babies and children, through a glass door so that the separation is not traumatic. Churches are so keen to attract new members that they will do almost anything to make it easier for people with cars or children. Vicars agonise about how to get younger people in. The vicar of Tokyngton near Wembley, John Metivier, said that he couldn't decide whether or not to abolish Prayer Book evensong on Sundays and replace it with something more attractive to twenty-five-year-olds. Only six people had come to evensong the previous Sunday: two of them were clergy and the other four had come in the morning. What of the other 4,994 people in the parish? How could they be lured? But wouldn't it be sad to get rid of the lovely service of evensong?

Twenty- to thirty-year-olds are harder to attract than children. Parish churches tend to have wonderful relationships with the nearby schools, and this means that vicars know far more children than grown-ups. If you go for a walk with a vicar round his parish you notice that children are always saying 'hello' while grown-ups don't recognise him. This was particularly striking in North Thamesmead, the marshy cul-de-sac of south-east London, beyond Woolwich, beyond everywhere, where newly built roundabouts peter out into nothing and leafy walkways connect the park to the houses and the houses to the wide river. On a hot July afternoon children were walking along the tame paths after school to buy ice-creams at the only shop. They all knew Christopher Byers, the team rector. He asked them how well they did on sports day. 'This isn't a churchgoing area,' he told me. 'I'm not out to get 'em into church. I am here as someone who is to build up the life of the community and of the people in the community, and to get this place to work. I think life is more than church. The C of E is at its best when it's living alongside and accompanying people.'

On a rainy Sunday in Wallsend two eight-year-old boys were to be baptised, and it was their own decision. Mark had decided to become Mark Peter. Their willing relatives and godparents came along, and St Luke's church was packed. In the same upside-down way that descendants of the Africans whom British missionaries converted to Christianity in the nineteenth century are coming back to re-convert us, eight-year-old children are now starting to convert their parents.

'This hasn't been a century of great congregations,' said Dick Lucas at St Helen's, Bishopsgate, arguing that great preachers cannot exist without large and spiritually hungry audiences. This was harsh. His own congregation seems large enough. Hundreds of City people in well-cut suits make for St Helen's at lunchtime on Tuesdays. The scene outside is like the rush hour at Cannon Street, except that no one is carrying a briefcase. They sit for a full forty-five minutes listening to a strong sermon, and only then, if they have put their names on a list first, can they have sandwiches and fruit from the trestle tables.

Great congregations exist, and you come upon them suddenly. St Luke's, Wallsend, has a great congregation. In fifteen minutes at the après-service in the church hall I met Olive, who runs the local Mothers' Union and sends aid overseas; Ada, an ex-church warden, who runs a bereavement service in the parish, visiting mourners; Brian in the navy, Brian's sister and their parents who have been coming for years; John, a Samaritan on three nights a month, who started coming to church because things were difficult at home and he needed forgiveness; and a woman in beige whose husband left her and who is now a dedicated lay member, doing the hymn boards. The atmosphere in the church hall was exhilarating. The vicar and his wife, John and Denise Inge, are exemplary in that they are neither stuffy nor prim but full of delight in parish life. Hymns and songs in the church are sung loudly, and this is a sign of high morale. Denise practised 'Meekness and Majesty' on the flute after breakfast.

When a good vicar leaves, congregations sometimes dwindle. The quality of one does to some extent depend on the quality of the other. The congregation of St Paul's, Deptford, in south London is still in shock after the sudden death of Fr David Diamond, who single-handedly converted most of them. I visited him six months before he died and he took me down the high street, pointing out his converts: the woman in the pie and mash shop, the woman in the launderette, those three boys loafing about. 'Come to the Festival Mass and you'll see them all. They all come – black, white and khaki.' He carried a large bunch of keys around, for opening vandal-proof doors to safes and store cupboards. 'You have to be like St Peter in this place. But last Sunday two petty car thieves sat in church next to the very officer who nicked them.'

'People in working-class parishes need colour.' I had always heard this. 'They're not interested in the theology of the Word. They want the sacraments, they want theatre, they want to *do* something.' Now I saw the theory at work. On the June evening of the Festival Mass at St Paul's, Deptford, we were in church from seven thirty till ten. It was packed to the galleries with gazing crowds: whole families, black people kissing white people, tiny yobs with crew cuts, friendly, fat women with thick necks and short grey hair, girls of baby-sitting age with bad teeth. At the entrance of 'Bishop Roy' of Southwark, everyone sang,

> Consider yourself at home,
> Consider yourself as one of the fami-lee.

There was supposed to be a performance of dancing from seven thirty till eight, but it went on till eight thirty because every nation had to have its turn: Africans, West Indians, Thai children, Thai sixth-formers in dazzling clothes.

The hard core stayed for Mass. The church was still packed but you could at least find a seat. Fr Diamond read the water-into-wine story from the Gospel, nodding his head every time he came to the word 'Jesus'. Bishop Roy's text was 'God has laid on a party, and I am invited'. He repeated the text at the end of each thought, in his warm Irish accent. 'God has laid on a party, and I am invited'.

Incense was swished upwards and downwards over everything. A little skinhead boatboy and a black boy were servers. A strict grown-up server pushed them about. Most of the time they were allowed to be like Wimbledon ballboys, sitting low on the side and watching.

There was a production-line air about the Eucharist itself. 'The Bread of Life, the Bread of Life, the Bread of Life,' you could hear the administering bishop saying, giving the open-mouthed receivers no time to say 'Amen' before the wafer was on their tongue and he was on to the next one. He pronounced Mass 'Marse' when he said it was ended. Then the Romford Children's Band marched in through the west door, playing 'Mine eyes have seen the glory of the coming of the Lord' and beating drums.

There aren't many slum priests of the 1890s kind left; Fr Diamond was one of the last. He actually called himself a slum priest, and devoted his life to converting his parishioners with cheap and cheerful sacramental religion. The most common way of being converted now is by the words and emotions of evangelicals rather than by the smells and tastes of Anglo-catholicism. To be converted through the evangelical channel you need to be quite mature because it requires experience of the cruel world. It helps if you are slightly sad and vulnerable, and have a deep need for rebirth. A Born Again congregation is a well-behaved and mature congregation, keen to learn and be reformed, keen to listen to other people's conversion experiences and to talk about Jesus after the service. The crowds at St Paul's, Deptford, would rather talk about pie and mash than about Jesus. But they believe, implicitly, that

> God was man in Palestine
> And lives today in bread and wine.

IO

Four Vignettes of Lay Life

*T*he first vignette illustrates different kinds of zeal. We see
the mattins-loving Anglican-from-childhood talking to the
fervent Born Again Christian who goes to an independent
church.

A. N. Wilson sent me to see Richard Adams. 'I have thought of
a distinguished lay person whom you *must* interview.' So I went
to lunch with the Adamses in Whitchurch. They live in a lovely
house with low ceilings and large windows.

'I can't think why he sent you to see me. You couldn't find a
more ordinary member of the church than I am.'

'Well, it's interesting to meet ordinary members. I've spent so
much time with vicars who are immersed in the Church and think
about nothing else. It's interesting to meet lay people who just go
to church. I want to find out what lay people think about things
like the ordination of women.'

'Controversy is a matter for the officers of the church. The
private soldier in the ranks has got no reason to enter into the
controversy. I'm sure many women would make excellent clergy,
energetic and enthusiastic. The sooner the better. I'm surprised
they didn't do it ages ago. Why on earth are people against it?'

'They say things like "Jesus only chose male apostles".'

'You can't restrict modern thinking to "what Jesus would

think". He didn't say anything about animal rights, but I regard my work with animal rights as an important part of my Christian life.'

'When you shut your eyes and think of God, what do you see?'

'I think God's within you. He certainly isn't anywhere else. It's harmful, this feeling that God is up in the sky, because it isn't true. D'you read Jung? Jung saw Christ as an archetype within the soul. He talked about the Christ figure within all of us. My secretary ought to join in this conversation. She's a Born Again Christian. Liz!'

Liz popped her head round the door.

'Come and talk to us about Christianity.'

'Oh, yes!' Liz was large, dark and beaming.

'Did you have a moment of conversion?' I asked her.

'I've written some testimonies. I'll send them to you if you give me your address. I can tell you the exact day. It was 11 December 1976, and I was up in the balcony of the church at an induction service. I felt a big, warm hand on my shoulder, and I turned round, and there was nobody there. I was stunned, and afterwards I told the new minister about it. He said calmly, "*I* saw the hand of the Lord on your shoulder." That was the beginning.'

'Do you still worship in the parish church?'

'I worship in a Christian fellowship now, actually.'

'D'you believe in miracles?'

'Miracles have *happened* to me. I had a chronic blood condition for years – I've written a testimony about this, too – and I was terribly ill, on steroids. Colin Urquhart came to lead Mission Newbury in 1985, and at one of the meetings he said this: "There is someone in this tent who has a chemical imbalance which affects the metabolism. The Lord is healing you now." I just knew that person was me. And it was. The next morning I was better: not shaking any more, not feeling ill. I haven't taken a steroid since that day. I've been completely healed by the Lord Jesus.'

'D'you really feel the Holy Spirit working?'

'Oh, yes! I was on a motorbike with my husband in 1987, and we had a Word of Knowledge that we were going to have an accident. We committed ourselves to the hand of God. I had a Peace about it.

I was thrown off the pillion seat and was unconscious for fifteen minutes. But not a single broken bone. You think of that.'

'Does the Holy Spirit tell *you* what's going to happen in that way?' I asked Richard Adams, who was listening to Liz with patience and astonishment.

'I can't say that he does. I think I'm less likely to feel the Holy Spirit than somebody like Liz.'

'Would you like the whole world to be Christian?'

'I've just been reading Margaret Mead, the American expert on the Polynesians and the South Seas. She *did* on the whole think it was a good thing that the Polynesians and the South Seas had discovered Christianity. [To Liz] Would you like Islam to be converted to Christianity?'

Liz: 'The Islamics don't know the Lord. I'm sorry but they don't. It's not through good works that people are saved.'

'Did you have a conversion experience like Liz?' I asked Richard.

'No, I can't say that I did. Christianity's the air I breathe. Prep school gave me a good grounding in the Gospel and Acts, and the story bits of the Old Testament. At public school I learned about the Prophets and St Paul. It was all very much taken for granted. My reason for believing in Jesus is what he said and what he did.'

'D'you believe in the bodily Resurrection?'

'I wouldn't say the Resurrection was the essence of my belief. Gods do rise from the dead. Isis does, for one.'

Liz: 'I think people should give a testimony as to how they came to know Jesus as their saviour and their Lord. I'm thinking of the Bishop of Durham.'

'What about music?' I asked them both. 'What effect do you think it has on worship?'

Liz: 'It lifts you up to the Lord.'

Richard: 'Well, people *like* singing. I very much regret the discontinuance of psalms and canticles. I can't remember when I was last called upon to sing the *Te Deum*. This is a generation of people who wouldn't know what to do with a canticle if they saw one. Psalms were of *great* importance at Bradfield. At seventeen, I didn't like the Holy Communion service. There wasn't enough for the congregation to do. I wouldn't say Holy Communion was my favourite service by any manner of means. Evensong's a nice service. When I was toying with becoming a Roman Catholic, my real reason for deciding not to was an emotional one. I *liked* the Anglican services. I went to Mass while fishing in the West of Ireland. The congregation just stood there.'

'D'you have Holy Communion in your fellowship?' I asked Liz.

Liz: 'Yes, we do, sometimes. Our fellowship uses non-alcoholic wine.'

Richard: 'I know a clergyman who gives claret at Holy Communion. He wouldn't give anything else.'

'Would you mind if you had a homosexual vicar?'

'I must say, I'm a bit of a child of my time on this subject. I do think it's wrong. I wouldn't feel a bit happy if an incumbent of my church was homosexual.'

Liz: 'It's an abomination. The Bible's clear about it. It's an abomination to the Lord. So is the occult. I used to be very involved in the occult. I was a medium and I did tarot cards, crystal ball, ouija boards, etc. Now I know that they're an abomination to the Lord. You can look it up in Deuteronomy, chapter 18. I wrote a fourteen-page letter of warning to Richard Grant who's heavily involved in the occult, but he didn't reply.'

'I can safely say,' said Richard, 'that I've never had a super-natural experience.'

Then we had lunch cooked by Mrs Adams. It was delicious chicken, and Chablis to drink. Liz was a vegetarian, and she drank water rather than Chablis. 'I can't think why A. N. Wilson sent you here,' Richard Adams said again.

Liz sent me her testimonies the next day, with a long letter which ended, 'I pray you find the strength, and will, to renounce your involvement in the occult. The freedom is great! Meanwhile, God bless you. Yours sincerely in the Lord Jesus Christ, Liz.'

Now, an evangelical children's camp on the north coast of Norfolk. Lay Christians, many of them schoolteachers, give up two weeks of their summer to run these camps. This one is called Dolphin Camp, and it has been happening on the same patch of Norfolk coast every August since 1919. *Andrew Makower, a Clerk of the House of Lords, invited me to stay at it when he was a tent officer in the Recess.*

'Safety belt done up?' Andrew asked in the car-park at West Runton station. 'Right. Camp's half a mile away. I've left Commy in charge of my shooting ploy, so we'd better hurry.'

'Who's Commy?' I asked. 'What's a ploy?'

'Commy's in charge of camp. Short for Commandant. A chemistry master at Christ's Hospital. Very nice chap. Small ploys are activities – things that campers get on with on free afternoons. But it's nearly tea now, so *you* won't have to join a ploy. But you will be expected to tell a funny story at tea. All visitors are. Have you thought of one?'

'No. I don't know any jokes.'

'Well, you'd better think of something. There's half an hour still to go.'

The car swung into a green field on the edge of the North Sea. On the field were four columns of white wigwam-shaped tents, as symmetrical and pretty as stationary ballerinas.

'So these are bell tents,' I said.

'And that's the upper marquee and that's the lower marquee. This is the gubbins bin. Up there are the latrines.'

'And what are they playing there?' Leaping children were facing each other on either side of a high net, throwing a small, dense rubber ring into the air, backwards and forwards.

'That's halo. Everyone plays it here.'

The halo pitch was in the middle of the camping ground, between the girls' lines and the boys' lines, and I couldn't stop thinking about the word. The game was invented after the First World War when these children's camps started, and it is fascinating to think that people were so steeped in religious symbol that the sight of a small, dense rubber ring should remind them of the circular golden aura on top of St Mary. It is the opposite inspiration to the one which calls a clergy collar a dog-collar: it gives the secular a religious name, rather than the other way round. You might as well call a frisbee a 'wafer', or lacrosse 'casting the nets'.

Dolphin Camp has hardly changed at all since 1919, except that twenty yards of the camping ground have fallen into the sea. The image of the eroding camping ground is often used in sermons in the lower marquee, to remind the children that they are citizens of no abiding city. The campers are aged between nine and thirteen: the age when they love jokes, and don't mind if the last word of a limerick is the same as the one at the end of the first line. They don't have a proper bath for two weeks. 'The sea is our bath,' said Andrew.

Adj said Grace in the upper marquee. The orderlies went off to collect our pink spam from the trestle tables. I sat next to a quiet, serene little girl aged nine called Anna Dunn who just ate slice after slice of white bread.

'*T and TPT*!' shouted ADC, when the plates had been cleared away.

'What's *T and TPT*?' I asked the tent officer on my table.

'The *Tent and Tent-peg Telegraph*. It's a running newspaper we have at the end of each day. Watch.'

One by one, Commy, Adj, ADC, Docko (the doctor), Andrew and a cook called Fiona stood at the front and were funny, in hats. They read out items in read-all-about-it voices, telling of results on the halo pitch, and making much of some very minor incidents in Tent Nine. The campers were riveted. Then the visitors were asked to stand up. The other visitor was a tall, athletic Christian wearing a tracksuit and a crucifix pendant. We found ourselves being bowed and curtseyed to by the children nearest to us.

'Now we're all going to sing to you, aren't we?' said ADC.

To the tune of the 'Ode to Joy', the high-pitched campers sang their loaded welcome.

> There are strangers in our presence,
> Let us greet them *with* a song . . .
> Now tell us a funny story,
> But make sure it's *not* too long.

The athletic Christian got up first and told a long story about tanks and soldiers which everyone loved. At the gruesome bits they all shouted 'Horriiid!' I had just been told about arrow prayers, and how you can shoot them up at moments of urgent need. I tried one.

'Please make me not have to tell a joke. Please. I beg you. Amen.'
It worked.

'Do please –' began Commy.

'Go!' chanted the campers. It is the code for the end of meals. The camp runs on running jokes which have been running since 1919.

'Been sucked into the holiness competition, have you?' Andrew asked when he came up behind the upper marquee and found me in a huge pair of industrial rubber gloves, scrubbing mug after mug and pouring left-overs into a smelly hole called the wet sump. I had, indeed, been sucked in. Being at Dolphin Camp makes you long to work harder than anyone else and make the mugs cleaner than they have ever been, in rows, ready for breakfast.

'OK. Anagrams for "wet sump",' said a steward.

We bent our minds to this new word game as steam from the buckets of hot, green water rose towards the pale sky. It was not nearly dark. In our tent, Libby and Hazel, two tent officers, were having a rest. They were exhausted from sleeping in a bell tent for a week, helping from dawn till dusk and going to the loo in disguised buckets. Libby's back was hurting because she had been playing too much halo with her tent. When I crawled in after the washing-up she was sprawled out on her mat with a biro, trying to write a limerick about being woken up in the night by what she thought was a caterpillar but turned out to be the toggle on her sleeping-bag.

But of course Jesus died, so camps like this can't all be fun. In the evening, gas lamps were slung up in the lower marquee and everyone shuffled in – eighty small campers and thirty big helpers – and took a copy of *Junior Praise*. Commy, in shorts, was standing at the front.

'We'll start with number 185,' he said.

Campers aged between nine and thirteen love the morbid, sad lines of choruses. They know them by heart and sing them with feeling, almost wailing:

> Bleeding, dying,
> Bleeding, dying . . .

An hour ago they had been listening, riveted, to the story about tanks and soldiers; now, again, they were being carried away by thoughts of agony and death. Commy spoke in his evening voice, softly and seriously. He began by giving a demonstration of not-fairness, with chocolate. 'When Christ died, it wasn't fair.' Then he told a terrible story about a family dying in a car crash, which again held the children riveted. 'What did it demonstrate?'

Hands shot up. 'Love.'

'Love. Yes. That was the sort of love God had for Jesus. When we get to the end here, what's going to happen? When we reach death it's very morbid – really terrible. And yet camp has just been singing praise songs to God, happy songs. Read what St Paul says in Colossians: "God has now brought you to life in Christ." God forgives us all our sins. Think: Tent 32, wasn't it yesterday, distinctly went against the rules.'

On the blackboard, Commy drew two boxes with a gap between them. One said 'Life on earth' and the other said 'Life in God'. 'I'm not an artist, I'm afraid. But God nailed our sin to the cross. Bang, bang, bang.' Commy nailed a cardboard cross into the gap. 'And you'll notice that I position this so that, with a bit of a step which you'll learn about in camp, you'll get through this gap. What did Mr Makower tell us last night in his talk about being lost at sea without Commy, when the campers had their intercommy but didn't know whether to use it?'

All the hands in the front row shot up.

'To holler for help is heroic.'

'Exactly. There *is* a way across that gap.'

It was bedtime for the campers. On the black lawn between the girls' lines and the boys' lines three T.O.s stood guard, telling the bell tents to pipe down. Later there was a prayer meeting for the grown-ups. The upper marquee still smelled of seconds, but the trestle tables had been cleared away and replaced with a circle of weathered chairs. Gas lamps hissed and we sat in silence, hanging our heads in prayer and drowsiness. The funny cook in plaits, who had waddled about during the *T and TPT*, speaking in a clownish, quacking voice and putting aside all her dignity for the sake of making the campers laugh, had become serious again, and seemed a different person.

'This one chokes me up whenever I sing it,' she said. 'Number 79.'

It was 'When I survey the wondrous cross'. Adj's wife played the guitar, watching her hardened fingers stretch and contort as they changed chords. The hymn was sung slowly, with lots of little twangy notes where you would usually have solid chunks of organ:

Demands my soul, my life, my all, *strum, strum, strummm.*

We plunged back into silence. People said impromptu prayers aloud, sending up thanks and confessions in fierce voices. 'Yes, Lord, oh, yes, yes, Lord,' the tent officer on my right whispered in agreement to other people's prayers.

Some tent officers fell asleep trying to prepare for the next day which was Sunday. On Sunday there was double the amount to eat, and a scavenger hunt and a crocker match. Crocker is a kind of Christian cricket, easy to do well at.

Other, greedier tent officers stayed awake for gannets, which is a late-night feast of left-overs in the mobile kitchen. Campers long to be tent officers when they grow up.

A parish pilgrimage to Walsingham in late June with the clergy and congregation of St Michael's, Brighton.

It took from seven o'clock till lunch-time to get from Brighton to Walsingham. The parishioners were prepared. They brought things to do on the coach. Prebendary Gerard Irvine was looking after me. He had sweets in his bag, and *The Tablet,* and his own old brown office book stuffed with pretty cards and holy bookmarks. He said Morning Prayer to himself on the M23, then offered sweets round, saying, 'Happy pilgrimage!' The parishioners were dressed in suitable clothes – hats and loose tops and sandals. Fr Freddie Jackson, the priest in charge of the pilgrimage, was nervous and shepherd-like, making sure we were all all right. The loo stop near Newmarket took three-quarters of an hour, because the tiny roadside conveniences were not designed for pilgrimage-sized groups. Roman Catholic and Anglican women queued up together. The Roman Catholics said, 'Are you going to Lerds this year?' to each other. The Anglicans said, 'Isn't it awful being a woman and having to queue for the loo?' We got back into the hot coach and went on for two more hours. At Walsingham we piled out, dazed, on to the blazing road beside the shrine.

The little Walsingham world is small and well-organised. Groups sit about on the lawn until the woman in charge of room allocations comes out and tells you where you are sleeping. The moment you find out you rush upstairs and sink into delicious privacy. I longed to wash my face but there was no towel, so I had to go to the Walsingham gift shop and buy a Walsingham tea-towel depicting the Slipper Chapel, the East Window Arch and the Pump House.

In the dining-room you help yourself with a tray and try to mingle with other pilgrim groups. I sat next to a group of old ladies from Durham who had taken even longer to drive here and were relieved. Then we went for a little walk. We walked round the mini-Calvary, which is a hillock with the three crosses wrongly close to the empty tomb, like Big Ben and the Tower of London in tourist advertisements which pretend they are in the same street. There are many little chapels to go into and think about the Queen of Heaven. She appeared here in the Middle Ages to Richeldis. The shrine itself is hot with candles and smells of melting wax. It is time to pray.

We went for a walk in the town, looking at the gift shops and the other pilgrims. There was a huge group from the Diocese of Trinidad and Tobago, milling about. Fr Irvine said 'hello' to them and 'happy pilgrimage!' The Methodist minister stood solitarily at the door of his plain chapel. I went in and was refreshed by the plainness. The shrine church can make you feel full up and sick, it is so thickly decorated and laden with symbols and plaques.

'Mass and procession', said our timetable, in the after-supper patch. The shrine church was so full that there was nowhere to sit down except on the floor. We couldn't see. The procession was a relief because we could go outside. The processional hymn lasts for twenty minutes and every verse has two lines and a refrain:

> Then lift high your voices, rehearse the glad tale
> Of Our Lady's appearing in Stiffkey's fair vale.
> Ave, Ave, Ave Maria, Ave, Ave, Ave Maria.

It is good to hear 'Stiffkey' in a hymn, when you have taken it for granted all your life that hymn place-names can only be Middle Eastern – Jordan's bank or the little town of Bethlehem. A photographer takes a snap of you as you shuffle round a corner in your crocodile. You can buy one the next day and you look unattractive, holding a candle and a hymn book with your mouth open. Far away in front, the statue of Our Lady is being carried high up, in sedan-chair fashion.

After the procession I sat up late talking to two of the parishioners about their difficult lives and their torments of remorse and disappointment. Walsingham makes conversations like this happen, and this is what makes people who in some ways loathe Walsingham feel fond of it. You really talk to people, and feel better the next day.

On the small rosy lawn straight after Mass and breakfast on Sunday, six of the St Michael's pilgrims lit up early-morning cigarettes. The people who like coming to Walsingham are often those who suffer and feel a bit of a mess and have yellow fingers from smoking. Priests are on standby to hear confessions. We walked to the Slipper Chapel, which you are supposed to do with no shoes on like the early pilgrims did. It is a long walk and the previous night's conversations carried on. The lanes were golden and hot. It felt Chaucerian to be listening to stories while moving towards a holy place. The Slipper Chapel is clean and quiet and you sit there, thirsty, praying for your friends and family.

On the way back to Brighton we said the Angelus on the stroke of six, then sang choruses. I was ill afterwards from the exhaustion of communal life.

Some vignettes of lay life in prison now. Convents, prisons and the Queen's bedroom are three places I have always longed to see inside. The first two came into the scope of this book.

'People just *say* they're Born Again Christians so they can get a lighter sentence,' a group of sallow prisoners in the canteen at Winson Green prison told me. The canteen is the enormous, whirring room up two flights of concrete stairs where the prisoners make mail-bags, hold-alls and horse blankets. They said, 'Hello, Miss' when I went up to talk to them. Hardly anyone calls anyone

'Miss' any more and I liked it. The politeness of prisoners is striking.

At the Bible class in the chaplain's office in the afternoon, Maggie from Prison Link, who took the class, had a more grating voice and manner than anyone else in the room. First she made us sing 'Holy, holy, holy' to a funny new tune.

'But I don't know that one,' said a confused prisoner. 'I know "Holy, holy ho-lee, Lord God almigh-tee".'

'No, it goes like this,' said Maggie. 'Holy, ho-lee, holy, ho-lee.' Everyone tried to join in. By the end they had nearly learnt it and one of them said, 'I *like* the new tune.'

Then Maggie said long prayers. 'We pray that you will meet us at the very point of our needs.' Then she told us that to be great is to be misunderstood. 'Paul was misunderstood, and he was a great man.' The prisoners listened in silence. The reading was Acts 21, verses 1 to 17 and 26. This made us go straight to verses 18 to 25 to see what had been left out. It was a complicated bit about Gentiles and purification.

'Let's read round the class. Why don't you start?'

The inmates took turns to read, very slowly. It was about Paul's third missionary journey. 'P-tole – P-tole –'

'Ptolemais,' Maggie corrected, dropping the 'P'.

'Pass,' said a Caliban-like prisoner when it was his turn to read. That was a sign that he didn't want to. He wasn't made to. Mark, a serious and scary-looking man, took over. He had a different version from ours and this was refreshing. He read slowly but beautifully. 'He must be in for fraud,' I thought. 'He's really clever.'

The room was stuffy and smelly. The tiny Victorian window was closed and steamed up. We were sleepy. Even Maggie said 'cavalry' when she meant 'Calvary'. She told us about St Paul, and what it must have been like to *be* St Paul.

At the end of the class an orderly called David said he had nearly cried during the Bible class, the reading was so beautiful. Mark, the scary-looking clever one, talked about the Holy Spirit in a serene way. He looked dazed by his new belief and I don't think he was just putting it on to get a lighter sentence. The next day he was being put into a van and driven to a prison in Leicester for a year and eight months. He was a sculptor, he said, and it was he that had sculpted the white Christ figure on top of the chaplain's filing cabinet. Earl fiddled with a rosary given to him by one of the Franciscans from the house down the road. He gave me a spare crucifix.

'Christmas here is as flat as a pancake,' said the chaplain, Bryan Gracie. 'It's permanent Easter Saturday here, waiting for the Resurrection of Sunday.'

The Anglican chapel at Winson Green is awful because it is a cinema most of the time. The prisoners think of it as a cinema. The unimaginative text for the embroidery on the wall is 'I was in prison and you visited me'. Prison chaplains talk about 'Strangeways' in the way that monks talk about 'Vatican 2'. It was a watershed in prison-chapel life, because that is where the riots started. Now inmates have to sign their name on a list if they want to be chapel-goers. Few do.

At Ford Open Prison near Arundel the chapel is smart and octagonal and smells new rather than old. The chaplain, Brian Barnes-Ceeny, is friendly and jolly and told me that only eight per cent of prisoners put 'nil' on the form which asks them what their religion is. The ones in doubt tend to put 'C of E'. When prisoners grumble he says, 'Don't do the crime if you can't do your time.' But he assures them that the wonderful thing about Christ is that he *seeks* the sinner. Other religions don't have the vital pinion of forgiveness at the centre.

Well-dressed City of London prisoners in polished brogues are the chapel orderlies.

'What did you do that makes you be here?' I dared to ask one of them, who was handsome and balding.

'Rather a lot of money went missing from a firm of solicitors in the City,' he said. 'I felt that the firm was treating me quite badly, and I took revenge by financing my passion, which is collecting pictures. For men like us it's the first and hopefully the last time we'll have to come to somewhere like this.'

'It's a time for reflection,' said Tony, who came from what he called 'a conventional background in Kent' and was in for stealing in order to keep his house. 'I had no time to reflect before. I was a social Christian. Now I really think about Christianity.'

'I was in a church choir as a boy, but I drifted away from church,' said the City man. 'Perhaps that's why I'm here.'

They took me to 'A' Wing to see Nick Young, the son of the late chaplain to the Queen, who was in for a financial offence. He was charming, and his job was to cook bacon and eggs for the officers, in a kitchen which stank of cooking oil. His cell a few doors down the corridor was neat and pretty, with a row of devotional books above the desk, and photographs of his beautiful wife (now ex-wife) and well-brought-up children. 'My faith has strengthened enormously since being here,' he said.

The chaplain had a box of Kleenex in his filing cabinet, and he gave me a wadge, out of pure generosity. I wasn't crying. 'A fair number of those who come to chapel are solicitors,' he said. 'We've only got one or two lifers that come.'

'You're considered a bit soft if you go to chapel here,' Tony said. 'You're not a real man.'

II

Nuns

Letters from clergymen come on thick white paper with a printed address at the top. They are usually typed and as you read them you can hear the voice of the dictating and overworked vicar making the most of his part-time secretary. These letters fall heavily on the mat. From the furthest corner of my bedroom I can hear a clergyman's letter arriving.

Letters from nuns, on the other hand, make no sound at all. You can go for hours without even realising that the post has come. My 'letters from nuns' file still feels pitifully thin, even though if I count them there are actually over twenty-five. A letter from a nun comes in a minute doormat-coloured envelope which has been used at least once before. It is written on a tiny sheet of paper – as small as the smallest Basildon Bond size you could possibly buy, and much thinner.

The neatness makes you sit up straight as you read. Yes, do come and stay; vespers is at four forty-five and supper at six fifteen. We will expect you at four o'clock. The letter is the opposite of dictated. The guest sister at West Malling Abbey in Kent has turned the clicking knob on her unelectric typewriter, forcing the small piece of paper round the trusty cylinder. She has worked out a system of indents, of line-spaces, of where to put the telephone number in relation to the address, and of where to put the important fact that you can't ring her up at any old time: 'Guest sister answers 7.0 – 7.15 p.m. daily.'

Some nuns write by hand but the neatness is just as striking. There is usually a calligraphic element in the handwriting: something about the 'd's and 'e's that makes you think of plainsong. When you arrive at the abbey at West Malling the first thing you read is the hand-painted sign on the gate with its pretty diphthong: 'ST MARY'S ABBEY. NO PARKING'.

You could live a long life as a regular and fulfilled churchgoer without ever finding out that the Church of England has monks and nuns. They don't make their presence felt in the way that Roman Catholic ones do. The back of the *Catholic Herald* always has fascinating advertisements where nuns advertise for more nuns at £5 per single-column centimetre. But Anglican nuns never advertise for new vocations in the *Church Times*, or anywhere. They just pray.

'Fulfil now, O Lord, the prayers of thy faithful people, as may be most expedient for them.' Thus such prayers end. When no new vocations come, and convents begin to die, God seems to be making it clear that it is most expedient for the convents if they do die. Nuns tend to be serene and philosophical about this. Shrinking communities shrink quietly and gracefully, until the final remaining nun is buried in the garden with her absent sisters. Their work is done.

A trickle of novitiate is all that is needed to keep a community going. Most Anglican communities have this trickle. Typical statistics for Anglican nuns in the *Benedictine Yearbook* would be: Nuns: 36. Novices: 2. Two is infinitely better than none. And when you think what it means to be one of those two novices, it seems amazing that any modern young woman should actually choose to become one. Yet they do. Rachel at Wantage, aged twenty-six, in her white veil with nothing of her own on but her old watch; Sister Seonaid at West Malling, missing being allowed to sit with her feet up reading a book with a mug of Nescafé: they are doing it, at this very moment. They really aren't going to hug a man ever again, or go to France.

There is certainly an element of voyeurism in the lay person's fascination for nuns. But, as the Bishop of Lancaster said to me when I admitted to a 'Thank goodness I am not one of them' sensation when I watch nuns processing blackly into compline, you must never feel guilty about having mixed motives. Mixed with the 'rather them than me' feeling is a strong 'thank goodness they exist' feeling.

People who don't know much about Anglican nuns say that they are marginal. People who do care and know about them say that they are important. Their constant prayer is important for the world. They set an example to the doubting passer-by: God has called them, so there must be such a thing as God. They provide an oasis of peace and regularity of life in a world where trains are cancelled due to an incident at Sandy.

Their importance used to be more outward and obvious than it is now. In the mid-nineteenth century intelligent, well-brought-up Anglican girls were itching to do good in a Christian way – to help reform prostitutes, for example – and religious houses were founded for them by kind vicars with the bishop's tentative approval. The Benedictine community which is now surviving but shrinking in a small country house in Leicestershire was founded in the London Docks in the 1850s when the parochial system was proving inadequate to minister to the ragged and ill poor of the lower Thames. The new sisterhoods provided work for the girls and lightened the burden of the vicar. The community at Wantage was similarly founded in order for women to be able to do active good in the world, rehabilitating the needy. Until very recently the Wantage nuns were still rehabilitating female alcoholics in Harpenden. But they have just withdrawn from the town. And ten years ago they withdrew from teaching at St Mary's, Wantage, so now the school is boringly lay, with not a habit in sight, just a new sports centre and a metal footbridge. The nuns live on the other side of the town. 'The days of highly skilled and experienced amateurs are over,' Mother Alleyne of Wantage explained to me. 'You have to have qualifications now, and a long training, and keep abreast of professional requirements.'

So, while vicars find that they have less and less time for private prayer and study, and have to spend more time than ever out at meetings, nuns find that they are sitting still and praying more and more.

The satisfaction of rehabilitating haggard female penitents has been replaced with the slightly less exciting task of providing hospitality to perfectly healthy people who come for retreats. Another aspect of the importance of religious houses is that tired lay people can go to stay at them and be quiet for days on end. You go to the daily offices, read a spiritual book or two and write letters on holy notelets which the nuns sell. Guests flock to Wantage; the convent is in danger of taking on a hotel-like air. 'Hospitality' is one of the things that nuns write on the leaflets about themselves: most communities seem to have a 'what the community does' leaflet. Printing is another of their activities. There is always a rack of home-made 'Come Holy Spirit' and 'I am the true vine' cards for sale: they are some of the cheapest objects in the whole Church of England, costing five pence, sometimes four pence.

Clergymen go on retreats: if you go to stay at a convent you nearly always find that one of the other guests is Fr someone, on his own, tired-looking, not wanting to talk. Clergymen and their wives who are having trouble with their marriages go to talk to nuns about how difficult marriage is and how when the telephone rings it is always for him. Nuns listen.

'Ours is essentially a hidden life.' Two of my thin calligraphic letters contain that very sentence. The whole point of enclosed nuns (battery nuns as opposed to free-range nuns, as they are sometimes called) is that they live a private life which you never see, behind walls. The curious visitor has to do a lot of tactful gleaning. Spying is instantly noticed: after lunch at Fairacres I lingered for a second in the hall outside the nuns' dining-room, reading the noticeboard. 'Are you lost?' the guest sister asked. '*That* way.' And I was back in the guest world, ousted from the enclosure.

Days of my Church of England year have been spent in silence at convents, waiting for the bell to ring for the next meal or the next office. Ding, ding, ding, it goes, exactly five minutes before the event. I put my glasses on, which is certainly a voyeuristic thing to do: it is not in order to read the psalms but in order to see clearly the faces of the distant nuns: their lines, the expressions on their faces, sometimes rigid, sometimes beatific.

Rempstone Hall, West Malling, Wantage and Fairacres were the four convents at which I stayed; at each, the gleaning was constant and vigilant. There were obvious similarities and differences. The similarities were noticeboards, words on the loo about how to flush it, birdsong before Lauds, the posh 'o' sound the nuns make when singing. The differences were in the manner of singing, the appearance of the buildings, the atmosphere of meals, wimple material, and the nuns I spoke to, all, of course, extremely different from each other, as human beings always are even when they are wearing the same clothes.

The sound of rubber-soled sandals on wooden herring-bone floors is a homely one: it is a sound you hear when shrinking communities move from their huge Victorian purpose-built pile to a small country house which fits them. What was once the drawing-room becomes the chapel. The herring-bone floor sound is to be heard at Elmore Abbey, the community of Anglican monks which used to be huge but has now moved to a small house near Newbury. It is also heard at the Convent of the Holy Cross, a Benedictine community of nuns who started as active do-gooders in the London Docks, lived for a century in an enormous brick convent in Haywards Heath, felt more and more drawn to the contemplative life, adopted the Benedictine Rule, became smaller, and in the 1970s moved to a bleak white house near Loughborough called Rempstone Hall.

At Rempstone there are eleven nuns and no novices. The house is dark and silent in the afternoon and the arriving visitor is taken to the guest-house where bright central lights are switched on one after the other. Sister Mary Bernadette, the guest sister, pointed to shortbread and to the bookshelf: 'You must need tea and a rest. Do read one of these books. How about something about animals?'

You often find books about animals in convent bookshelves; they are a safe subject. So is pond life. After a train journey you probably don't want to read about the Kingdom or the Weight of Glory, so they have thoughtfully put *Tarka the Otter* instead.

The inventories for guest bedrooms in Anglican convents would hardly vary at all. Bed, chest of drawers with extra blanket in bottom drawer, wardrobe with enough hangers, basin, little glass shelf, high-up mirror, set of clean sheets and a notice asking you to change them when you leave, fire regulations, cross on the wall, times of meals and offices, and (this is cheering) always a means of switching the light on and off without getting out of bed. Usually it is a string which controls the blinding central light; bedside lights are rare. At West Malling the simple comfort is ruined by the sheets being made of bri-nylon, that slippery material which makes you wake up sweating. The wimples at West Malling are made of the same stuff and it can't be healthy.

Mother Mary Luke is the new Reverend Mother at Rempstone Convent and she talked to me in one of those dreary downstairs rooms they have at convents, belonging to no one, with no one's belongings in them, just two common-room chairs and a table, and an 'engaged' sign in calligraphy on the outer door-handle. Mother Mary Luke gave me more of a feeling of what it is really like to be a nun than any other to whom I spoke. She is in her forties and has been at Rempstone Convent for seventeen years. She is pale and wears glasses, as all the nuns at Rempstone do, except for the completely blind nun who no longer needs to. She dared to give examples; so many nuns speak in general terms about belonging to God but hardly ever provide a single concrete detail.

She had been an air-hostess. For years she had had a fascination with nuns, mixed with horror; she went to see *The Nun's Story* six times. All her friends were getting married and she wasn't. 'I knew there was something wrong with my life. It seemed as if whatever happened no man was going to be there. I started to ask, "What do you want of me, Lord?" Then I was sent to New York on a standby. I had to sit in my hotel room from two till eight, and I bought *This House of Brede* by Rumer Godden. As I read it, this conviction came over me: "You are going to be a Benedictine nun." I picked up the Gideon Bible which they always have in hotel rooms. The Holy Spirit only needs a tiny chink and by golly, he's in.'

The shallower the trigger, the deeper the effect: vocations often seem to come suddenly, and a lush novel read in a hotel room can be just as powerful as a sermon about Julian of Norwich listened to in a pew. The first moment of certainty that 'I am going to be a nun' – the direct invitation from God – is something that all nuns seem to remember vividly; likewise, the days afterwards, when doors seem to open, when the right person sends you to the right community, and it feels like coming home. Parents are nearly always horrified. They think that their daughter becoming a nun is hardly better than her stepping into her coffin. They are right, in a way: taking final vows *is* 'a kind of funeral', as Ronald Knox stated at a nun's profession once. Nuns' funerals, on the other hand, are like weddings: everyone rejoices that the sister has at last arrived at the place prepared for her.

Mother Mary Luke remembers the hot-water bottle she found in her bed when she first came to stay at the Convent of the Holy Cross. She thought it the most caring thing ever. 'I want to be one of these people!' God seemed to be taking a hand in making it happen: '"All right, Lord, I'll do as you say, but not until my stepfather's dead. I've got to look after him."' The stepfather died three weeks later. '"All right, Lord. You mean it."'

The last days in the outside world remain vividly in nuns' memories. Words spoken to them in their postulancy resound in their heads for the rest of their untalkative lives. Dame Mary John Marshall, now Mother Abbess of West Malling, came widely travelled to the abbey thirty years ago and was worried about not being allowed to travel any more. The Mother Abbess reassured her: 'But, darling, there's no place to go but up.'

It is good to think of the Mother Abbess calling her novice 'darling'. It is a motherly expression and at homesick moments one would need it. All I have ever heard nuns calling each other is 'Sister'. 'Are you actually *friends* with one another?' I occasionally asked in the course of intense conversations in downstairs rooms. There was never an eager answer such as, 'Oh, yes. I couldn't stand it here without Sister Mary Philomena!' Instead, the response was unemotional. 'We relate very much in silence.' 'A religious community is a community of reconciliation.' 'We have formal recreation two or three times a week.' 'On Feast Days and Solemnities,' the Bursar of Rempstone Convent Sister Mary Lawrence told me, 'you can go for a walk with someone or play Scrabble. Spiritual talk between A and B is not encouraged. If you were having problems you'd speak to the Reverend Mother or the Warden.'

'What do you *talk* about during Recreation?'

'Oh, we laugh. We knit and sew and paint cards. The sisters tell stories about when they were postulants – the daft things they used to do. We talk about what other people think of us. And about our nephews and nieces. You find you adopt other people's families.'

The moment something is called 'Recreation', any chance it had of being really good fun vanishes. The outward sign of the limitedness of recreational fun is the gramophone that you see standing in the corner of nuns' common rooms. It is a mono gramophone with its lid closed, and next to it are two neat cases of thick LPs, caught in the 1970s.

But of course fun isn't the point, and the only way in which women can possibly live together without going mad is by spending most of their time in silence. At West Malling the nuns are allowed to talk for forty minutes a day. All the subjects that make secular women's conversations so delicious – men's handwriting, the use of dill in cooking, the yearning for thinness, Fogal tights at nineteen pounds a pair – are irrelevant in the Religious Life where there is no wooing, salt and pepper are the only flavouring, diets are not allowed and you go around with bare legs, only putting on pop-socks in cold weather.

'What we're trying to do,' Mother Mary Luke explained, 'is attack the root causes of sin. Where do egotism and hatred begin? Me! If we have a row with a sister in the community it's the same row that triggers schisms in the Church and war among nations. It *is* trivial. But every good thing I do adds to the pool of good and every bad thing adds to the pool of bad. You do steam up, of course. But give me a novice who's got a fiery temper rather than someone who wouldn't say "boo" to a goose – you've got something to work on.'

'Doesn't sexual desire make a novice's life agony?'

'You don't quench your sexual desire: you transmute it. Then you've got something to offer to God. He doesn't want a sexless neuter but a woman, with all her passion. Give me a novice who's got a capacity for loving. We want full-blooded people, real people. The ideal age to enter is between twenty-five and forty-five: you know what the world's about, you've been in love. But if God wants a woman in a community he cannot *allow* her to have a happy love affair.'

It is all very well saying 'Give me a novice who . . .' but at the moment God doesn't seem to be giving Mother Mary Luke any novices at all. 'If God wants us to survive, he'll send us the vocations,' she said. He has sent a few postulants and novices along but they don't seem to have staying power. 'There's what I call a postulant's hump and a novice's hurdle,' Mother Mary Luke said. 'Your methods of coping with things in the world don't work in the Religious Life. Here is an example story: a novice comes who has always fasted on Fridays. That's not what we do here, so we tell her she shouldn't, but she insists. So we allow her to fast on Friday. And she faints. "Why did that happen?" she asks. "I never fainted before." *Conversion of manners* is one of the Benedictine rules. I've known one novice who went absolutely berserk when I suggested that instead of dramatic fasting why didn't she go for a week without salt and pepper? *She* didn't last.'

Nuns live to an average age of eighty-nine, so life in religious communities often involves a great deal of looking after old nuns, wheeling them about and helping them to get in and out of the bath. It is a test of charity and niceness. The thought of such tasks is off-putting to people who might otherwise have nunnish leanings. When young women go to Diocesan Directors of Ordinands and ask for advice about what to do with their vocation the Religious Life doesn't even enter the conversation. Mother Mary Luke said: 'I said to our Diocesan Bishop when I last saw him, "Can you get it through to the DDOs to *think* Religious Life?"'

Instead of saying 'all kinds of things', Mother Mary Luke uses the expression 'this, that, t'other and t'which'. She speaks in a way which is not serene or beautiful, but which is direct and takes the Religious Life off any pedestal it might have put itself on. 'This is what it is like to be a nun: you fall down, and you get up again, and you fall down, and you get up again.'

The impression one gets at Rempstone Hall is of women praying for the world and struggling to batter sin. At West Malling Abbey the guest is more likely to be struck by beauty. It is also a Benedictine abbey, but so enclosed that once a nun enters she never leaves the grounds again except for urgent medical necessity. The Advisory Council for Religious Communities recommends people take three weeks' holiday a year, and most Religious take this advice and go to stay at other religious communities, or with their blood-mother or blood-sister. But not the West Malling nuns. They take the word 'enclosed' literally. The Mother Abbess doesn't even go to the annual meeting of the Union of Monastic Superiors. She is greatly missed.

Catchy expressions have no way of insinuating themselves into a community if the community is totally enclosed. The voices of the West Malling nuns are caught in time. You hear them reading the lessons and they sound like the Mistress of a Cambridge college before the war: the words are hard, cold, slow, rigid and carefully but lifelessly pronounced. Introducing a new word to these nuns makes you feel as guilty as introducing the common cold to the Eskimos. I polluted Sister Mary Paul's vocabulary and still deeply regret it. She asked me what kind of articles I wrote. 'Features,' I said. I had to explain what a feature was and it suddenly seemed a silly word from a silly magaziny world. 'I hope all your features go well,' Sister Mary Paul said when I left, emphasising the word as one does when mastering a new one.

The beauty of West Malling Abbey lies partly in its oldness. It started being an abbey of Benedictine nuns in 1090, and the building which faces you as you come through the gate is a humble Norman tower, half-ruined, its interlocking arches smoothed by rain and wind. It stopped being an abbey at the Reformation, and considering how few things ever revert to their original use it is astonishing that it is now an abbey of Benedictine nuns again – albeit Anglican ones this time – approved by the Bishop and frequently stayed at by the Reformed canons of Westminster Abbey.

It looks exactly as an abbey ought to look. The wide, long lawn is clipped at the edges, and no weeds grow in the flower-beds, only rich heather and unshowy Kentish flowers. Apple trees, lovingly pruned, form a small orchard in the far corner, their blossom in May giving the visitor something to stare at and meditate on in the long ten minutes before Sext.

In the morning you might see a sister at work with a wheelbarrow and a spade. That is a beautiful sight. Over her black habit and face-covering wimple she is wearing a plain blue apron, the neck-ties of which pull on the back of her veil and make it look like a loose hood. The effect is Vermeer-like: a girl interrupted at her musick.

Utter regularity of life and utter identicalness in clothing among a large group of people are hard to achieve and fascinating to witness. There they all are at Lauds, processing into the chapel, turning and bowing towards the altar, Mother Abbess last, tall and serene and bowing more deeply than anyone; there they all are again at Terce, Sext and None, at vespers and at compline; after each office they turn east at the two little knocks of the Mother Abbess's hammer and file out through their own door into their own cloister, black figures, hooded and indistinguishable, vanishing into the distance.

They really pray. It is never long before the next office. From nine till twelve every morning there is a three-hour gap so work can get done, but in the afternoon there is no long officeless stretch. Glasses on, I scoured the nuns' faces for signs of deep boredom, as they filed in yet again to sing more psalms, so often Psalm 119, which goes on and on and says I will not forget thy testimonies. But there was no audible sighing or visible frowning, just a strong sense of peace. Guests don't even sit in the main part of the chapel but round a corner, so unless you sit in the front row on the left you can't see anyone. But at Eucharist every morning you are invited into the sanctuary to stand in a large circle (Choir nuns: 30. Novices: 2) and this is a wonderful occasion. The West Malling nuns have designed their own Eucharist based on early liturgies and it was this that Mother Abbess talked about when I saw her in the downstairs room: she did not talk about salt and pepper or steaming up. 'We were very drawn to the early Greek Fathers, and we built a simple Eucharistic rite. It *begins* with the Kiss of Peace, then comes the Sursum Corda, and it *ends* with the Sanctus. We find it completely satisfying, and that's been going on since 1963. When I came the liturgy was still in Latin. In the 1960s we asked, "Is it time to recover our Anglican roots?" We started changing to English. And I would say to a man – to a nun – we're happy with what we did.'

The celebrating priest at Eucharist is not the parish priest of West Malling but an Anglican Cistercian monk called Fr Aelred Arnesen. He is the only Anglican Cistercian in the world. Ewell Monastery, where he lives, is at the other end of the nuns' private vegetable garden; he worships in a converted medieval barn. 'Monks:

1,' the *Benedictine Yearbook* says. But the blurb about the monastery still bravely speaks in the plural: 'The monks follow the contemplative monastic tradition without interruption, living by the work of their hands.' Sometimes the count does go up, briefly: 'Monks: 1. Novices: 1'. But the next year it goes down again. Fr Aelred is said to be prickly and difficult to live with.

Holy Communion has a particularly powerful effect when you take it before breakfast – when you are really hungry. 'God became as tangible and physical a man as this bread and wine are tangible and tastable.' It hits you hard. Communion bread at West Malling is brown and home-made: at the offertory it is a bap and the priest breaks it up into bits. The wine is so sweet and strong it makes your eyes water.

The nuns sing beautifully. It seems effortless; but if you listen to the singing in other religious communities you realise how hard it is to make a pure and lovely sound in plainsong. Wailing Spanish Poor Clares behind grilles are the worst I have heard, followed by bored Cistercian monks near Burgos who gave up trying soon after Vatican 2. But even in the small world of Anglican Religious standards vary. At Fairacres in Oxford you hear a squeaky sound at each change of chant as the nuns agree on the note; at Rempstone, Sister Mary Bernadette's mouth organ starts everyone off. But at West Malling the sound seems to come out of the air. The nuns sing completely in tune and in time with one another, and their voices are pure and sweet. Projection is not their aim, and the 'o' sound is the opposite of full and operatic: it is enclosed and well-brought-up. The phrase 'Let me not eat of their dainties' has stayed in my mind. It is sung at vespers on Fridays and Saturdays, and is the second half of a psalm verse. The final syllable of 'dainties' is short and light. The nuns wouldn't dream of eating anyone else's dainties, and it seems right that they should sing this prim, ungreedy little verse.

A quiet novice called Sister Seonaid talked to me in the down-stairs room, and afterwards wrote me a thin calligraphic note full of love and prayers. She talked about the growing need for prayer in the world, and the need for places like this abbey which point beyond themselves. 'If these places died out, who would point towards what everybody is looking for? I realised that if I went to look after Mum and Dad I would be narrowing my horizons. If I stayed here I could pray for them as well as for all the other people who need praying for.'

'Do you *ever* have free time?'

'After vespers on a Sunday we do: we have an hour and a quarter. There's a community record-player and you can ask for a record to be played.'

She works in the laundry and in the printing department, making booklets and cards with a treadle printer given to the community in 1926. She described the early-morning routine: 'From five twenty-five till Lauds we have prayer time or spiritual reading. We have our pittance after Vigils on a Sunday but normally it's after the liturgy – '

'Pittance?'

'That's our word for breakfast.'

'It sounds a bit meagre.'

'Oh, no. You can *stuff* yourself on pittance.'

I spent Easter at West Malling and we were in silence from Maundy Thursday evening until after Terce on Easter Sunday. Most of the other guests were oblates: you could tell them by their green 'Pax' badges. Being an oblate means that you live under a vow and are associates with the community, without in any way having to be a nun. You have an oblate sister whom you can talk to about spiritual matters, and out in the world you must say three offices a day. Vocations to the Religious Life in the Church of England are diminishing in numbers but the number of oblates is rising fast. At Elmore Abbey in Berkshire there are now only thirteen monks left but there are 350 keen and loyal oblates. They just don't quite want to live together.

Oblates talk about diets and when the Great Silence fell it was a relief. We, like the nuns, started to 'relate very much in silence', making 'Would you like some more bread?' gestures at countless silent meals. The sense of mourning on Good Friday was strong. At the service of commemoration we stood in a circle and passed a rough-hewn cross round, pressing it to our bosom turn by turn. Meals got earlier and earlier and we sank into a deeper silence. Every now and then I needed to get out: drunk on routine, I found a walk which took exactly an hour if you went at marching pace. It was along the charming, normal, creosote-smelling, stinging-nettle-lined footpaths of secular West Malling. Every back garden was a fascinating reminder of what people do when they are not nuns: they make huts, play ping-pong, take dry shirts off the line, put out the deck-chairs, tell the dog to shut up. The walk became a daily urge.

'Easter Sunday. 3.45 a.m.: Rise. 4 a.m.: Hot drink on the landing.' Having stared at the noticeboard for days, I longed for that hot drink on the landing. It was tea, in the dark. Then we had to assemble in St Gandulf. That sounded exciting, but St Gandulf turned out to be the dreariest downstairs room ever, with the sad gramophone in the corner. We took a candle each, and waited. Then we were ushered into the cloister, which is part of the unseen enclosure that you long to get a glimpse of. There it is, utterly familiar to the nuns and utterly unfamiliar to the guests. At four twenty, the flame was lit. 'The Lord is risen. Alleluia.' The nuns broke into harmony. We took light from each other's candles and soon the cloister was aglow with bright half-hidden faces. We processed into the chapel and went back to our guests' corner for the two-hour Paschal vigil. A minute later we came to the stark words in the liturgy folder: 'Candles are extinguished.' With short blows, they were. It was back to electric lights. The vigil was a dawn lesson on God's plan for his people, with readings from the oldest Old Testament to the newest New.

'What are monks and nuns *doing* in the Church of England? Wasn't the whole point of the Reformation that it did away with monasteries?' This is what many Roman Catholics say when you tell them you are going to spend Easter with Anglican Benedictines. But when you go to one of these houses, you don't think, 'How odd. Why aren't they Roman Catholics?' They just aren't. They are steeped in Anglicanism. They pray for N our Bishop and M our Visitor. They sing the Office in English and are proud of it. Four of them sit on the General Synod. Some of them do pray daily for the Pope and talk frequently to Mary, but it is never soppy and rarely in an Irish accent. They are not called the Little Sisters of This or the Little Sisters of That, but have staunch Victorian names chosen by their Oxford

Movement founders: the Sisters of the Love of God, the Society of St Margaret.

Mother Alleyne of the Convent of St Mary the Virgin, Wantage, sat with me in the downstairs room and said, 'We're very much a Prayer Book community. We're very Anglican, which means we take a lot from different strands.' William John Butler, the Bishop of Oxford, started the community in the 1840s, when Wantage was so riddled with poverty, disease and prostitution that it was known as 'Black Wantage'. The sisters are not Benedictines; they have their own rule, which is inspired by a mixture of St Augustine, St Francis de Sales, St Vincent de Paul and Jane de Chantal. They used to wear black but changed because sewing black habits with black cotton is bad for the eyes. 'Now,' Mother Alleyne said, 'you'll see sisters in Black Traditional, Blue-Grey Traditional and Blue-Grey Modified, which Sister Valeria is wearing.'

From the outside the convent looks churchy and Anglo-catholic. The new chapel is a low-budget Pearson with a Comper window and the old chapel is a Street. They are Pevsner-worthy. Inside it is like a women's college in the early days, with red tiles, polish, noticeboards and corridors. The nuns stand about in the corridors and chat, which is a shock after West Malling. To get to the chapel you turn right at the icons.

There are six novices, which brightens the place up and gives hope for the future. Thirty years ago there were forty novices and 300 sisters in all; now there are 120 sisters. The old, hunch-backed nuns are fascinating to look at: serene and dogged. They have had active lives. There is still a branch house in India and there used to be one in South Africa as well, in the Transkei. Nuns were sent out to work on the mission there with the Cowley Fathers. Sister Mary Jennifer, who lives at the branch house in Clapham Old Town, spent years in the Transkei, helping in the parish and teaching Africans to do the books and type. Both the Cowley Fathers and the Wantage sisters have withdrawn from South Africa now. They have Transkei reunions in London sometimes.

Running an old-people's home in Wantage is less romantic than riding about on horses in the Transkei, but this the Wantage sisters now do. They are not as active as they used to be but they are not inactive. In the Clapham branch house Sister Mary Jennifer visits

St Thomas's Hospital and Wandsworth Prison and prays hard for the ill or sorry inmates. Sister Jean Mary helps to run the parish Sunday school. Sister Francis Honor does spiritual direction and individually given retreats. Sister Lorna does some visiting and some clowning. As well as all this, they have two hours of private prayer a day, four offices and the Eucharist. 'Most active Roman Catholic sisters don't have such long hours of offices and prayers as we do,' Sister Mary Jennifer said.

The cleanness and tidiness of Anglican nuns is frightening. At West Malling, the four drawing-pins at the corner of the tiny notices are all exactly forty-five degrees and the same number of millimetres in from each corner. Notices are clear. Loos say 'Toilet' on the door and at Rempstone Hall even the towels say 'Toilet' on them, woven in like the name of a hotel. There is no possibility of not knowing where something is or what something is inside a tupperware box. It is all labelled. This is necessary for silent retreats. But at Wantage the utter cleanness in the guest kitchen can make the guest feel lonely. All the surfaces are scrubbed and smell of scrubbing. Everything is put away: spoons in the spoon drawer and the sealed cornflake bucket in the cereal cupboard.

A delightful young sister called Sister Barbara Anne talked to me, first in the downstairs room and then in the chilly grounds. She is an artist and a cowshed is her studio. She is making the Stations of the Cross for a Scottish church. She was realistic about the toughness of the Religious Life. Of novices, she said, 'They only have to be here for two weeks and the tears flow.' Of sexuality: 'There is so much more to being feminine than the sexual act. You feel differently about your sexuality at twenty, at forty, at sixty. We have to learn not to splash all our maternal feelings over the other sisters.' Of arguments: 'We are women: the feeling-level is high. One question, such as when and where to be silent, can be a tremendous hot potato.' Lots of people from 'out there', 'society', 'the world', come for spiritual direction and help with their cluttered lives and the Wantage sisters are not cut off or out of touch. They radiate self-sacrifice and compassion.

A hermit lives in the grounds, in an outhouse. The young sisters don't see her very much but she smiles broadly when she does appear. She comes to Mass but not to the offices. Raw food is taken to her and she cooks it.

The Sisters of the Love of God have hermits in the grounds of their branch house at Staplehurst in Kent; but I went to see them at their mother house which is some way up the Iffley Road in Oxford. They are contemplative and *sui generis*. A Cowley Father, Fr Lucius Cary, founded them at the beginning of this century and his aim was not to copy any of the other orders. The first Fairacres nuns were Oxford undergraduates, and even now people who interview Fairacres nuns nearly always ask, 'Are you an intellectual community?' They see this question coming and are fed up with it. But it is a justifiable question. The nuns do look clever and they publish the *Fairacres Chronicle* every year which contains exquisitely researched essays about mystics and divines.

Daily life is tough at Fairacres, and you would have to be pretty intellectually self-sufficient to put up with it. Hours of every day are spent in solitude and contemplative silence, and the nuns get up for a whole hour in the middle of the night to go to the Night Office. The prioress, sister Edna Monica, told me the timetable: lights out, nine-thirty. Called at one forty-five. Back to bed a couple of minutes after three unless it's a saint's day in which case the office goes on a bit longer. Up again at five thirty. The norm is to attend the Night Office on four days out of five; on the fifth you say the office alone before bed and, blissfully, sleep through till morning.

Even vespers doesn't last an hour. It seems cruel that the longest office of all should be the one in the middle of the night when you are most yearning to be horizontal and between sheets. There are lots of psalms, sung in a monotone; a hymn is sung and there is a long biblical reading and a long patristic reading. Sister Edna Monica has been a Sister of the Love of God since 1960. 'You must be rather fond of getting up in the middle of the night,' I suggested brightly. 'Fond?' she said. 'That's not exactly a word I'd use. I still find it very hard to break the sleep rhythm. But I'm aware of how needed our night prayers are: it means a lot to people. One's really got to be doing it for the glory of God: one is even willing to break one's sleep for him.'

Sister Benedicta Ward SLG is the famous Fairacres nun. The rule about being enclosed is lifted slightly for her. She is a member of the Theology faculty at Oxford and teaches spirituality and church history to undergraduates, who love her and never forget her. It is thanks to her that they have any understanding at all about what Julian of Norwich was really like, and why she was one of the great English women of prayer. So close in spirit to Julian of Norwich is Sister Benedicta Ward that undergraduates start to think that she *is* Julian of Norwich.

'I live basically in the twelfth century,' she said, when I asked her whether she thought women ought to be priests. 'I would not find it useful or edifying. I would go by image and likeness.' That was the end of that subject. She drifted back through the centuries, out past the birth of Christ into the desert before him, where the desert fathers roamed. 'The monastic instinct is a human instinct. Monastic life in 5000 BC had the same framework as ours. We just put the lens of the Gospel over it.'

A small triangle of face was all that was visible; the tight, non-nylon wimple shut everything else out. ('The nuns cut their own hair,' Sister Edna Monica told me. That is about the most unvain thing a woman can do.) Sister Benedicta's eyes and mouth shone with life and quizzical joy all the more brightly for being confined. She told me about St Philip Neri's bad temper, and the understandable bad tempers of nuns ('We scrap among ourselves *terribly*'); St Teresa of Avila; St Christina of Markyate; St Augustine and King Ethelbert; St Aidan and King Oswald; King Edwin and his thanes.

Meals in convents are unforgettable. What you have to eat at them will be dealt with separately in chapter 14, where the questions of why Anglicans do or do not drink alcohol, and do or do not eat too much, will be examined properly. The *aura* of meals at different convents is striking. Sometimes guests eat on their own, presided over by one of the sisters who says Grace. At Wantage, Sister Lynne ate with us and, between courses, became silently absorbed in an article about foxes from a nature magazine. At West Malling, all meals are eaten in silence apart from lunch, when Sister Mary Paul reads a book aloud, in her clear, authoritative voice. At the beginning of December, the book was *A Walk to Jerusalem* by

Gerard Hughes. Keeping an eye on us all, she read about the man's walk to Jerusalem: amusing episode after amusing episode. At the last scrape of pudding she finished a paragraph and said, 'I'm afraid we'll have to leave him in that predicament.' The man had just read a notice in a foreign language and didn't know whether it meant 'These are the safe hours' or 'These are the dangerous hours'.

What you long to do is to eat in the same room as the nuns. At West Malling you never see a nun eat except at Holy Communion, but at Rempstone Hall and, surprisingly, at Fairacres, you are allowed into the refectory. At Rempstone Hall there is a lectern at which one of the sisters stands and reads aloud at lunch. First she reads a passage from the Rule of St Benedict. On the Wednesday in November when I was there it was about welcoming guests; you must treat all guests as if they were Jesus himself, sometimes even prostrating yourself on the ground. Then she read from the biography of Donald Coggan and it happened to be the chapter about his worldwide travels. He took aeroplanes everywhere; he took seven or eight aeroplanes in that single extract, flying about from continent to continent. It was strange to hear about so much motion in a place where no one travels more than fifty yards.

Lunch at Fairacres was the most riveting of all. The Fairacres nuns are beautiful to look at, with rosy cheeks, brown habits and black veils kept slightly away from their foreheads. Brueghel rather than Vermeer is the Old Master who comes to mind. They process in, slowly, as if into chapel and sit on long wooden benches. Then the New Testament lesson is read aloud; on the Sunday when I was there it was the same lesson as we had had at Eucharist a few hours ago: 'Feed my sheep'. 'Tend my lambs'. Then the reading nun said, in a firm, clear voice, 'And the record is . . .' The record? Perhaps we were going to hear something about Early English nuns and benefactors, in the way that Roman Catholics read aloud from the Martyrology. 'And the record is James Galway playing Mozart's Flute Concerto in D.'

There, to my amazement, was the gramophone. It was not shut and tucked into a corner, like so many convent gramophones; but open and exposed, on a table. On went the record, and we listened to the comforting opening chords. Then the eating part of lunch started. We ate not off plates but out of large wooden bowls. Guests are given knives and forks, but the nuns eat with a spoon only, which makes them look even more like hungry Brueghel wives who are being greedy and thankful after hard harvesting. To the scratchy sound of James Galway, and not talking, we sawed away at our pork, the guests with knives, the nuns with the blunt edges of their spoons.

Habits and conventions develop slowly in enclosed institutions so that they seem natural to the inmates. Often they take the guest by surprise. Active orders of Anglican nuns tend not to have such unchanging and unlikely ways of doing things. Their noticeboards are messier. At St Saviour's Priory in Haggerston, near Hackney, single drawing-pins hold up floppy and creased notices about urgent needs in Tower Hamlets. The nuns are out and about, on bicycles. They have half-days off and vespers on Tuesday is thinly attended but none the less moving, in a charming early-twentieth-century vaulted chapel. A row of rusty prams is kept in the inner courtyard – slightly odd and unlikely, but prams have proved to be a sensible and practical way of carrying things round the parish. The assistant superior, Anna, does not insist on being called Sister Anna, and she bicycles off to St Mary's, Bourne Street, to see her confessor. Pam helps with the children at All Saints. But prayer and the saying of the Daily Office is still a major part of their life. Sister Denzil, at the Community of St Andrew in Kensington, helps in two parish churches as well as being a member of her own community. Sunday mornings involve a glut of praying as she dashes from the inside world to the outside world and back again.

'We have one novice at the moment.' 'We've got one novice and one postulant and we've got an aspirant coming in October.' 'One' is a much-used number in admitting the state of affairs concerning novices. Statistics for the whole country, diocese by diocese, about the number of Religious make bleak reading because there are so many noughts. Sheffield: professed men: nought; male novices: one; professed women: nought; female novices: nought. But suddenly you come to professed lay women in the Oxford diocese: 216. Altogether there are about 900 Anglicans Religious in England, spending very little indeed on clothes. At any time of the day you can look at your watch, imagine one of the 864 nuns and think, 'Now she is praying' or 'Now she is about to pray because it is five minutes before None.'

12

Interiors

'Their churches look like houses and their houses look like churches.' Discuss.

The proposition is an interesting one, but too simple. As so often, generalisations are inaccurate. The spectrum must be taken into account. In my experience of Church of England churches and vicarages, the first half of the proposition is sometimes true at the lower end of the spectrum and the second half is sometimes true at the higher end.

'We've put a new kitchen in here, and a room for sitting and meeting in here, and a hatch here so you can pass the plates through. There are two new loos through there. We've put carpets down, as you can see. And we've made a lovely new room upstairs.'

The scene of that tour was Christchurch, Fulham. It is an example of a house-like church. The church hall was sold and is now a recording studio. The money raised was spent on refurbishing the main building. The same trend that is making liturgical language casual and hymn music Radio 2-like is making evangelical churches as unchurchy as possible. The aim is to attract, rather than repel, the unchurched. Hatches and fitted carpets remind visitors of home and give churches a relaxing air. Kitchens are useful because they make the organising of the après-service easy, and good après-service is an important attracting agent.

The sad fact is that even the best architect is unable to transform a slice of dark church into anything very pretty or cheerful. These divided-off bits of church tend to be ill-proportioned and not to have enough windows. The room for talking and Bible study at Christchurch, Fulham, was windowless and had stackable chairs in a circle. It was neither church-like nor house-like: it had no features at all. I found it sinister.

Anglican catholics like to keep their churches churchy. A sense of mystery must be preserved. But even they have been affected by the de-pompifying movement. The introduction of the nave altar is a visible sign of this. The altar at the far east end is, in many churches, no longer used except on Christmas Day and Easter Day. It is too far away, and has no space to stand behind so you can face the people. Now a second altar stands three feet away from the front pews. It is a small altar and often has no pall or frontal at all, just a white cloth, so it is more similar to a kitchen table than to the unmovable and draped block of marble in the sanctuary. The domestic habit of eating in the kitchen rather than going all the way to the unfamiliar dining-room has its corollary in worship.

In the way that dog-owners come to look like their dogs, you occasionally find that a church and its vicarage come to resemble one another, because the vicar makes thousands of journeys from one to the other. You find secular junk in the church and religious junk in the house. This was particularly striking at All Saints, Haggerston, where I did the Stations of the Cross in Holy Week. When you walk round a church slowly, stopping fourteen times to meditate on pictures of agony, you get a chance to examine its interior properly. The pictures of agony weren't very good or absorbing and I found my eyes wandering. I was in front of an old Pampers box. We shuffled on to the next Station: Tippex bottles. The next Station: a ladder. Then, a heap of jumble-sale clothes, a pile of stacked chairs, another cardboard box.

Robby Pearson, the vicar, had long hair in a pigtail with a bobble, and a frayed hem on his cassock. His wife Brandy had lots of clothes on and a cold. They were delightful and invited me to milky coffee at the vicarage. The drawing-room was full of crucifixes. You had to take hymn books off the chair to sit down.

Parish priests with an eye for beauty notice stained-glass windows and church furniture for sale at architectural salvage yards and can't resist buying them. 'Take a pew,' they say when you arrive at their house, and they mean it. A pew looks good against a vicarage drawing-room wall.

Furniture tends to look good if it comes from a larger building. The fashion for making curtains four inches too long so that they bunch up on the floor is an example of the urge to dabble in large proportions. Church proportions can be even larger than stately-home proportions, and some of the most attractive drawing-rooms I have seen are clergy drawing-rooms enriched with pairs of gilded cherubs. Prebendary Gerard Irvine, the retired vicar of St Matthew's, Westminster, lives in a Regency house in Brighton rich with churchy elements. He has huge carved angels above his bed. Even the spare room has angels on the wall. The walls are bright orange and bright deep green, and bits of church look magnificent against them.

'Come and see my oratory,' he said. It was in the space under the front steps of the house, low, cavern-like and painted white. Fr Irvine says the Divine Office there every morning and evening, kneeling on an upholstered prie-dieu which has two deep dips in it made by the knees of generations. He looks at a little shelf where there are lighted candles and icons from places which mean something to him. On his left is a row of prayer-books, shabby with use. He needs visual aids in order to pray properly, and he is not ashamed to admit it.

It would be useful if *Crockford's Clerical Directory*, among its many abbreviated nuggets of information, told you whether the entry was married (m), single (s), celibate and homosexual (c and h) or plain homosexual (h). Instead of being told it you have to glean it. Interiors sometimes help. In general I have found that young single heterosexual men take less interest in their vicarages than either (c and h) or (h). You see terrible bachelor bareness in some places, where it is obvious that the man is longing for a wife. You look in the visitors' book and see that only one page has been filled, and that all the guests have his surname because they are either his parents or his siblings. You see bathrooms of other single vicars well painted, with the bottles neatly arranged. These are the only data to go on. I still have no idea whether half the single men I interviewed are (s) or (h). I was too polite to ask, and unless there are joint invitations on the chimneypiece you have to make do with guessing by the feel of the place.

Young women deacons bring a new flavour to clergy interiors. So far, unless they are married to vicars, they have had to live in curates' houses rather than vicarages: these are usually small and in an ugly street, adequate but cramped. Celia Thomson, a curate at St Barnabas's, Southfields, and overjoyed at the Synod vote, lives in a modern little house which is charming inside. I first met her eight months before the vote when she was still feeling that her vocation to the priesthood was being smothered. There was a piano, open and recently played, with a music stand next to it; and, on the table we sat at in the living-room, a bowl of apples and satsumas on an Ordnance Survey tray. It showed a peaceful delight in good, simple things: music, fruit and the English countryside. It was a waiting house, though. It yearned to be as messy as a real vicarage.

Julie Childs's house in Kinsbrook Green near Harpenden *was* as messy as a vicarage, in the week before the final Synod vote. As well as being a curate-in-charge of a small church she was a campaigner for the ordination of women, and the house was littered with piles of letters and cuttings that she was trying to tidy up. She gave me some to read while she listened to the answering machine. 'Here's a booklet by the women deacons in the Ely diocese. This is a little cutting about me from the local paper. And here's a letter I've sent to every single member of the Synod. Some of them will drive down the M1 next week to Church House, and they'll see the turn-off to Kinsbrook Green. They'll remember it. All these things are blessings.' I read avidly, clutching a brown mug of coffee. The next week she was photographed in the national papers, smiling and praising God. A new layer of cuttings fluttered on to her heaps.

When the answer is neither (s) nor (h) but (m), gleaning is easy. Wedding photographs, a wedding ring, vases of flowers, full jars in the kitchen – all tell you that a vicar is married. Variations on these elements suggest divorce or widowhood. Sometimes he takes you into his poky study, which smells of photocopying chemicals. The wastepaper basket is overflowing with sheets of A4 paper crumpled up in frustration when they have come out too dark or too light. Being taken to the study may be a sign that he has children and wants to spare you the potties, the toys and the noise.

The Church Commissioners have published a Parsonage Design Guide, and page twenty-eight is all about the parson's study. Wheelchairs must be able to reach it. It must be not less than 170 square feet if separate storage space is provided for robes. It should have a pleasant outlook and be as quiet as possible. Shelving (why not 'shelves'?) should be provided, and space for office equipment. Morning sunlight is suggested; so is sound insulation, a temperature of 70 degrees and a hard-wearing, low-maintenance floor finish for use without carpet. At the bottom of the page there are two diagrams, one of a successful design, where a matchstick parson has got a tree to look at out of the window, coat-hangers in the room next to him and suitcases in the room above him; and the other of a bad design, where sound waves are shown to be impinging from all sides: a WC is being flushed in the room next to him, visitors are waiting by the window, another WC is being flushed, and a matchstick child, a teddy bear and a pair of quavers are standing side by side in the children's bedroom directly above. The poor matchstick parson is trying to write his sermon.

Category one in the Design Guide is where the essentials for design are put. Categories two and three are more detailed and suggestive. The essentials for modern parsonage design are, among other things, two reception rooms, two double bedrooms and two single bedrooms, a utility room or laundry area, a garage, a garden, and a paved area for sitting out and children's outdoor play. It is all quite generous.

It needs to be. Clergy children tend to come in threes, and they make a terrible mess. I have been to one or two curates' houses which were hopelessly inadequate to contain the screams and gumboots of the offspring. Grown-ups tripped over toys and children tripped over handbags. I have come across discarded vests and inside-out pants just lying there next to the dining-room table, untouched for hours. I have seen hysterical tears over which child should be allowed to say Grace. In the way that some parents let their figures go some let their houses go. Clergy are so busy keeping the parish in order and organising the maintenance of the church that some seem to have no willpower left for maintaining the house. Clergy kitchens are often dishwasherless (there is no mention of dishwashers in Category one, two or three of 'Kitchen' in the Parsonage Design Book), so it is as much as a vicar and his wife can do to wash up the most recently used plates and mugs. Even that seems to take ages.

Hardly any vicarages or rectories I have visited in my year have been lovely old houses that have been parsonages for centuries. I have not particularly *tried* to find old vicarages: it was the inhabitant rather than the dwelling that was my quest. I can think of one very old vicarage, and that was in Helmsley in North Yorkshire, where David Senior has been vicar since 1955. The house is called Canon's Garth. He sat in the inglenook and called his wife 'dear'. She brought us coffee and thin biscuits on pretty plates. I grilled him about why he was against the ordination of women. But nuns lived in the house in the nineteenth century, and it has only recently become the official vicarage, so it doesn't quite count. The Rectory in Grantham is a handsome eighteenth-century house, and it does count, because it has only ever been a rectory. It is thirty yards from the magnificent church with its loud peal of bells. But apart from those, there was almost nothing earlier than late Victorian in my whole random sample. It shows how small the fraction of un-sold-off parsonages has become. I have come to expect an adequate-but-dull box. The Church Commissioners publish a glossy pamphlet showing the winners of the most recent Parsonage Design Award. There are prizes for alterations as well as for new designs: not all parsonages are sold off. Some are handsomely altered. All Saints, Kings Cliffe, in the diocese of Peterborough, won first prize in 1988. The panelling in the drawing-room was restored, and extensions were built on. I happened not to visit it.

Of the adequate-but-dull boxes I have seen, by far the most attractive inside was John and Denise Inges' in Wallsend. Denise cried when she first saw the house, with its monotone bricks and unbeautiful proportions, but they quickly got to work with imagination, optimism and a few good old pieces of furniture which belonged to their grandparents. The dullness of the basic building faded away quickly: ugliness is now dwarfed by beauty. There is a grand piano in the drawing-room, played rather than unplayed. After supper the candles are taken there and you sit in flickering light among pictures and rugs. The kitchen is bright with jars, bowls of fruit and plants on the windowsill. It smells of fresh homemade bread. Even the spare room is pretty, and that is rare in vicarages. I have slept in some where the only element of character is the colour of the duvet. But at the Inges' the beds are high, and there are books you want to read, a good bedside light and a jug and basin on the chest of drawers. Denise tries with the garden. The house is full of flowers from it. She gives lots away, and has discovered (from the pruning process) how true it is that the more you give the more you have.

Evangelicals don't much like ornate church furniture studded with jewels. But strangely enough it is they, rather than catholics, who talk about arriving at the pearly gates. It is a witty, unembarrassing way of talking about arriving in Heaven. Imaginary conversations happen there, between the unlocking angel and the newly arrived Christian. Earthly rather than heavenly ornateness is what preoccupies catholics. They don't talk about going to Heaven or being saved as much as evangelicals do. They get on with basking in earthly creation, trying to do it to the glory of God.

The person who knows more than anyone about church taste is Elizabeth Hoare, the director of the London firm of church furnishers Watts & Co. Her grandfather, George Gilbert Scott Jnr, was one of the three founders of the firm in 1874, and Mrs Hoare has spent her life hooked on church interiors. She rescued hundreds of Victorian frontals and vestments from destruction during the anti-Victorian era in the 1950s and '60s, when gold and turquoise fishes became the rage. She hoarded the rescued objects, and now they are on display in Liverpool Cathedral, which was designed by her uncle.

She and her assistant David Gazeley took me down to Lancing, the boys' public school in Sussex, where the new chaplain, Fr

Ian Forrester, was longing to restore the interior of the splendid chapel to its previous state of beauty. On the train they told me why carpets ought to be taken out of churches. 'I spend *lots* of time telling people to take carpets out,' said Mrs Hoare. 'A church should not look like a drawing-room.' We went past Hove. 'So *boring*, those skyscrapers, aren't they? No fun in them at all.'

Lancing Chapel was freezing. It was cold enough to deserve a place on my chart:

Extreme temperatures in Church of England Interiors

Very cold
Lancing Chapel, much too cold even when you have hats, coats and gloves on. Must put boys off church for life.
Wells Cathedral, kept at 54 degrees, which is 16 degrees cooler than the stipulated temperature of a parson's study.
Ballet classroom above St Michael's church hall, Lewes.

Very hot
St Luke's Hospital for the Clergy. Even hotter than most hospitals for the laity.
Guest room at West Malling Abbey. But then nuns are generous about heating.
Shrine of Our Lady of Walsingham – hot with too many candles.

The only warm room in Lancing Chapel was the vestry. We spent a long time there, looking through the vestments. 'Look at what I have to make do with,' said the chaplain. The vestments were olive-green and made of napkin material by J & M Sewing Services of Newcastle-upon-Tyne.

We carried on opening drawers and looking. Of a dull vestment, David said, '*Très ordinaire*'.

'It was embroidered by a former master. This one's ink-stained. Look.'

'Yes,' said David. 'It's perfectly serviceable for a little low Mass in a side chapel, but not much more. Now, *that's* what I call a vestment!' It was a pink one, heavy and embroidered.

'Do I dare tell you,' said Fr Ian, 'that I wear it as purple?'

'It moves well,' said David. 'And who made this one?'

'I'm not sure. If there's no label it's quite possibly nuns.'

'Look!' said David. 'Tomato Cathedral!'

That unlikely pair of words needed explaining. 'Cathedral' was the name of one of Watts's original fabric designs. Incense and fabrics are the two products which have catchy names given to them like 'Basilica', 'Tudor' and 'Cloister'. 'Tomato' was the subtle red colour that the sample of Cathedral came in.

In the main body of the chapel, our hands lazy with cold, we examined what needed to be done: new frontals, new fringes, new palls. 'Some of these frontals are as limp as *handkerchiefs*,' said Mrs Hoare. The chaplain nodded. He was delighted to discuss his burdens and dreams with two people who spoke his language.

Well-off lay people go to Watts and buy wallpaper and fabrics to make their houses rich with colour and Victorian designs. Clergy don't usually have enough income to allow such extravagance. The only reason why parish priests envy prison chaplains is that they are paid by the Home Office rather than by the Church. *They* could probably afford a few yards of Tomato Cathedral. The smallness of the ecclesiastical income affects the interiors of parish priests' houses and even some canons' residences. Houses are big but bare. In some of the most elegant drawing-rooms in cathedral closes, with alcoves and sloping floors, you see sparse and cheap furniture which will fit all too well into the eventual retirement bungalow. Books, thank goodness, do furnish a room, and there are, always, books.

A final vignette: Canon Colin Semper, Canon Treasurer of Westminster Abbey, lives in the Little Cloister at the Abbey. His study is on the ground floor and its window gives on to the cloister with its small arches and its fountain in the middle: inspiration, you would think, for any sermon-preparer or budget-decider. But he has put obscure glass in the window panes.

'Why?' I asked.

'So I keep my nose to the grindstone.'

Of all the forms of penance I have come across in the Church of England, this was the most subtle.

13

Monks and Friars

nglican monks smoke and watch television more than
nuns do. They are not as neat or tidy. They are often
easier to talk to than nuns: less anxious, more relaxed
and amused. Their gardens are messier and they can't tell you
what all the flowers are called.

It seems unfair that celibate women are more prone to becoming
dried-up than celibate men. Women are strict on themselves and
rejoice in extreme self-negation. Monks are quite strict with
themselves, but they allow their human failings to show. Dom
Boniface at Elmore Abbey watches *The Clothes Show* as often
as he can, and chuckles. Nearly all the monks I have spoken
to have a wireless in their bedroom and listen to Radio 4. It
is an 'ad usum' wireless – in other words, it doesn't belong to
the monk but is simply used by him – but it is a wireless none
the less.

The Religious Life is waning in the Church of England. There is
too much to give up now if you go into a community and few feel
called in the clear tone of voice in which people were called fifty
years ago. The growing area of the Religious Life is the Franciscan
area. Franciscans are to the Religious Life what evangelicals are
to the secular Church of England: the vigorous, young, unstuffy
branch. If you go to a Franciscan community you find that some

of the novices have modern names like Wayne. You will find no such names at Mirfield.

Many of the male communities are remnants of what they once were. Anglican nuns now outnumber Anglican monks by five or six to one. Where there were once 100 monks floating about in the enormous abbey called Nashdom there are now fourteen, many of them old and carrying large handkerchiefs, in a small house near Newbury. Nashdom was nearly bought by Peter de Savary, but he pulled out: the building has been vandalised and the fireplaces ripped out. Trevor Huddleston, sent out from Mirfield in the 1950s, made South Africa a better place and was thin and heroic. Now the Mirfield Fathers stay at home at the House of the Resurrection, praying, studying, running retreats, listening to their wireless sets and sometimes going by train to stay with grand dons and college chaplains. The Cowley Fathers were outgoing and housemasterly in India and Africa for years but they withdrew. ('We withdrew' is a common phrase among religious communities. It suggests a shrinking, a closing in of the ranks.) Now the Cowley Fathers are delightful old men, eight of them living at St Edward's House behind Westminster Abbey, four in a small branch house on the Iffley Road in Oxford with their dog, called Jane.

One of the things that cheers them all up is that there are more and more oblates. It is the same phenomenon as the one I discovered at the Swan pub at Chappel: the modern English public do not actually want to *be* monks, but they would hate the monks not to be there. Normal married people find that they feel called to have a firm but not imprisoning connection with a religious house. The monks of Elmore Abbey have been so cheered by the dramatic growth in oblate numbers that one of them has written a book about oblates and how to be one. It has got calligraphic writing on the front and pen-and-ink drawings by an oblate inside. The Superior of the Society of St John the Evangelist (the Cowley Fathers), Fr James Naters SSJE, is similarly delighted about the growing numbers of Fellows of the Society, who give alms and live a rule of life suggested by him.

The appetite for retreats is growing in England. You can buy a book with the sickly title *Away From It All* which lists retreat houses throughout the country; but parish priests trying to book a weekend in which to take their parishioners away to a place of prayer and quietness find that retreat houses are booked up months in advance. I went on a retreat in August at Launde Abbey in Leicestershire, conducted by Dr Martin Israel, and I just got in by booking in January. There are no monks at Launde Abbey, only a supervising priest and some excellent cooks, gardeners and banister-polishers; but it satisfies a craving among the laity for a corporate silent existence, if only a two-day one.

In Cambridge, Massachussetts, the Society of St John the Evangelist is flourishing. The Society's magazine is full of photographs of young, laughing American monks. 'Why aren't you flourishing here?' I asked Fr James Naters, in a dreary talking-room at St Edward's House. 'I don't know,' he said. 'It's mysterious. If you have young people in a community, more young people will come.'

I told him I knew a few men with monkly leanings.

'If you do, please send them along,' he said. 'We're getting very old here, I'm afraid. The Superior before me thought our work was done. He didn't much encourage new vocations.'

Fr Naters does, and has changed the rules, so that you can now come and live in the community for three years, and you don't have to promise to do anything for life. This is realistic, and it might work. But monks in other communities think that a vocation is for life, not just for Christmas, and that a man must either be a monk completely or not be a monk at all.

Men together create an aura, and it is the aura of male communities that I want to describe. These are the elements that create the aura of St Edward's House. The bell for offices and meals makes a burglar-alarm noise, which makes you jump. The chapel is plain with pews round the walls, and in the pew-shelf you might find a rusty, battered spectacle case with a label on it. Possessions are few, and they are possessed for years. The offices are short and peaceful. The public is invited but hardly anyone comes, even though the chapel is one minute's walk from the Houses of Parliament. Times of services and confessions are printed on a board outside, and the word 'SEXT' always has a newly painted 'T', repairing a vandal's job. At the first muffled stroke of Big Ben, the office starts. There is one hymn, sung surprisingly well to a plainsong tune, with an 'A-a-a-*me*-en' ending. Psalms are said, each side taking turns with the verses. There are rubber mats rather than hassocks to kneel on.

In the house, there are floor tiles, not table-mats, to eat off. Monks' cloaks and woolly berets are hung up in the hall on a row of hooks, and if a monk goes out he hangs a little cardboard clockface on his hook and moves the hands to the hour at which he expects to return. There are pigeonholes with names in Dymo tape, and clothes-brushes on top. The hall smells of mince and washing-up water.

But on top of the building you come upon one of the most luxurious and covetable roof gardens in central London. Fr James is proud of it, and tends it well. Produce ripens in the greenhouse. It is taunting, if you are searching Westminster for a quiet spot to have a sandwich in the middle of a hot day, to know that there is an inaccessible, high-up haven a few yards away.

The silence in the house all day is deep. The monks disappear to their rooms and reappear when the bell goes. They pray and read. The library is well stocked and even the new books have grey-edged pages. When the General Synod is on, the building is full of guests. It is a hospitable house, and it leaves its visitors alone in the long in-between hours.

The Fathers are water-conscious, as is everyone with a historical imagination who lives in this patch of London. They have a map of what the Abbey looked like when it was first built. It was moated. There is still a Thorney Island Society, and inhabitants of the patch belong to it. 'We're still on a tributary,' said Fr Naters. 'We had to dig down sixteen feet before reaching solid ground to build the lift.'

What is now St Stephen's House theological college in Oxford used to be the mother house of the Cowley Fathers. One of the ordinands I talked to there said, 'This study used to be the morgue of the Cowley Fathers, where they sang psalms round freshly dead bodies.' The remnant feeling in Oxford is strong now. Four men and a dog live in a little house further up the Iffley Road: Fr Alan, Brother Anselm, Brother Gerald, Brother Alban and Jane. They are friendly and pleased to see you, and talk to and about the dog. They wear slippers in the daytime. Their chapel is a converted garage, small, square and harshly lit. You sit on box-shaped stools round the edge and the dog wanders in and out. One of the brothers has a long white beard and holds the Bible close to his face while reading. The monks eat in a cramped Oxfordy drawing-room with a globe in the corner and lots of books, all old and improving. A tape reads to them. When I went it was *Set in a Silver Sea* by Arthur Bryant.

They have *done* all their active good, these men. They have been in Bombay and Poona, running Christian hostels. Now they are resting and living a plain and regular life, day after day.

Old men together are anecdotal, and communities of monks tend to have a men's-clubbish air about them. At Mirfield, during the talking hours, such as at lunch and supper, guests sit round the tables with the monks and listen to their stories. Obituaries of deceased monks, written by still-living ones, are rich with specific anecdotes rather than vague generalisations about how good the person was. Breakfast and elevenses are silent and you see how the antisocial urge and the social urge can exist side by side in the same people. Mirfield is also clubbish in that it tends to reject prospective monks unless they are obviously made for Mirfield: preferably ordained, clever and with a suitable sense of humour. A few of the young friars at Hilfield Friary were Mirfield rejects. 'The Mirfield monks told me, "You're a Franciscan",' said a postulant at Hilfield. 'So I came here.' It was clear to me that he would not have fitted into Mirfield at all. He was young, long-haired and angry, and not at all posh or clubbish. He was keen on the beer kitty.

When a monk takes you on a tour of the premises, you have to brace yourself for the cemetery. It is part of the garden. A recently deceased Mirfield Father wanted to be the hundredth to die, but died too soon. This ambition was written in his obituary in the quarterly review. Fr Benedict Green took me to the pretty cemetery and showed me a mulberry tree which he saw being planted when he arrived at the community in the 1960s. Now it is large and they make ice-cream and jam from the berries. The Superior at Elmore Abbey, Dom Basil OSB, told me that one of the monks was depressed and kept going up to the cemetery to choose his patch of ground. 'The monastic institution depends on *some* making a life commitment,' said Dom Basil. 'It's my hope and the hope of all my brethren to be buried in the cemetery here.'

At some abbeys you are taken to see the incense works. Alton Abbey and Elmore Abbey, both Benedictine, make incense which you can buy, handsomely packaged, for £12 a box at holy shops. The incense workshop at Elmore Abbey is spick and span, beautifully organised, with labels on everything. At Alton Abbey, Dom Bede makes incense in a freezing cowshed which is in a deep mess of the kind that only unmarried men make. Trays of drying resin, shovels, cardboard boxes, stained secret recipe books and one of those chimney-shaped gas heaters on wheels make it impossible to move. But Dom Bede delights in his work and makes several flavours of incense, of which Rosa Mystica is the most famous and the most craved by clergy. Abbeys make money out of this sort of homely industry. But their main source of income is money from the past well invested.

In the dining-room at Mirfield, Fr Benedict Green said to me, 'For a short time we tried queuing for our food, but we didn't like it. It was a bit, er, er – '

'Canteeny?'

'Exactly. So we went back to having the tables like this.'

'How long did you try the canteen arrangement for?'

'Fifteen years.'

Fifteen years is a short time in a religious community, but you also find that monks are highly sensitive to minutes. The bell at Mirfield goes not ten but nine minutes before the office. Fr Benedict arranges to meet you at a fire door at four minutes to. At Sunday tea at Elmore Abbey Dom Mark, who joined the community in 1946, told me energetically how he had once laid the tables for the whole community in thirteen minutes flat so that he could watch a programme on television. If you don't interrupt a monk, it is interesting to see how he changes the subject to *his* subject: his sister's son, or the cat, or St Matthew's Gospel, or the nineteenth-century divine he has been reading about.

You can talk to Dom Basil about the sexual urge, and he won't pretend that it doesn't exist. 'I'm heterosexual', he said, 'and I couldn't be in a mixed community. There's a good balance here between heterosexuals and homosexuals. Some communities are almost totally homosexual.' He is bright-eyed and realistic; he used to work for the *Daily Mirror*. A monk from the Abbey ran off with a nun in the 1980s, and that caused a deluge of disenchanted departures. But now the community is holding together in a firm but smaller way, saying the offices at even times of day: eight, ten, twelve, two, four and six. Men can go and stay there on retreats but women can't, because there aren't enough facilities.

The trend for being examined by outsiders has spread not only to cathedrals but also to abbeys. 'Two Sisters of the Church at Ham came here to do a personality study,' said Dom Basil. 'Psychological profiling, it's called. It was good, actually. I felt like murdering one of my brethren, but now I understand how he works, so it's got much better.'

When I asked a young Franciscan novice why he was one, he said, 'Where I was in my life wasn't where I was supposed to be.' Another said, 'I think it's a very exciting mix of the being/doing thing.' There is a way-outness about Franciscans. The young ones speak rather like the Beatles did in their late 'Lucy-in-the-Sky' phase. Some of the postulants at Hilfield Friary in Dorset wear potters' smocks, which make them look more like bread-making artists than psalm-saying holy men. Franciscans are all called 'Brother' now, even the ones who are priests and therefore of 'Father' status. The young ones spend a lot of time arguing about whether they are really living in poverty. Some say they have never been as comfortable in their lives.

Hilfield Friary is tucked away in the hills of Dorset and hard to get to even by train and car, but wayfarers and tramps somehow manage, and when they arrive they are given food and a bed for three nights. Everyone has meals together, but non-tramp guests sleep in a different wing from tramp guests. The tramps watch television in the afternoon if they don't feel like helping with the gardening. They can go to offices in the chapel if they want to but they generally don't. The non-tramp guests do. The friars have to. Morning Prayer and Eucharist before breakfast are an hour long. The chapel is cheaply built. During my Anglican monastic travels I counted the lengths of the gaps in the middle of psalm verses at the different institutions. Hilfield had the longest of all. It is a medieval tradition to go,

2. 'O let mine ears consider well:
   [very long gap]
   the voice of my complaint.
   [no gap at all]
3. If thou, Lord, mark only what I have done amiss:
   [very long gap]

and so on; in other words, to have the gap exactly where it would not be in ordinary speech. There is a good reason for this, say justifying monks. The two sides of the chapel take turns singing the verses, and the singing side needs time to breathe in the middle of its turn. The other side can come straight in as soon as the verse is finished. That might have been true for singing, where breath control is important, but psalms are said now in many religious houses, and the gap system remains. People are fond of it, even though it detracts from the sense of the words. It feels medieval and rhythmical. At Hilfield the gap was four whole seconds long. Silence fell in the middle of sentences, where the colon happened to be. At the Franciscan house in Plaistow, though, the gap was only two seconds long, so it is obviously not a rule, just a habit.

The Anglican Franciscan presence in England has been strong ever since its revival in the late nineteenth century. There are fifteen Franciscan houses. The Brothers steep themselves in poverty and immerse themselves in life with the poor and needy. In Balaam Street, Plaistow, in east London, a street lined with chip shops and crash repairers, the Franciscans live in the house which used to be the headquarters of the Society of the Divine Compassion. It has a huge, hidden garden with a chapel at the end. The door of the house is always open and anyone can come in for tea and biscuits. 'The soap goes and the loo-paper goes,' said Brother Edward, who lives there. 'The other day we went down to the kitchen and the whole Sunday joint had gone. This place has the lowest O-level pass rate in the country. The people smoke heavily, drink, take drugs and so on. Into this, we come and work. It's what Mother

Teresa does: washing the feet of the world. That's what we try to do. St Francis believed that the only way *through* was identification with the poor.'

The personality of St Francis – bird-loving, sun-warmed, funny, magnetic – has infected the whole movement and, just in the way that Sister Benedicta Ward is mistaken for Julian of Norwich, some contemporary Franciscans are so bound up with St Francis that they almost *are* St Francis. Brother Angelo was the first Franciscan I met. He was staying at Freeland with the Anglican Poor Clares – enclosed female Franciscans – and being their chaplain. He danced about after lunch, doing the washing-up and refusing to let anyone help, and singing. He loves leaves and insects and the stones of Assisi, but he is also grave and acquainted with sadness in the way that funny people often are. He used to be a hairdresser.

I was unconvinced about the poverty at Hilfield. Brother Raphael talked at length about the joys of hitch-hiking, and the miracles and God-given coincidences that had happened to him in lay-bys round the country. 'In the security of their own car, people open up to you if you're a Franciscan. They ask questions and pour out their problems. The miracles I've known!' But on the train back to London, who should be in my carriage but a ticket-holding friar?

The postulant driving me back to Sherborne said, 'We've just had a workshop called "Dealing with Anger". A woman came down from London to do it. She charges £300 a day to companies in the City. That's one of the good things about poverty: you get wonderful things free.' Brother Raphael, talking about the time when he lived at the Franciscan house in Llandudno and was a university chaplain, said, 'I didn't have to pay for concerts or the canteen.'

When 'poverty' means 'getting things free', it is not quite poverty. The Franciscans live on generous donations and covenants from guests and Tertiaries (members of the Third Order – the Franciscan equivalent of oblates). The number of Tertiaries in the country has grown from 400 to 2,000 in ten years, another sign of the lay hunger for half-monasticism. Brother Edward in Plaistow is chaplain to the Tertiaries. 'I've got a little car which they pay for,' he said, 'and I drive all over the country.' The Benedictines never ask for money from their visitors. The Franciscans at Hilfield suggest £12 a night for non-tramp guests.

Monks, friars and nuns have heard of each other. 'Oh, I know Brother Raphael.' 'Oh, I know Dom Basil.' 'Oh, I know Mother Mary John.' They are always saying this when you drop the name of another order. The Anglican Religious Life is a little world in itself on the edge of the Church of England. Its hangers-on increase while its life members decrease, or at the most remain stable. Religious communities pray for each other, as well as for the suffering world.

14

Food and Drink

K now-your-Bible sermons are popular with evangelicals. The congregation is encouraged to participate. 'How many meals can you name in the New Testament?' my converting friend Andrew asked when he was preaching at St Stephen's, South Lambeth.

People in the pews put their hands up. They liked the quiz-programme atmosphere.

'The feeding of the five thousand.'

'Grilled fish on the beach.'

'The feeding of the four thousand.' (This was clever, and showed thorough knowledge. 'Yes,' said Andrew. 'Same miracle, different occasion.')

'That time when Martha was cooking and Mary was sitting at Jesus's feet.'

'The Last Supper.'

'The wedding at Cana.'

'Jesus was always eating,' said Andrew. 'The Gospels are really one feed after another.'

He had done his prep and jotted down more meals: meal eaten with Zachius; fish eaten in the Upper Room to prove himself not a ghost; meal served by Peter's mother-in-law; husks of grain chewed by disciples on a sabbath; banquet and feast imagery in parables; 'I am the bread of life'; 'I am the true vine'; Jesus describing Heaven as a banquet; main sacrament itself a meal. He wove a sermon out of all this, about the character of Jesus.

It was with the congregation of St Stephen's, South Lambeth, that I first became fascinated by what Anglicans eat and drink. I wanted to get to the bottom of the pallor of some fervent Christians and the podginess of others. They took me on Christian outings: a weekend in a cottage on the coast of Dorset; a weekend sailing on the Norfolk Broads; a Spring Harvest weekend in Devon. I noticed that I always came back fatter, but also that I never actually ate or drank anything wicked or rich. Much of my Church of England year has been spent being highly alert to food and drink, because meals are what Christians have, three or four times a day. Jesus's own eating habits are justification enough for this. No John the Baptist he, living on locusts and wild honey. I have been struck by the different habits of evangelicals, Anglo-catholics, old-fashioned Prayer Book Anglicans and monks and nuns.

Anglicanness is what they all have in common. It means sitting round a table with others, trying not to be greedy, having proper Sunday lunch and being loyal to the produce of England. I have been well looked after by Anglicans all over the country, and never came away hungry. Anglican food is, in general, unfussy and made of plain, wholesome ingredients such as flour, free-range eggs, apples from someone's orchard, the soft fruits of August, milk, sugar, cheddar cheese, ham and potatoes. This means that it is usually rather good and makes you feel well rather than sick or sluggish. There is a lack of Frenchness, a lack of sauces made with cream. The lubrication, if there is any, tends to be gravy.

Anglican meals are early rather than late. If a priest or bishop is busy all evening he will have supper at six rather than at ten. Breakfast, sometimes called 'a bite of breakfast', happens promptly after Morning Prayer. If you go out to supper with active and fervent Christians seven thirty is the time to arrive, not eight thirty. The puritanical belief that late nights are morally dubious lingers in the Anglican consciousness.

Grace is to be expected in Anglican households. I have learned not to babble before meals, because if you are the last person to speak before the hostess says to her husband, 'You say Grace and then we can start', your secular words echo into the prayerful silence. In chatty evangelical Grace on the Norfolk Broads, food was the last item to be mentioned. 'Lord, we thank you for this lovely weather and for giving us a chance to be together on this special day. And we thank you for this food before us. Amen.' In good Christian households, the standard Grace is 'For these and all thy mercies, Lord, we give thee thanks. Amen.' It is interesting that food is not specifically mentioned in this Grace; it is classed as just one mercy among many. I have never heard anyone say, 'We thank you, Lord, for this delicious roast chicken.' Specific dishes are a taboo subject in Grace. The Stancliffes in Portsmouth only say Grace when there are potatoes: this is the sign that it is a proper meal rather than just a snack. When I went we had a jolly Grace with 'Alleluia' at the end rather than 'Amen'. The Anglo-catholic priests and curates in Sunderland said, '*Benedictus, benedicat, per Jesum Christum Dominum nostrum*, Amen' before their dinner party: Latin but boring. The higher the churchmanship the shorter the Grace. At the very top end, men just cross themselves, so quickly that their hand doesn't touch their forehead or chest.

Weak coffee the colour of tea is something you drink a lot of if you are steeped in the Church of England. You have to sip it to know which it is. Only in the households of a few Franco- and Italophile Anglicans have I found strong, brown coffee made with freshly ground beans. What is the psychological force that makes Anglican coffee weak? There is more than one force at work. Disapproval of drugs is one. Coffee is a drug, and the less you have the better. A woman putting spoonful after spoonful of instant coffee into rows of weightless cups at the back of a church finds that shallow spoonfuls make a jar last longer. She also puts milk into them, before the hot water; and this means that there is too much milk, because she has nothing to measure it against. The Church of England boycotted Nescafé when Nestlé was found to be giving powdered milk to babies in the Third World. Other brands of instant coffee were adopted, and they tended to be weaker. Coffee is seen by the Church of England not as an intoxicating and craved liquid but as a comforting hot milky drink, like Ovaltine.

But Anglicanness is too varied to generalise about for long. The spectrum makes its presence felt in almost every aspect of

Anglican eating and drinking. The simple meal of breakfast, for example – cereals, toast and marmalade, and tea or coffee – is quite different in an evangelical household and a high-church household. Evangelicals do not expect beauty or superior quality in their breakfast. Adequacy will do. The cereal will be cornflakes, or muesli decanted into a plastic tub with a snapping lid; the toast will be from a sliced loaf in the freezer, warmed with the toaster on the snowflake setting; the butter may well not be butter at all but Clover or Flora; the marmalade will tend to be thin-cut rather than thick-cut; and the hot drink will be milky. At Fr Gerard Irvine's house in Brighton I realised for the first time how wrong it is to cling to the theory that Anglican food is safe and unfrivolous. Breakfast was in the dining-room rather than the kitchen, and that is rare among Anglicans, who generally like eating as close as possible to the washing-up bowl. 'Have some of these,' said Gerard. 'They're frightfully good.' They were mad, brightly coloured fruit-flavoured cereals newly brought out by Kellogg's. Gerard had a craze for them. The toast was thick, the butter unsalted and the marmalade heavy with orange peel. It was eaten the smart way – not spread all at once but broken into fragments and individually loaded. The coffee was almost too strong to drink.

Lunch with Paul Weston in his house at Oak Hill Theological College was fascinatingly evangelical by contrast. I arrived at one o'clock and we sat straight down to eat in the kitchen. On the table were: a plate of ham sandwiches made with white bread, a bowl of un-dressed lettuce, a tub of Sunflower margarine, two bottles of bought salad dressing, a plate of salted peanuts, a plate of Club biscuits, a bowl of apples and a jug of tap water. Paul said a long and informal Grace then, 'Help yourself. I'm not eating, myself, I've been eating already, but go ahead.'

The characteristics of evangelical food and drink we see illustrated here are:

1) No drinks before meals. There is no point, if water is what you are having and lunch is what you have come for. The peanuts that would normally be nibbles are eaten as part of the main meal.

2) No drenching of salad ingredients. This means that nothing is wasted. The evangelical palate doesn't notice that salad actually

tastes nicer if it is tossed in a large bowl first. The whole lettuce is used, not just the crisp middle. The healthy, picnicking childhood of evangelical families causes children to be brought up addicted to transportable food such as whole tomatoes, plums and hard-boiled eggs.

3) Wine is not necessary. Nor is mineral water. We live in a country where the tap water is drinkable, so why not drink it?

4) No pomp where pomp is not necessary. The lack of pomp in church is echoed by the lack of it at the lunch table. Prayer is the essential item and happens at a fixed moment. The rest is left to choice. You can have a Club biscuit and go back to ham sandwiches if you want to.

In private houses, the difference between high- and low-church food is more marked than it is in church halls. Parish food is of much the same quality wherever you go. Lunch at the parish reunion at St Cuthbert's, Philbeach Gardens, for example, I expected to be delicious and beautifully presented, in keeping with the finery and pomp of the parish Mass. But it was exactly what I have had too much of this year: help-yourself Christian salad. Christian salad is laid out on a trestle table and you walk round with a paper plate. It consists of:

> chicken drumsticks in breadcrumbs
> slices of ham with white edges
> grated carrot
> raw sliced onions in a dish on their own
> thick slices of cucumber with peel
> quarters of tomato
> dark green lettuce leaves
> strong coleslaw
> chunks of French stick

At least Anglo-catholics give you wine to wash the parish food down with. In lower-church parish halls it is all too often orange squash. Grown-ups in the non-church world rarely drink orange squash, unless they are Scottish dancing, and it has been a shock to find so much squash in the Church of England. The White-Thompsons gave me Ribena at twelve. The young evangelical couple I stayed with in Market Harborough had a jug of squash on the table with supper. They were pure, young and recently married and we had fish for supper cooked with herbs from their young garden. The non-church world has left orange squash behind and moved on to bottles of the juice of at least ten oranges. I have never seen one of these bottles on a Christian supper table. It is too expensive and pleasure-giving.

The food you get at parish bunfights such as parties after inductions, when it is not salad on a plate, is a low form of drinks-party food. There are sausage rolls, lukewarm and hard; cheese and pineapple on sticks; cubes of cold quiche; and triangular sandwiches. 'These are salmon', the woman explains, meaning salmon paste from a jar. There are no dips because dips are sensual.

Secular food has become health-conscious, and dips are an example of this. At drinks parties, oblongs of celery and carrot are what people cluster round. Church food has not caught up. After sausage rolls in a church hall, you go on to jam tarts. On a Christian picnic in Devon, at which we had had two rolls each, as well as crisps and a tomato, a girl said, 'Pudding!' It was a fruit cake which she had baked herself and put in a Family Assortment tin. Cake for pudding is an Anglican phenomenon. Christians love baking, because it is homely and you can share what you have made. Homemade fruit cake is not wicked, but it is fattening and you are given a large wedge. Fussiness is frowned upon. You accept what you are given and eat it all up.

'I don't need any more' is the evangelical way of saying 'I don't want any more'. 'Who's going to polish that off?' means 'Can I have the last slice?' Duty comes before desire.

I have been struck by the Italianate character of Anglo-catholic eating and drinking. As well as having maps of Florence and Rome on the bathroom wall, Anglo-catholic clergy I have met like pasta for supper and a big bottle of Frascati. They love Italy and you often get those Amaretti biscuits afterwards, with wrappers which shoot up to the ceiling when set fire to. This is a topic of conversation.

As well as high-church and low-church food, there is plain old-fashioned Anglican food. The Bishop of Newcastle wrote in his letter to me, 'Why not come and see me at eleven thirty on the 1st July? I will give you some simple lunch.' I was longing to find out what 'simple lunch' meant. We had sherry first, from a decanter in the drawing-room, then went to the bare kitchen. Our lunch had been cooked for us by a woman who comes and cooks (the Bishop is an elderly and abstemious bachelor). The table was laid with a blue cloth, and our food was waiting for us, already on our plates, with a metal lid over each one. We lifted the lids. It was a lamb chop and a sausage. It is very old-fashioned to have a sausage with your meat. With it we had roast potatoes and just enough peas. I had to ask the Bishop for water half-way through: no drink was provided at all. Later he went to the large, empty refrigerator and got out a small orange pudding made of tinned mandarin oranges and sponge.

It was a bit nursery-foodish. It is well known that old English men without women love nursery food, and I have seen a lot of nursery eating at bachelors' residences and men's religious communities. At St Edward's House where the Cowley Fathers live, lunch consists of soup as thick as the sauce on spaghetti, then pilchards and salad. The monks tend to take fairly small helpings of all this, then to fill up on bread and peanut butter. At Mirfield the monks are creative with the given substances. I saw marmalade and cheese eaten together at breakfast. Supper was pork pie and baked beans and a mug of tea, then left-overs: left-over bread, eaten with lemon curd and margarine from a scoop; and left-over bread and butter pudding, with milk because there was no cream.

Nuns' food is much more delicious than monks' and friars' food. At West Malling the food in the guest dining-room is exactly what you feel like eating. On Maundy Thursday evening it was:

Butter-bean and onion stew

Curranty malt loaf with
homemade strawberry jam

A piece of Cheshire cheese and
a Cox's orange pippin

The only sadness was that there was margarine on the table

instead of butter. It is a small but keenly felt feature, as disappointing as the nylon sheets upstairs. You can't say, 'This is delicious!' or
even 'Mmm!' because meals are in silence. Your inner delight has
to be concealed beneath an expression of devout concentration.

At the Convent of St Mary the Virgin in Wantage we had a
baked macaroni dish with a flour and water sauce for supper.
There was bread and a choice of butter or margarine, and Sister
Lynne, our presiding sister, actually chose margarine. I have met
some hardy Anglicans who prefer hard loo paper to soft. It shows
the same self-punishing urge. Pudding was rhubarb and porridge.
You helped yourself from the sideboard. The porridge had to have
a sign next to it saying 'Porridge', just in case you didn't believe it.
In a silent dining-room, explanations must be printed rather than
vocalised.

Hilfield food was the most disgusting I had in the whole year.
The friars cook it themselves, and this is worthy: they are trying
to live in poverty. Most monks get someone in to do the cooking:
it is a luxury they allow themselves. In the kitchen at Hilfield in
the morning, the friars on duty pour wholesale ingredients into
enormous saucepans. I saw an oven-proof glass bowl of cold
mashed potato with a label on it saying 'Tues'. It looked as if
it had been made on Sat or Sun. Supper was greasy beefburgers
and baked beans. It was not in silence so at least you could take
your mind off the food by chatting.

Wine is drunk at Mirfield on red-letter saints' days. At Rempstone Convent, the nuns are sometimes given a bottle of wine by
a cheerful visitor. They share it out among the eleven sisters and
drink it out of egg-cups.

For most clergy and their families, Marks & Spencer's food is too
expensive. Only in Winchester have I been given it, consistently, by
both lay and ordained hosts. 'Now your fish course,' said Canon
Roger Job, giving me prawn and mayonnaise on brown. 'Now your
meat course': chicken tikka and lettuce on granary. In cathedral
towns, it is impossible to resist the delights of Marks & Spencer
two minutes' walk from the Close.

The best food I have had in a clergy household is at the Provost's
House in Portsmouth. The *Church Times* has done well to snap up
the Provost's wife Sarah Stancliffe as its cookery columnist. She

does use cream, herbs and all sorts of France- and Italy-inspired ingredients. Her risotto is saffron-coloured and seems, at the time of eating, the best you have had. Her bread is heavy and homemade. She understands that salad should be eaten in large amounts, with salad dressing made of at least eight elements. Her prose style is straightforward and sensible.

The Stancliffes have pudding on Sundays only. The boys and monks at the Society of the Sacred Mission have puddings on solemnities. The special-treat mentality is popular among gastronomic and austere Anglicans alike.

Cathedral-restaurant food has more in common with museum food than with vicar food. This is fortunate. The cathedral-going public are as hungry after an hour of plaques and effigies as the museum-going public after an hour of statues. They flock to the warm cathedral restaurant for expensive food that is worth the expense: butter-bean and onion bake, asparagus quiche, hunks of red Leicester, cheese scones, country apple juice, chocolate brownies and filter coffee. Cathedral food is Anglican in the best sense: respectful of God's creation but knowing how to use it so that it gives pleasure. Self-denial food does not sell.

Anglican pallor is rarely caused by fasting. In the 1950s it was still the done thing to fast before Holy Communion, which is why it had to be in the morning. Aged Anglicans who have lived in hot countries remember the feeling of faintness and thirst before tropical Mass. But now, even for the strictest Anglo-catholic, an hour's fast before Mass is considered enough. Lenten fasting for the clergy has become as playful as it has for the laity: it consists of giving up an addictive luxury. Some clergy actually preach against Lenten fasting, saying that it can make you arrogant. I have been told by evangelicals that fasting is bad for you because it means that in church you think about lunch rather than about God.

So, what *is* the reason for the pallor? I am thinking of fervent thirty-year-old Christians who read the lesson and say the prayers which start, 'Basically, Lord . . .' Perhaps they would be pale anyway, even if they were agnostics. Pale and shy young men are more likely to hear the Gospel message than swaggering film stars. But Christianity keeps them pale. The reasons can only be these: too much indoor life, eating biscuits with other Christians at prayer meetings; the natural pallor of insecurity; the lack of alcohol; the lack of vanity which makes others go to the gym.

I have met more overweight clergy than underweight ones, and have been scouring their philosophy and life-styles to understand it. These, I think, are the forces at work.

1) The inability to say 'No' when parishioners offer you toasted tea-cakes. For young clergy, especially in the north of England, this is a real problem. One of the topics of conversation at the Sunderland dinner party was how much weight the two young priests had put on since working there, and how enormous the teas were when they went parish visiting.

2) Disapproval of dieting: only vain people go on diets.

3) Among more puritanical Anglicans, the need for an outlet. If you don't have too much sex or too much drink or too much fun, you have got to have too much something. Food is the least wicked form that over-indulgence can take.

4) Five Christmas lunches in December. The first roast-turkey dinner can be as early as the fourth. One parish institution after another invites you and it would be churlish to refuse.

Christians try to be as convivial as Jesus was, and conviviality is cemented by food and drink. Rather than saying, 'Can we come to your house?' Christians after church say, 'Will you put the kettle on for us?' It means the same thing.

15

Prayer

Anglican prayer *looks* different from how it used to look in our grandparents' day. Far less kneeling goes on. When the minister says, 'Let us pray', in a parish church a few stern people yank their hassock towards them with both feet and sink on to it. They rest their elbows on the hymn-book shelf, clasp their hands together and close their eyes. But the majority of the congregation stays sitting pretty much in the listening-to-readings position. All they do is drag their weight a few inches forward towards the edge of the pew, and look down. This is much more comfortable than kneeling. The widespread use of contact lenses means that the shutting of the eyes for prayer is becoming less common, because less possible. It hurts if you shut your eyes for long with your lenses in. Vicars who start to wear contact lenses notice the change it brings to their prayer life.

The discomfort and squatness of kneeling remind us that we are not worthy so much as to gather up the crumbs under the table of the figure we are praying to. The injunction to make your confession 'meekly kneeling upon your knees' is one of the most resonant tautologies of the Book of Common Prayer. In the Alternative Service Book, the posture of prayer is not mentioned. Individual ministers decide what to say. 'Let us sit or kneel to pray' is most common. One of the things that Book of Common Prayer-lovers hate about the Alternative Service Book is the dilution of the old self-chastising words of the confession,

> We do earnestly repent, And are heartily sorry for these our misdoings; The remembrance of them is grievous unto us; The burden of them is intolerable

to the much weaker-sounding

> We are truly sorry
> and repent of all our sins.

You can say the new words without even noticing you are doing so. And if you are not even kneeling or shutting your eyes, the whole confessing process becomes as unmomentous as apologising for standing on someone's toe. Rather than wallowing in your own sinfulness in a grovelling position you just say sorry sitting down. Church of England niceness has seeped into the liturgy.

God hasn't changed. He is no more merciful or merciless than he ever was. But human beings, trying to get in touch with him and do his bidding, have developed new tones of voice.

> Lamb of God, that takest away the sins of the world: have mercy upon us

has become, in Rite A of the Alternative Service Book,

> Lamb of God, you take away the sins of the world: have mercy on us.

The small changes are momentous in effect. Some old clergymen have never got used to addressing God or the Lamb of God as 'you'. 'When "you" came in, awe went out,' said Dean Ian White-Thompson, who has not only been the Dean of Canterbury but also the Domestic Chaplain to Cosmo Gordon Lang, William Temple and Geoffrey Fisher in his long, church-steeped life. 'I still find it extremely difficult – I can't, in fact, refer to God as "you".

Michael Ramsay said to me, "Don't worry. People are going to get used to this." It's true that most people have. It's a question of mateyness versus awe. If I had to choose, I'd go for awe. Jesus did say, "When you pray, say Our Father". But let nothing minimise the tremendous fact that you and I can speak to the creator of all that is, seen and unseen. It sometimes seems so tremendous that I don't want to preach about anything but that: communion with God.'

The second change to the 'Lamb of God', 'you take' replacing 'that takest', is even more offensive to some, because it allows us human beings to tell God what he does, as if he needs to be told. It is committee writing. 'Lamb of God, *who take* away the sins . . .' sounded not quite right to the modern English ear, and the problem was solved by changing 'who' to 'you'. The effect is that the delicate relative clause is destroyed, and that instead of reminding *ourselves* that Jesus bears our sins, we are reminding *him*. In such small linguistic alterations the tone of prayer subtly changes from supplication to chat.

There is one striking element of prayer grammar that distinguishes an evangelical prayer from a non-evangelical one. It is the construction, 'Lord, we pray that you *would*'. 'We pray that you would intervene in the situation in Northern Ireland.' 'We pray that you would help us to draw closer to you.' 'We pray that you would' sounds less greedy and demanding than 'we pray that you will' and less archaic than 'we pray that you might'. It is polite, but not as polite as 'Grant to us, thy humble servants, we beseech thee'. The collects in the Book of Common Prayer are nearly all built round a lowly and aweful clause like that.

'And finally, Lord, regarding the General Election . . .' is the most aweless opening to a prayer that I have heard in a long year of hunched sitting. It was at Holy Trinity, Brompton, and the leader prayed not for 'the candidates' but for 'the Christian candidates'. 'Lord, it's amazing, too good to be true . . .' was another opening. When a prayer leader, on a platform of microphones, has his eyes shut and is lost in prayer, relying on the Holy Spirit to make him say the right things, the words might be deeply felt but they lack the concision and elegance of prayers which have been written in tranquillity.

It is generally true that if you pray that a dying person whom you love might not die but get better the person dies all the same. Perhaps, if you had not prayed, the person might have died sooner or in more agony. You never know how much worse the world might be if the seemingly failed prayers of millions were not happening. Evangelical churches are packed with people who believe and proclaim that God really has answered their prayers: he has healed them, or sent them a new job, or found them someone to marry, or rescued them from a narrow scrape on a pedestrian crossing. The optimism of these evangelicals is in many ways an enviable trait: they have an ability to praise God for good things but not blame him for bad things. Non-evangelicals worry that such optimism can't last, and that a faith which relies on miracles will be shattered to bits as soon as anything really awful happens.

Not a single clergyman or woman I talked to said, 'I'm rather good at praying, actually.' Every now and then I asked, exasperated by my inability to hear the faintest squeak of God's voice during the intercessions, 'Does praying get any easier?' What I discovered was that the clergy are no better at praying than the laity. We think they must be better at it, because they have systems and cycles of prayer, and do it every day. They are better at concentrating. But everyone, from the most devout monk to the most casual godparent, struggles with frustration and boredom during prayer.

A rich supply of justifications for being bad at praying has built up in the Anglican conscience. Dr Peter Ball, the former Bishop of Gloucester, when he finds it hard to pray thinks, 'St Francis didn't feel the presence once for two years.' The chaplain of Selwyn College, Cambridge, thinks of the Archbishop Ramsey anecdote. 'How long do you pray for every day?' 'For one minute,' said the Archbishop. 'One minute? *That's* not very long.' 'No. But it takes me an hour to prepare for that minute.' (Three clergy have told me that anecdote.) 'People don't talk about the Religious Life as the way of perfection any more,' said Brother James at Hilfield Friary. 'Sometimes my mind drifts off during the Eucharist and I've stopped feeling guilty about it.' 'It's just one of those relationships where you're not chattering all the time,' said Andrew Makower, who has always admitted to being a bad pray-er.

There is also a rich supply of advice, and of definitions of what prayer is. 'Just ask God, "What is the next step I should take?"' said Canon Alan Page at the end of a confirmation class. 'Don't try to take too many steps at once.' *Listen* is what clergy tell you to do. Learn to say, 'Speak, Lord, for thy servant heareth' rather than 'Hear, Lord, for thy servant speaketh.' If you find it hard to communicate with the smiling father figure whom you see when you shut your eyes – for me God is still the Hieronymus Bosch God-in-the-clouds that I first saw on the back of *Flemish Painting* at the age of three – don't try to get his mouth to move. Just talk to yourself frankly in the *presence* of God. What all this advice is trying to do is to persuade us that we should not be frightened of prayer, and that every little bit helps. 'You come to know more deeply that prayer is a crucial thing,' said Dr Peter Ball, 'crucial for the whole church and the world. Even in the deadness you know it's crucial.' You do not get good at it; you just see more and more that it is important.

The dull ache of trying to concentrate during the prayers is one of the most familiar sensations of the Anglican worshipper. The intercessions in the Eucharist are something to be got through. You do not look forward to them, because you are at the mercy of the leader. Like the sermon, the intercessions can vary in length, and you can't relax in the sight of the ending as you can with a hymn.

> Strengthen N our bishop and all your Church in the service
> of Christ; that those who confess your name may be united
> in your truth, live together in your love, and reveal your glory
> in the world. Lord, in your mercy,
> All: Hear our prayer.

In the new *Oxford Dictionary of Quotations*, the Book of Common Prayer has eighteen pages and the Alternative Service Book does not get a single entry. Its words are too inoffensive to be memorable. They lack storminess. But they are fair and full of kindness: you can't hate them. Between each printed paragraph of the kind quoted above the leader speaks his own words that he has carefully composed the day before, checking the newspapers for trouble spots of the world. Your mind darts about the globe, from summit meeting to famine to guerrilla war. After each specially written paragraph, you go back to the cushion of the printed words which show you how many more sections there still are to go. By the end, you seem to have prayed, in a general way, for every single person in the world.

Why is it all such an effort, and so unsatisfying? It must be that blanket prayers of this kind are too enormous and vague for the human mind. Scanning the globe from the Amazon to Siberia, and goading your imagination, you see love pouring into the hearts of terrorists, greed vanishing from drug barons, cancerous cells blossoming into healthy ones, sacks of food arriving in starved villages, dictators turning into old-age pensioners. The prayers end and you are weighed down by the dull awareness that nothing has changed at all.

The Church of England likes to be seen to be praying for everyone, not just for the local ill few. It is niceness again. 'And in the Anglican Cycle of Prayer we pray this week for the Diocese of Nord Kivu in Zaire, and for Methusela Musubaho the Bishop.' It is kind to pray for each Anglican diocese in turn, but it puts the praying public to the strain of having to imagine an African bishop in his hot and remote habitat. Prayer of this kind is a formality: it is good manners. Sometimes you wish the person leading the prayers would stop talking, so you could pray your own prayers rather than the good-manners prayers being read out. It is sad that corporate silence plays such a small part in parish worship. One lay person I talked to said that the only time in the whole church year that he managed to pray properly was during the two minutes' silence on Remembrance Sunday. With 120 seconds to himself he could marshal his thoughts of repentance and supplication. Corporate silence is encouraged at theological colleges, where you are meant to sit in the chapel together before Morning Prayer. But it does not often spread out from there to parishes. The public is thought to require a constant stream of words.

The few pockets of deep corporate prayerfulness that I have come across in the Church of England have all involved silence. Some priests give midweek intercessions after the weekday Mass. These seem to be less global than Sunday intercessions, and less talkative. The tiny congregation of parishioners who are free at ten thirty on a weekday morning are *led* by the priest but are given minutes of silence between each prayer for contemplation and private additions. The monastic office of compline lasts only ten minutes; but it is extraordinary how much more intensely you can pray in this short, ancient office of psalms and responses than you can in a whole hour of noisy Sunday worship. Because compline lasts only ten minutes, you arrive ten minutes early, in order not to be late, and the silence deepens in those ten minutes of waiting. Compline has not spread from its revival in the Anglican Religious Life into parishes, except where there is a medievalist vicar who likes that kind of thing. You have to live near an abbey or a convent if you crave it. At the Edington Festival in August, held in a small village in Wiltshire, compline happens by candlelight late every evening for a week, sung in perfect plainsong that some think exquisite and others think prissy.

Lay people lead the parish intercessions more than they used to, and this is a good way of making a congregation feel not left out; but the quality of spoken prayers can suffer. Humphrey Southern said, while still in his second curacy in Liverpool, 'Lay intercessions are sometimes terribly bad, like a kind of sermon. One parishioner only needs to have *heard* of a sick baby and he gets carried away. It's embarrassing, it's sentimental, it's cringe-making.' When people say, 'The C of E's a very *busy* little church' in a patronising way, you sometimes see what they mean. They mean partly, 'It ought to stop talking'.

I asked Richard Ames-Lewis, the vicar of St Mary's, Barnes, what he found most helpful at the Southwark Diocesan Conference held at Butlin's Holiday Camp at Caister for three days in April. I expected him to say 'Listening to Bishop Spong' or 'Meeting other vicars'. But he said, 'My high point at Caister was realising I could pray with clay. You really can pray by making a model. Let your fingers free on it, and the clay starts to talk to you, to tell you about you.'

There obviously is a hunger for non-verbal prayer in the Church of England. Lay people find that they have to take the law into their own hands and make their own rules about what prayer is. They decide that hoovering is a kind of prayer, and so is washing up or arranging flowers. I was told of a hospital worker who decided that buffing up the floor so that it shone was his idea of prayer. Anything, anything, but sitting hunched up on a pew, not quite kneeling and not quite shutting the eyes, and being force-fed with the prayers of another.

If you read one of those evangelical success-story books, about 'how our congregation grew from twelve to 600', one of the most striking elements in the story is the variety and agility of the prayer that helped it happen. Prayer is welcomed into every activity, mental and physical. 'So we prayed about it for a while.' 'We prayed it over.' 'We prayed it through.' 'We instantly called a prayer meeting.' Prayer and thought seem to mean one and the same thing. When Dr Carey became Archbishop of Canterbury, his book *The Church in the Market Place* was reissued to show us what kind of man we would have as Archbishop for the 1990s. The book is full of praying things through. The chapter called 'Pull out – it's madness!' is about the difficult time when the congregation of his parish church, St Nicholas's, Durham, had managed to raise £101,500 on a gift day for the renovation of the building, and then been told that the target amount had doubled. Dr Carey explains how prayer kept the project going, how bewilderment turned to praise, how despondency was overcome. The result was that there was another gift day, and the building work could at last begin. It is painful to read about the poor congregation being bled twice like this, and being persuaded by the Holy Spirit to give up their money. The vocabulary of prayer and the vocabulary of business (numbers with noughts on the end) look incongruous on the same page. But the church in Durham is now large, warm and rich with facilities. Business prayers of this kind are becoming more common as money for renovation is more desperately needed. The congregation's pocket is where the money must come from, and if it won't be brought out it must be *prayed* out.

But, of all fashionable forms of prayer, arrow prayers are the most popular. You simply shoot one up the moment you want something to happen. Clergy and laity alike start using arrow prayers as soon as they have heard of them. Arrow prayers have always existed, of course, but now they have a respectable name and you are told it at Christian Basics classes. These prayers require neither intellect nor eloquence, just faith. What you are requesting is usually something small and instant, and it is more often than not granted.

Praying for wars to cease is more thankless. It is not arrow-prayer material. We don't know how much or how little our parish prayers that 'men may honour one another, and seek the common good' are doing. But the Church of England's worthy policy about thankless prayer is simply to keep at it; or, as evangelicals say, to bash on with it.

16

Music

S mall patches of Bible are lifted to a prominence far beyond their authors' intentions when tradition makes them part of the liturgy. The joyful outburst of the obscure character in Jerusalem called Simeon, for example, when he saw Jesus being brought to the Temple by his parents, is now known as 'the Nunc' (pronounced 'Nunk') by countless evensong attenders in the Church of England. His delighted words 'And to be the glory of thy people Israel' have taxed the imaginations of the best composers in the land. Each one has tried to set that climactic phrase slightly differently. Few have managed to avoid the most obvious word-painting: 'glory' is usually a few notes higher and five times louder than 'and to be the'. Herbert Howells alone set the phrase twenty-two times. Stanford set it in A, in F, in B flat and in G. An experienced chorister or lay clerk could sing you any 'and to be the glory' that you asked for, and get it right.

The inner landscape of someone who has been in a good Anglican choir has fascinated me ever since I shared a study at school with ex-trebles of King's College, Cambridge, who used psalm language in everyday speech. They told me to commune with my own heart upon my bed and be still. They said they didn't have the wherewithal to go to lessons. They said, 'My fart is igniting with a loud clatter', echoing 'My heart is inditing of a good matter'. They were capable and funny and sensitive, and they listened to *The World of King's* and *The Sound of King's* after games.

Now they are lawyers, but they still sing in the bath. On the fifteenth evening, years later, they are still aware that it is the evening for Psalm 78, which has seventy-two verses and four chants, by Mann, Cooke, Nares and Stanford. While so much in the Church of England is changing and getting slightly worse, the tradition of music in cathedrals and Oxford and Cambridge colleges is being both preserved and perfected. Psalm 78 *is* still being sung on the fifteenth evening in King's Chapel, to precisely those chants. A generation of boys born in the 1980s is now singing it, watching the beating hands of the choral scholars in the back row.

Traditions can die overnight, if they get into rough hands. Four miles from Rochester Cathedral, where daily psalms are sung by the choir, the man in charge of music at St Mark's, Gillingham, Simon Heathfield, talks about how cathedrals need to have 'a big rethink' about what they are trying to do in the 1990s. He would like to see more congregational participation at cathedral services, less passive listening. The sight of a robed choir singing psalms to twelve people on a weekday evening depresses him: an evangelical opportunity is being missed. 'The cathedral where they do music well is Bradford,' he said. 'I would say this, because it's an evangelical cathedral, and they have a music group. Cathedral music ought to reflect what's going on in the parishes.'

Fear of pollution is a strong emotion, and you come across it a great deal in the world of Anglican music. Cathedral musicians dread being polluted by evangelical choruses, and evangelicals with drums and guitars dread being polluted by the lifelessness of performed anthems. The two sides scoff at each other across a chasm. They imitate each other: cathedral musicians go 'Jesus, Jesus, yeah, I love you, I want you' with imaginary guitars, and evangelicals mimic the worst Victorian hymns in vibrato voices. Cathedral musicians imagine that evangelical churches are in the grip of the music group; evangelicals imagine that cathedral choirs are in the grip of the dean. Cathedrals where daily psalms are sung become fortress-like in their fear of being infected by the charismatic movement. Trendy canons are not offered jobs. Evangelical churches loathe the way diocesan music committees don't even mention evangelical music: to them, 'music' means anthems and psalms and responses.

Actually, both sides are doing good in their own way, and if they would only stop trying to invade each other and being rude about each other the Church of England would be a happier institution. Some people (I am one of them) are brought to Christianity by the sound of a cathedral choir singing psalms, which lifts the spirit up to the vaulting and beyond. Others are converted by singing worship songs by Graham Kendrick. We are lucky to have a Church which gives us a choice. I am going to take aspects of church music and examine them turn by turn.

The familiarity of hymns

Schoolgirls love the hymn which goes, 'For those in peril *on* the sea'. It has an exciting, seasick tune and makes you think of distressed sailors with pails and wet ropes on deck. They also love the slightly foody hymn, 'Jerusalem the golden, with milk and honey blest', and the soppy one towards the end of the hymn-book which goes, 'But thy couch was the sod, O thou son of God, in the desert of Galilee'. Number one in the hymn charts at the moment is 'Dear Lord and Father of mankind', which has a violent decrescendo in the last verse, from 'earthquake, wind and fire' to 'O still small voice of calm, O still small voice of calm'. What is the drug that makes these hymns popular? What is really going on in the mind of the carried-away singer?

The theology is not the drug. You can sing a hymn for years, and love it, and crave it, without once examining the words for meaning. 'Praise to the holiest in the height' has always been a favourite of mine, but only in my late twenties did I try to untangle the verse

> O generous love, that He, Who smote
> In Man for man the foe,
> The double agony in Man
> For man should undergo.

The tune was what I craved, and the way you had to work out, on the spot, where to put the emphasis in the last line: 'For ma-an *should* u-u-undergo'. It was satisfying. Music is so powerful that it dwarfs words. The doggerel rhymes of favourite hymns are comforting to sing and they make the mouth feel good. But the meaning just washes over you. Holy thought after holy thought, carefully worked out by the Victorian author, are relished not for their meaning but for their sound and mood. The most popular and craved hymns are ones which sound the most delicious; where violently contrasting emotions are pulled together by rhyme and music.

We love with a deep love what we sang in our childhood. We got the giggles about 'And lowliness become mine inner clothing' long before we understood or cared what lowliness was. The hymn went straight into our consciousness without pausing at the intellect. Part of the reason why hymn-lovers feel so threatened by the seepage of evangelical songs into Anglican worship is that they think their childhood is being tampered with. It is like being told that Marmite has been bad for you all these years: you feel insulted and upset. The thought that the next generation of children may grow up without lines like 'Ransom'd, healed, restored, forgiven' singing away in their subconscious is too much for hymn-lovers to bear.

Evangelical ten-year-olds are just as fond of 'Led like a lamb to the slaughter, in silence and shame' as we were of 'Jerusalem the golden'. The refrain goes

> You're alive!
> You're alive!
> You have risen!
> Alleluia!
> And the glory
> Is given
> Alleluia!
> Jesus to you.

It is number 151 in *Junior Praise*, and children love it for its violent changes of mood from mourning to joy. A whole tradition of childhood favourites is building up in the evangelical world; it is just as powerful as the Victorian hymn tradition. That one is by Graham Kendrick, who is the genius among Christian song-writers. He is not an Anglican; he belongs to the Icthus Fellowship, which is an independent church based in south London. Lyrics pour out of him, and a melody comes with them. He asks friends to arrange the melody in an attractive, jazzy way which will catch on. His ideas for songs are simple but they strike a chord: they are emotional without being soppy, and there is always something about the tune which makes it addictive. 'The Servant King' is another favourite: the title itself is touching, and people love the mixture of grandeur and lowliness.

> From Heaven you came,
> Helpless babe,
> Entered our world,
> Your glory veiled;
> Not to be served
> But to serve,
> And give Your life
> That we might live.

The tune is slow and people sing it with their arms in the air, carried away by adoration. They are mouthing profound truths, simply expressed.

A time of worship

'We'll pray for a little bit longer, and then we'll look to the Lord in worship.' Leaders of evangelical services say this, and it is confusing the first time you hear it. Soon you realise that 'look to the Lord in worship' means 'sing'. When someone in a jersey comes up to you after the service and says, 'Hi. I'm in charge of worship here,' he means, 'I'm in charge of the music'. Rather like 'gay', the word is past saving. It has taken on a new specialised meaning, and even those who regret this have given in.

Evangelical services usually begin and end with a time of worship. There is no hymn board. The man with the guitar just starts playing a different song and the person in charge of the overhead projector nudges the next piece of plastic into place. The songs to be sung have been chosen by the worship group and agreed by the vicar; they vaguely coincide with the readings for the day. You sing for twenty minutes on end. The songs usually go from happy to sad to happy to sad, so by the end you have loosened up all your emotions.

I have been trying to analyse the different psychological effects of singing in a time of worship, and singing hymns in the old-fashioned way. I don't think you *could* sing old-fashioned hymns for twenty minutes without stopping. It would be too exhausting. There is too much vocabulary: old-fashioned hymns are stuffed with elliptical thought.

> These, though we bring them in trembling and fearfulness,
> He will accept for the name that is dear;
> Mornings of joy give for evenings of tearfulness,
> Trust for our trembling and hope for our fear.

One hymn at a time is quite enough. Worship songs, on the other hand, are generally one-thought songs. They are slighter than hymns. When you have finished one you still feel that you have hardly said anything. Number 284 in *Songs and Hymns of Fellowship*, for example, goes:

> Jesus, Jesus, Jesus,
> Your love has melted my heart.
> Jesus, Jesus, Jesus,
> Your love has melted my heart.

That is all. Your appetite is whetted: you need more. The Purcell anthem 'Rejoice in the Lord alway' expands on the opening words. 'Let your moderation be known unto all men . . . By prayer and supplication with thanksgiving, let your requests be made known unto God.' The equivalent song 'Rejoice in the Lord always' in *Songs and Hymns of Fellowship* just goes:

> Rejoice in the Lord always
> And again I say rejoice.
> Rejoice in the Lord always
> And again I say rejoice.
> Rejoice, rejoice,
> And again I say rejoice.
> Rejoice, rejoice,
> And again I say rejoice.

The thought is not enlarged upon. Again, you need more.

Evangelical music is easier to sing when you are in the mood for it than when you are not. You can plod your way through 'O worship the Lord in the beauty of holiness' even when you are feeling antisocial and sour. All you have to do is read the words and sing the tune. But to sing a syncopated worship song, such as

> Rejoice! Rejoice!
> Christ is in you,
> The hope of glory
> In our hearts.
> He lives! He lives!
> His breath is in you . . .

you need to be feeling active and uninhibited. It is very pop-songish, and it helps if you sing it in a slightly American accent rather than in a clipped English one. One reason why the time of worship needs to go on for twenty minutes is that a mood must be created, and once it has been created it seems a pity to bring it to a premature end.

Sixty-seven of the songs in *Songs and Hymns of Fellowship* begin with the pronoun 'I'. There is nothing wrong with that. Lots of psalms begin with 'I', and evangelicals work on the principle that if it's allowed in the Bible it's allowed today. Many worship songs consist of chunks of psalm, simplified and modernised:

> I will enter his gates with thanksgiving in my heart,
> I will enter his courts with praise.

'A good teaching resource,' say music-group leaders. The songs are not stuffed with technological language. There was a time in the 1970s when the threat was very real that new hymns would all start saying, 'God of concrete, God of steel'. But it didn't last. Modern carried-away singers *like* old biblical words like 'extol', 'magnify', 'glorify' and 'exalt'. Weak songs are made poetic by boosts from biblical vocabulary.

> It's so good, my Lord, living my life in You,
> For Your yoke is easy and Your burden is light
> Feels so good, my Lord, living my life in You . . .

Archaic forms of common words – 'liveth', 'thee', 'o'er' – are still used in modern worship-song writing. They make a thought sound holy.

But some of the songs that begin 'I' are gooey and self-indulgent. They are known as 'teenage crush songs' by sceptics. They are love songs to Jesus. 'I want to sing until I am lost in your love.' 'I will run after you with all my heart.' The time of worship, unless it is well controlled, can all too easily become a rapturous and soggy occasion. Some songs are almost sexual:

> Take me deep, deep,
> Deeper into You,
> Lord I want to know You
> Much more than I do . . .

The capital 'Y' for 'You' ensures a respectful distance, but only just.

Some songs are hardly longer than the copyright details above them. The four-line song,

> There is none as holy as the Lord,
> There is none beside Thee,
> Neither is there any rock like our God.
> There is none as holy as the Lord.

has, written above it, 'Gary Garrett. Copyright C Scripture in Song/Thankyou Music 1976, 1980.' Is it really worth locking such a meagre creation in strict laws? The outrage is much the same kind as you feel in the Tate Gallery about a picture called *White on White*. Pictures ought to be hard to paint, and hymns ought to be hard to write. A few craftsmanlike old hymns find their way into new worship-song books, and the names of their authors – Augustus Montague Toplady, John Ernest Bode – stand out among their casual modern neighbours – Dave Fellingham, Steve Young, Lynn DeShazzo, Wayne Drain.

The chorister spirit

Is there any overlap between all this arms-in-the-air music and anthems sung by cathedral choirs? Both kinds of music are trying to worship, glorify, exalt and extol God, and this is a bond. But extremists on each side insist that God doesn't much enjoy the other kind. 'I'm sure God enjoys the *occasional* choral evensong,' said Simon Heathfield, in a disparaging way. 'I'm sure God blocks his ears when he hears all those guitar noises,' say disapproving lay people.

The overlap is the enthusiasm of the singers and players. Bible-bashing Christians, who can't bear élitism, tell you that cathedral music is far removed from the Gospel: the singers are too busy getting the notes right to take any notice of the words, and the congregation is allowed to vegetate. What is actually happening is this. The singers and players are concentrating hard on not making mistakes, and this does stop them from taking much notice of the words at the moment of performance. But the very feelings of fear and total concentration produce, afterwards, a feeling of deep delight. A beautiful sound has been made, and beauty on earth provides a glimpse of Heaven. The achievement of performing a difficult piece of music is so satisfying that performers become fond of the music, and long to sing it again. The listeners are not vegetating but marvelling.

The enthusiasm of the singing evangelicals is visible: you can see it in their smiles, their closed eyes, their raised arms, their swaying torsos. The enthusiasm of choristers is hidden. Sometimes it is mixed with deep dislike, and a longing for the holidays. I spoke to one chorister at Wells, who was taking me round the Cathedral School and showing me the classrooms. I asked him which was his favourite Magnificat, and he said he didn't have a favourite. He just wanted to play cricket every afternoon, and being in the choir meant he couldn't. It was bad PR on the part of the school to give me that boy of all boys to talk to. But later I talked to two other choristers, Nathaniel Cromer and Michael Eccleshall, both aged eleven and in shorts. They longed to be allowed to wear trousers. They told me how, at the last service of the year, the leaving boys can choose the anthem. Last year it was 'The Twelve' by Walton, difficult but fun. Both boys hated Howells, who is the favourite composer of grown-ups in London choirs. Nathaniel said 'The Song of Wisdom' by Elgar was his favourite piece of all.

'And d'you like Psalm 78?'

'That's the fifteenth evening, isn't it? It's six pages long. We've missed it for the last four months. Once it was an exeat, once it was special psalms, and twice it was on a Wednesday when we don't sing. The longest fifteenth evening was two years ago with Mr Byrne. The psalm took nearly half an hour.'

It was not rapturous enthusiasm, but it was an expression of their priorities and trains of thought. They can tell you longest psalm, the hardest anthem, the funniest line in a psalm, the least favourite set of responses, the most popular canticle: in a small, hard-working group of young boys, a lore is built up. Anthems and canticles have nicknames. Wood in the Phrygian Mode is 'Wood in the Fridge'. 'Insanae et Vanae Curae' is 'The Insane and Vain Curate'. If you have five minutes on your own in a cathedral song school, where the music is kept, have a quick look at a copy of 'My Beloved Spake' by Hadley. Above the line 'And the vines with the tender roots give a good smell', you will find the name of a poor boy who smells.

Boys have honest reactions. They love pieces and they hate pieces. Stanford has gone out of fashion among choristers. 'People used to like Stanford,' the boys at Wells told me, 'but we're getting bored of Stanford now. You can sing it with your eyes closed and your copy closed.'

'Boys are great romantics,' said David Hill, the organist of Winchester Cathedral. 'They love "Blest Pair of Sirens" by Parry. [That is nicknamed 'Best Pair of Nylons'.] They love Langlais,

Bruckner, Elgar and Duruflé. They don't get over-strung-up about Howells, and they have an intense dislike of Palestrina and Byrd. They were furious when I put the Byrd Four- and Five-part Masses down on consecutive weeks. But they love the Tye *"Euge Bone"* Mass, with its irregular rhythms and lush chording.'

The sight of ten-year-old children sight-reading Elgar is an uplifting one. It reminds you how capable children can be. They might find psalms boring, but in five years' time they discover how enriched they are by verses which they know by heart, about locusts and Egypt and the little hill of Hermon. Years later, they are still vaguely wondering what on earth the verse 'One deep calleth another, because of the noise of the water-pipes' actually means. Enthusiasm and deep fondness sometimes take a long time to come. But one reason why the cathedral tradition of music is so resilient is that organists and directors of music were often themselves choristers in their youth: they are steeped in the tradition and want to uphold it, not destroy it.

Girls now sing in Salisbury Cathedral, three times a week, and they look enchanting, in tabards. They don't make as strong a sound as the boys, but it is just as sweet and pure. Of all the choristers I talked to these girls were the most enthusiastic. It is all exciting and new for them: singing in cathedral choirs has always been something brothers were allowed to do but sisters weren't. Richard Seale, the director of music, dared to be the pioneer in England of girls in cathedral choirs, and at the moment the other cathedrals are just watching, waiting for results. Lots of parents had said to Richard Seale, 'I wish our daughter could sing in the choir. *She's* the musical one.' One mother said, 'Please give our daughter an audition, just so she can know that if she had been a boy she could have got in.' He auditioned her, and was deeply impressed. He came back to Salisbury on a train one afternoon after a meeting at Westminster Abbey, and by the time he arrived, his heart was set on having girls in the choir. 'The Lord's guided us to where we've got,' he said. 'Every single door that could have been locked has been wide open. Everyone who could have said "No" – the Dean and Chapter, the choir school, the gentlemen of the choir – said "Yes, give it a go".'

I talked to three little girls, Amy Russell, Emily Rolt and Kelly

Green, after evensong. They stamped their feet with excitement at the mention of the Advent carol service. 'It's darkness into light. The cathedral's completely dark and then you light candles one by one.' They spoke with music critics' eloquence about the sound they made: 'The boys' sound has got more depth. Ours is not screechy, but sort of more fluty.' Unlike many choristers, they love Stanford: Stanford in A, F, G and B flat were hammered into them on arrival. 'Some of the Magnificats we sing are so *weird*,' said Emily. Amy, aged ten, said, 'Latin is lovely to sing in once you know it well. I would hate to sing "*Ave Verum*" in English.'

The parish sound

We have, so far, been examining extremes. If you go at random into parish churches on Sunday mornings you discover how varied and unpredictable the standards of music are in the country. You come across pockets of excellence, pockets of mediocrity and pockets of dreadfulness. An inspiring vicar and a magnetic organist can make all the difference. A dull vicar, and an organist who has been at the church since before the vicar was born, can cause a stultifying musical atmosphere.

Vicars who are trying to please everyone allow a little bit of everything in their services. The music menu at a middle-of-the-road parish church in a Sunday morning Eucharist might well go as follows:

A Handel sonata on the organ, pretty, with one sharp. The organist learned it forty years ago and it has served him well.

The opening hymn, 'Praise to the Lord, the Almighty, the King of creation', grand and safe. The procession happens during this: two candle-holding youths, three grey-haired women in cassocks and surplices who make for the choir stalls, the parish deacon holding up the lectionary, and the vicar in heavy vestments.

The parish setting of the Eucharist. There are hundreds of

these to choose from and they are all easy for congregations to learn. 'Glory to God-in-the *high*-est, and peace-to-his people on *earth*', two, three, one, two, three. It brightens up a service to have sung bits like this, even though the music is usually so easy that it is completely lacking in beauty. If you don't know the setting you feel left out. But the regular congregation likes having music of its own, to get better and better at every week. A 'Gloria' sung to the tune of *EastEnders* is the new craze in some churches. If you look shocked, you are told, 'But Wesley picked up lots of his hymn tunes from pubs'. That is a much-used weapon of justification for cheap and cheerful church music.

At the end of the Gospel reading: 'This is the Gospel of Christ.' All (singing): 'Praise to Christ our Lord.' A short burst of music, with a cue from the organ. The regular congregation sees it coming, and can't help looking a bit smug.

The offertory hymn, 'O Jesus, I have promised'. It is long enough to be still going on by the time the two money-collectors are carrying the heavy bags to the altar.

More bits of Eucharist sung by the congregation. 'Holy, Holy, Holy, Lord, God of power and might', two, three, four.

The hymn board has five hymns on it. 'Oh, no,' you think. 'The service is going to be endless.' It is a relief to discover that two of the hymns are sung by the grey-haired women of the choir only, while the congregation is shuffling up to the altar for the bread and wine. The two hymns sound weak and faint.

'And now our final hymn, "Morning has broken".' This has found its way into serious hymn books, and embarrassable people wince. They hate 'Blackbird has spoken, like the first bird'. 'Blackbird' ought to have a definite article in front of it. It sounds silly on its own. But the children who have come into church from the Sunday school downstairs love this hymn.

A slow, chordy piece on the organ for the final procession towards the vestry. It does not go on for very long: you soon see the organ being switched off, and the organist changing his shoes.

The childless choirstall is one of the bleak sights of modern England. If it suddenly becomes uncool in a parish for boys to sing in the church choir, even the most optimistic organist can find it impossible to make it cool again. The boys have better things to do on a Sunday morning. Girls are less worried about coolness than boys, and in many choirstalls where you used to find little boys you now find little girls. But they don't usually sing very well. They can just about manage a hymn sung in harmony, helped along by loud men and women in the back row doing alto, tenor and bass.

A seam of excellence exists in the Midlands. At the parish church in Grantham, for example, there is a full robed choir of boys and men, singing proper anthems. These boys love singing in the choir: some do it against their parents' wishes, and walk in from the far outskirts for rehearsals and services. They are paid £3 a quarter, and they earn Royal School of Church Music ribbons for high achievement. The keenest ones stay in the choir after their voices break, and become tenors. The organists of the East Midlands are so pleased with their choirs that they have started an East Midlands Choir Festival. It is held once a year, and parish choirs from Nottingham, Louth, Boston, Newark, Ashbourne in the Derbyshire Dales and Mansfield have all joined. An orchestra accompanies them, and there is a fanfare of trumpets.

Parish organists are paid pitifully little. Advertisements in the *Church Times* for organists make dreary reading. The salary is in hundreds rather than thousands of pounds. Good organists crave cathedrals, or try to live in London where they can do lots of depping (organists' word for taking over when the regular organist is away).

The composer John Rutter is both cheerful and gloomy. I visited him in Cambridgeshire one afternoon to talk about music in the Church of England, and we sat in his study surrounded by large sheets of manuscript paper. 'At the apex of the musical tradition', he said, 'things have never been better. Taste has improved, and organists and singers are better educated musically. While other skills are dying, this skill is alive. A renaissance is going on, and it's very exciting to be part of it. But the tradition is dying at the roots. In the 1950s you could say that what was going on in cathedrals was better than but similar to what was going on in parish churches; now there is hardly any overlap at all. I don't think an apex can continue to exist if it's not supported by a base.'

The causes of the renaissance that he gave were these: King's College Choir blossomed in the 1950s and '60s, and this coincided with the long-playing-record boom. The public became educated and expected high standards. Women started singing in college choirs, in clear, blending voices rather than sticking-out operatic ones. Pools of adult professional singers now exist and form excellent choirs like the Tallis Scholars and The Sixteen. There has been an early music revival, and choirs thrive on this.

The causes of the dying-at-the-roots were these: people travel more than they used to, and people who would previously have sung in a parish choir now go away at the weekend. There is a strong body of clergy and laity who don't want choral music in church. It's possible to run a choir if you feel wanted; it's impossible if the management makes it plain that you are not wanted. Choirs are demoralised out of existence, and a music group takes over. The generation of trendy vicars trained in the '60s is working its way up the career ladder, and the '60s spirit of congregational participation is lowering the standards of parish-church music. Theological colleges give inadequate musical training to their ordinands. Many go into the Church ignorant of the musical heritage and tradition which will die if it is not handled with care.

'Nailing my colours to the mast', said John Rutter, 'I've yet to come across *any* evangelical music that I personally like or would want to hear more than once.' The one good musical thing evangelicals *have* done, he thinks, is to introduce other instruments than the organ into church. 'The so-called organist at St Michael-le-Belfry in York is much more like a kapellmeister of the eighteenth century, who has the role of organising groups of instruments and occasionally doing a bit of composing. I don't think *that's* a bad thing.'

'Do you think it's actually doing harm to people, this arm-waving and getting carried away in rapturous singing?' I asked.

'It's probably harmless when OAPs dance around in Hawkwell, Essex,' he said. 'It's probably not much more than fun. That's a pity when it could be so much more.'

Why organists give us hope

Bach preludes and fugues sing from the organ pipes of England. They are incredibly difficult, and to play them you need to be highly intelligent, agile, obsessive, strong-fingered and patient. When an organist meets another organist at a party the two talk together, standing near the peanuts, until they are prised apart by the host hours later. They discuss the organs they have played and the pieces that they have a craze on at the moment. The enthusiasm and talent of organists give energy to Church of England music. The best organists are put in charge of the best cathedral choirs, and their enthusiasm is catching. Out of their element, English organists are shy and tongue-tied, but in their element they are funny and magnetic. Children laugh at their jokes. They are knowledgeable about organs – where the good new ones are, who they were built by and what stops they have got. A good organist has not only heard of the new organ in Kingston Parish Church built by the Danish organ-builders Frobenius; he has had a Danish pastry in Denmark with Mr Frobenius himself.

If remote and hard-up parishes could afford to pay organists a decent salary, this small body of enthusiasm and excellence might spread through the country and bring new life to dying choirs.

Anglicans are ready with arguments which strike at the heart of your prejudices. If you say, 'But I like listening to the Anglican chant sung by a choir. I would hate it to be abolished,' disagreeing people are armed with cutting replies: 'The church is not there as a musical club.' 'I'm not sure how much all that has got to do with the Gospel.' Musical traditionalists, when asked, 'Why are you so élitist? Why can't you do music that everyone can sing, not just the select few?' reply, 'Whether it likes it or not, the Church of England is the custodian of a great cultural heritage. It may not want the job, but it comes with being the C of E.'

There is deafness on both sides. Taste in music is so strongly felt that it all too easily becomes a matter of what is right and what is wrong. The least tetchy Anglicans say, 'There's no musical style that is inherently evil. It's all redeemable for God.'

17

Whether or Not to be Gloomy

S hort, naked nouns have been the titles of many of the
chapters of this book. In each chapter I have scrutinised
the Church of England through a different lens: the niceness
lens, the cleverness lens, the food and drink lens, the sense of
humour lens, and so on. With will power, it is possible to extract
single characteristics from a confusing scene and examine them
separately. At the Albert Hall, sitting high up at a Prom, you
can train your eye to notice all the red clothes in the audience;
then, when you think 'blue', the red fades away and a sea of
blue emerges. Writing this book has felt like that Albert Hall
experiment. The difference is that instead of just being a visual
exercise this one has involved all the senses, both of the scrutinised
and of the scrutiniser.

Each noun has been dressed in turn with description, examples
and comment. And many of the nouns have had to fight with
their opposites, or with their least flattering implications. Over
the chapter 'Niceness and Goodness', for example, the spectre of
wetness hung. Over 'The Brain' loomed dimness. Humourlessness
had its part to play in 'The Sense of Humour', and pointlessness
in 'The Point of Cathedrals'.

At each moment of scrutiny the question of whether or not to
be gloomy has been swaying in the balance. One dim ordinand can

make you depressed about the future of the Church of England; one delightful vicar can make your heart sing. The smallest thing can make you change your mind. At Sunday services in parish churches you can find yourself alternating from delight to despair at five-minute intervals. 'What a lovely hymn we are singing, and look at all these people who have bothered to come. They're not all old, either. But the vicar has a weak voice and a weak face. His sermon was about the pop star Bono and the Gifts of the Spirit. It didn't make sense. Sunlight has been slanting in through those high windows since 1280. The church is old but profoundly healthy.'

If you put a magnifying glass over a small patch of the Church of England map you see how reasons to be cheerful jostle with reasons to be gloomy. In neighbouring parishes you can come to violently contrasting conclusions. In Wallsend, for example, I was astonished by the fullness of St Luke's Church and the energy and gumption of John Inge the vicar. He took me to the patronal festival Mass at St Peter's, Wallsend, half a mile away, and there hope turned to gloom. It would probably be the last patronal festival St Peter's would ever have. The diocese had recommended the church for closure. The east end was sinking and needed £100,000 spent on it. People from the next-door parish had come to the service to boost the church's morale, but it was still not even half-full. The lights were on and the vestments bright: the church was still alive, and there is a big difference between being about to die and being dead. Facing the sinking east end, we sang 'Christ is made the sure foundation'. We said, 'Christ has died, Christ is risen, CHRIST WILL COME AGAIN' with fervour. But the service in this doomed church was sad. The celebrant was the ex-Bishop of Masasi, who had been vicar of St Peter's a long, long time ago. He was very ill. He missed out chunks of the Eucharistic Prayer and administered the sacrament in Swahili.

The magnifying-glass method of examination is useful for pouncing on vignettes of life as it is lived in parishes. But if you spend all the time burrowing about with a magnifying glass you lose sight of the whole picture: the Church of England as an institution. The hovering method of examination must also be used in order to get an accurate picture. Hovering means looking down at the Church of England from a height, and surveying its sweeping trends.

I tried to interview the chief hoverer, the Archbishop of Canterbury. The questions I wanted to ask him were the following:

1) (to go in the 'Busyness' chapter). 'What do you do all day?'

2) (to go in 'Prayer'). 'How would you advise someone who was bad at praying to get better at it?'

3) (to go in this chapter). 'Are you or are you not gloomy?'

I wrote the first letter to him in early April, and heard nothing. Lambeth Palace had lost it. I sent a photocopy, and was invited to see the press secretary, Lesley Perry, in June. She said I might be able to see the Archbishop in November if there were a cancellation. She put me on the Lambeth Palace mailing list, and from then on, every week or so, a heavy envelope landed on my mat, containing the Archbishop's sermons and wooden descriptions of what he was going to do in the next fortnight.

2.30 The Archbishop will present the Lambeth Diploma of Student in Theology to two people – the Revd Ann Gurney and the Revd Michael Harley.

7.00 The Archbishop will be the guest speaker at the Directors' Network Dinner, at the National Liberal Club.

This did not bring the man to life.

The Bishop of Edinburgh wrote identical letters to John and George our Archbishops, asking them to see me. Prompted and reminded, Lesley Perry wrote to me asking for a second letter explaining 'how the book was shaping up', and 'what questions I might be asking the Archbishop'. I replied in early December, and in mid-January got her letter saying that 'with his present diary pressures' the Archbishop would not have time to do my request justice. At the end of January she rang up to convey the Archbishop's humble apologies, and to ask if I would like the transcript of his Lent article on prayer.

The Archbishop in the flesh was what I longed for. His inaccessibility was a reason itself for gloom. Great people manage to combine loftiness with availability. The word 'diary' had already become my least favourite word in clergy parlance, and now it was further blackened. How *can* an Archbishop be in touch with the present moment in his Church if he is booked up a year ahead?

The Archbishop of York's reaction was quite different. He wrote back to the Bishop of Edinburgh two days after receiving his letter, and said I should get in touch with him and he would find time for an interview. His secretary was a bit off-putting: 'We've done his diary for 1993, and we're just about to close his diary for 1994.' But clearly *his* diary, even when officially full, has room in it for spontaneity. There was a free hour on Thursday week.

In the palace in the flat, wet landscape outside York where the Archbishops of York have lived for 750 years I laid my agenda of potential gloom before John Habgood. He was charming, eloquent and convincing in his quelling of each fear. Of the talk of disestablishment, he said that if you look back over the last 200 years you see how every now and then disestablishment has come to the top of the agenda, and then talk of it has died away. 'The vociferous group that is calling for disestablishment is quite a *small* group.'

Of the Church of England's desperate need for money he said, 'I think poverty's a short-term crisis. The problem has been exacerbated by the Church Commissioners, who haven't been terribly clever in their investment policies, I don't think. It has been extraordinary to see how in twenty years we have moved from the whole of the clergy stipend being paid by the Church Commissioners to sixty per cent of it being paid by parishes. This has had a negative and a positive effect. The negative is that it has led to a sharper contrast between the committed and the uncommitted. The committed resent the uncommitted, and this can lead to a church turning in on itself. But it has been good to learn that you can't be an effective Christian without putting your hand in your pocket.'

Of the Archbishop of Canterbury's busyness and rigid publicity machine, he said that actually the Archbishop of Canterbury was very generous – too generous – with his time, and that he needed a team of people to protect him and make sure he only does what can't be done by somebody else. 'Everyone wants to see the Archbishop of Canterbury in person. There is a tendency nowadays to believe that you can only get the real thing by going to the top.'

Archbishops have to book up their diaries two years ahead because most of their engagements involve hundreds of other people, many of them foreign and with diaries of their own. The Archbishops are busy keeping in touch with the world Church so that the English Church knows what context it is making decisions in. 'I've just seen the Archbishop of Canterbury's programme for 1993, and was almost asking, "When's he going to be in England?"'

'Are your journeys really necessary?' I asked.

He didn't laugh. 'Yes, they are. For example, I've been going to Brussels and Strasbourg recently. The European Commission is very concerned that the Christian voice should be heard. At national level as well, it's surprising how much one's advice is asked. The Lord Chancellor has been asking us about the new divorce proposals. The Education Bill required an enormous amount of episcopal involvement. And the Church's voice will have a large part to play in the Asylum Bill.' High above parish life, these leaders are being diplomatists for the Anglican Christian cause.

Of the fear of schism over women priests, he said, 'After the vote, I invited all the dismayed clergy in the diocese to come here for a discussion. Eighty came. My overall impression was that here was a body of men who were longing to remain loyal to the C of E. I think the vast majority of clergy will take what's on offer. Some won't. In London, some people are quite implacable on the issue.'

Since I started researching this book in October 1991 gloom has shifted from those in favour of the ordination of women to those against. It is the turn of women deacons who feel called to the priesthood to jump about with excitement, and the turn of traditionalists and classical evangelicals (both of those expressions imply againstness) to worry about whether the Church of England is worth saving.

If you are in favour of the ordination of women, as I am, you can rejoice in the new dawn. My reasons for being in favour, as well as a simple gut feeling, are the following:

1) I have met wonderful women deacons who do *not* have nasal voices or militant tendencies. They will make marvellous priests.

Any movement needs its loud Mrs Pankhurst characters to get itself heard, but the strident element will die away when it is no longer needed.

2) If they are all making such a fuss about the priesting of women, why didn't they make a fuss in 1987 when women were first made deacons? It suggests that what people are *really* against is not the ecclesiological question of whether women should be allowed to join the threefold order but the idea of having women celebrating the Eucharist, because it doesn't feel right. It also shows that the diaconate is not respected as an order: it is just seen as a stepping-stone, rather like a Cambridge BA which can be automatically turned into an MA a few years later.

3) It is not as if the Creed has been changed.

When you really care about something your wrists hurt, and this women question is a wrist-hurting issue. Your blood pressure goes up as soon as you enter into an argument. It has been fascinating seeing how this question has been dealt with by the hundreds of people I have interviewed. I asked each one of them (unless they told me first) whether they were for or against the ordination of women, and found there was no pattern in the answers. It was like asking, 'Do you like oysters?' The answers were as unpredictable, as instant and as strongly felt. Their source seemed to be the gut rather than the intellect. Argument was used as decoration, just as it is with oysters. ('No! They're alive, lemon makes them flinch, I had a bad one once', or 'Yes! They're delicious, they slip down the throat, the Romans ate them.') The violence of feeling on the subject was remarkable. At the same drinks party a whole non-churchgoing family told me that they were furious about the result of the vote, and a strong, witty lay woman told me that she was a subscribing member of Women Against the Ordination of Women.

'Are your reasons theological or emotional?' I asked.

'Twenty per cent theological and eighty per cent emotional,' she replied.

Lay people, I found, admitted that their feeling was predominantly a gut one. The clergy, or the very churchy laity, were more euphemistic. Not a single clergyman ever said, 'It just wouldn't feel right to have women priests.' They used scores of arguments, but not the gut one. David Senior, the vicar of Helmsley in North Yorkshire, won points for honesty when he said, 'No doubt I should find myself intensely uncomfortable at the altar.' He continued, 'On the whole, when you get women in headship positions, it goes wrong. Maggie Thatcher was an example in a way. That's not to imply seniority or juniority; it's just that we're made differently. It worries me that this is such a modern idea. Why should the Holy Spirit suddenly change his line?'

It was a panicky argument, and a clear-thinking campaigner could knock holes in it with gusto. But at least I felt that a human being was speaking, not a disguised human being. He was honestly scared that we would soon have rows of Mrs Thatchers consecrating the bread and wine.

Some arguments against women priests are so euphemistic and subtle that you can't understand them. They are about sacramentality, sacrifice and headship. The Greek word for 'headship' tends to be used. You are left worrying that perhaps you are not clever enough to understand why the priesting of women is wrong. It is a genuine worry. The clever Bishop of Newcastle, and the clever Fr Peter Geldard, have thought it through and are convinced that it is wrong, and if we only had their intellect and ecclesiastical knowledge we would see that it is wrong too. But my wrists hurt when I read incomprehensible articles full of abstract nouns, written to make those in favour feel stupid.

Deafness is the religious believer's disability. You care about something so much, and are so sure you are right, that you become closed to persuasion. What you care about seems of infinite importance, and you can't just laugh it off. The Church of England has managed to hold together in spite of the worsening deafness of its extremists. The anguish of the lay person, watching the Church of England stagger and gasp for breath in its new post-vote state, is similar to the anguish of a child listening to its parents arguing. There is the same yearning for reconciliation, the same fear of divorce, the same longing to say, 'Please stop: it's not *that* important'. The Bishop of Sheffield deciding not to resign after all was a step towards the healing of the wound. Ann Widdecombe's hasty and loud departure seemed a petty gesture by comparison.

In the week after the Synod vote on women, ordinands at St Stephen's House in Oxford were seen picking up their forks in the college dining-room and saying, 'We might as well ordain *that*.'

'I wouldn't care if people like that left the Church of England,' a horrified layman said to me when he heard about this. 'Good riddance to them.'

Actually, I would care. I would hate the spiky high end of the Church of England to be chipped off. 'Forward in Faith', the euphemistically named organisation for Anglican catholics opposed to the priesting of women, has been waving the number '3,500 clergy' around. This number constitutes a whole, vigorous limb. Losing it would be not only crippling but also dulling. Horrid though bigoted Anglican catholics can be, they bring wit, colour, brains and fun to the Church of England. Misogynists can be pastors. They can run excellent churches and do good works. Their candle-lit, incense-filled services bring colour and a sense of mystery into people's lives. If they stomped off to Rome there would be a gradual drifting downwards of the Church of England's character; it would become tamer, more middle-of-the-road, sleepier.

One of the most high-blood-pressure interviews I had was with the youth pastor and music-group leader of St Mark's, Gillingham, Simon Heathfield. He was against the ordination of women for the fundamentalist evangelical reason: 'The whole thrust of the Bible, from Genesis onwards', he said, 'is that women are the helpers.' He gave me soup from a dehydrated packet, two slices of hard toast from the freezer and margarine. This didn't help. The Bible was his sole point of reference for what was right and what was wrong, and he had no time for clergy from other wings of the Church of England, whom he thought were living unbiblically.

'Would you like the Church of England to be disestablished?' I asked.

'Yeah, I wouldn't mind.'

'Why would it be a good thing?'

'Well, it would mean we wouldn't have to baptise hypocrites any more.'

I thought him self-righteous. He belongs to the Proclamation Trust, which is a mostly male Christian group run by Dick Lucas, the rector of St Helen's, Bishopsgate. Its Bible is the Bible, and its members are opposed to the ordination of women. They go to conferences and learn to preach the Bible and nothing but the Bible. But even these people, smug though they can be, are brightening up the lives of the English youth whose pastors they often are. All these extremists need is a chink in their armour of certainty that they are right.

The trends are undeniable and worrying. The theological colleges which are bursting are the ones which produce people who sing trance-like songs to Jesus, treat the Bible as a manual, 'have difficulty with' homosexuality, and wouldn't mind if the Church of England were disestablished. The churches which are fullest are the ones which are run by such people. You can't park anywhere near Holy Trinity, Brompton, on a Sunday evening at six thirty. The kind of worship the church offers is what the young of London crave. You have prayers about current affairs led by a man in a suit; twenty minutes of singing led by a guitarist who speaks so like a dazed rock-star that you can't hear him; a reading; half an hour of sermon given by another man in a suit; and then more hypnotic singing. This is the kind of Christianity that spreads. It is pompless, relaxing and sure of itself, and it moves people. They take notes in their Filofaxes.

While churches like St Peter's, Wallsend, are being closed down for lack of money and smallness of electoral roll, churches like Holy Trinity, Brompton, are re-seeding themselves. They are so overcrowded that they have to pray for a new venue. Their prayers are answered, and off a hundred of their members go. Within six months, the new hundred becomes 400. Empty Gothic churches are resuscitated. Microphones and loudspeakers are put in the sanctuary, and stackable chairs supplement the pews. You feel sorry for the dead people named in the memorial stones: they must be shocked, rather like past headmistresses on the wall of a school assembly room where a disco is happening. The Church Commissioners have closed, on average, a church a week for twenty years. There was an average of a church plant a fortnight in 1990.

Hovering over the Church of England and watching this, you can be filled with gloom. It is like watching mile-a-minute Russian vine swamping a garden and smothering the weaker shrubs. Russian vine is green and vigorous, but it all looks the same.

The evangelical wing of the Church of England likes to divide people into Christians and non-Christians. The clamour for disestablishment is getting louder, partly because of a general disenchantment with the Royal Family, partly because more and more clergy are of the kind who like people to be either in or out. A disestablished church would mean that churches wouldn't have to baptise, marry or take funerals for everybody in the parish. St Mark's, Gillingham, is already moving in that direction with baptisms: the policy now is that the parents and godparents must all be regular churchgoing Christians. The more this checking for credentials happens the more the Church of England will become a sect. That is an emotive little word waved around both by anti-ordination of women people (who feel the Church of England is no longer part of the Catholic Church) and by anti-disestablishmentarians. The callers for disestablishment wouldn't mind if the Church of England became a sect: at least it would be rid of all those agnostics who just want a church wedding.

The established Church, like the House of Lords, is difficult to defend on paper, except by saying that it works. Its essence is not the Prime Minister deciding who is going to be bishop. He doesn't, anyway: ask the secretary of the Crown Appointments Commission, Hector Maclean, who will give you a detailed explanation of the lengths to which the Commission goes to find the perfect man for a vacant see, asking 150 people for advice and praying for months. The Prime Minister is not brought in until the shortlist has been whittled down to two. Nor is the essence the Queen nodding her head at the sight of a name presented to her on a piece of paper. Her role is not one of power so much as one of presence. Since the first breath of Christianity in England, State and Church have worked together. Sister Benedicta Ward, the sparkling Oxford nun, delighted in reflecting on this, in the vivid historic present tense: 'Augustine lands at Thanet and can't start a church without King Ethelbert's permission; Aidan can't start without King Oswald. Edwin, another north-country king, sits down with his thanes and they decide to *take the gift*.' The Sovereign's influence is a stabilising one.

The one way in which the established Church makes itself felt is in the system whereby every citizen belongs to a parish and has a right to be baptised, married and buried in it. This is about as Christian as a system can be. All the kinds of people whom Jesus particularly liked – sinners, non-churchgoers, adulterers, tax collectors, fishermen – can come in and celebrate the most important moments of their lives without having to show a Christian identity card. It is a system which gives people the benefit of the doubt: they might only come twice in their lives but at those times they really might be experiencing a tremor of faith. Only God can be the judge of that.

Shooting up the M1, you go through a parish a minute. In the bland motorway landscape this is a comforting thought. Even hard shoulders have an address. Place names that would otherwise die in the climate of centralisation are kept alive by being the names of living parishes. Even in London, where I live, I have come across two places I had never heard of, Tokyngton and Furzedown. Tokyngton is near Wembley and Furzedown is near Streatham. Their clergy strive to do good and to make these places better and happier places.

Reasons for gloom about the Church of England are abundant. It falls short of its ideals in every aspect: millions of people remain unreached by the Christian message; canons give sandwiches to tramps but do not have them to stay; members of the clergy despise each other; fanaticism is rife; by trying to please everybody the Church of England manages to annoy everybody. Though many of its members are far from hesitant in their beliefs and prejudices, as an institution hesitancy is one of the Church of England's most striking characteristics. Rather than making swift and visionary decisions, it shilly-shallies.

'Hesitancy is both a weakness and a strength.' That was one of the sentences I used too many times in my year of research, end-lessly explaining that my title *The Church Hesitant* wasn't meant to be damning. All the wetness and lack-of-sense-of-direction that hesitancy brings is balanced by hesitancy's other implications:

modesty, unbossiness, humility, a sense of inadequacy when faced with decisions which relate to other people's souls. In all the chapters in this book the Church of England has been seen to be under strain. On important questions – whether to be wordly or unworldly, firm or malleable, lavish or sparse, self-indulgent or self-denying, poised or spontaneous – the Church of England as an institution takes no firm line. Individuals must decide for themselves.

So, after all the hovering, we can come back to burrowing again. What are these individuals actually *like*, on average? The main reason why my final stance is one of guarded hope rather than one of gloom is that the human beings I have met while writing this book have been, on the whole, delightful. Fanatical clergy exist at extreme ends of the spectrum, but in the middle calm and diligent people are trying to get on with their jobs. Bad-tempered lay people exist, disrupting the PCC and thriving on church politics, but the average churchgoer is a good sort, trying hard to become a better sort.

Far more often I have come away from visits and services tingling with delight than weighed down with gloom. There is one band of the spectrum which I particularly like, and it is quite a large band. It is clergy of a catholic disposition who are in favour of the ordination of women and who have no difficulty at all with homosexuality. The nicest people in 'Niceness and Goodness' and the funniest people in 'The Sense of Humour' fell into this category.

Every now and then a feeling of pure non-gloom swept over me. At special services such as patronal festivals and inductions, when the church was full and the choir was trying something ambitious with an orchestral accompaniment, I felt, 'It's all going to be all right.' The sight of rows of widows in the front pews was also uplifting: the Church of England is laughed at for being full of old ladies in hats, but isn't it good that the Church supports them in their lonely old age? Schoolchildren talking to the team rector of Thamesmead; the female curate in Southfields and her vicar beaming at each other with joy at the end of a service; the Precentor's children not quite sitting still in Norwich Cathedral; the high standard of oratory at the General Synod debate on the ordination of women; the eloquence and magnanimity of the House of Bishops' statements on emotive subjects; the fact that when you go to weddings or funerals they are done well rather than badly; these are all signs of hope.

But the flitting is over. I must settle down into a parish, as clergy keep telling me. 'It's not what you get, it's what you give.' Which church will it be? As soon as I have decided, the skiving urge will start to creep over me. Something about the church – the temperature, or the smell, or the vicar's way of emphasising pronouns, or the tune they sing 'Holy, holy, holy' to – will start to grate. That will be the test.

The Church of England is a treasure spurned. Reasons for spurning it are all too easy to list. Treasuring it requires stamina. But every gesture of loyalty lifts its shrivelled morale and makes it more worthy of treasuring.

Index

Names of churches in the London area are entered under London rather than the name of their districts